Legitimacy and History

Legitimacy and History

Self-Government in
American Constitutional Theory

Paul W. Kahn

YALE UNIVERSITY PRESS

NEW HAVEN & LONDON

Published with assistance from the
Louis Stern Memorial Fund.

Designed by James J. Johnson and set in
Adobe Caslon Roman types by Rainsford
Type, Danbury, Conn.

Printed in the United States of America by
Vail-Ballou Press, Binghamton, N.Y.

A catalogue record for this book is available
from the British Library.

The paper in this book meets the guidelines
for permanence and durability of the
Committee on Production Guidelines for
Book Longevity of the Council on Library
Resources.

10   9   8   7   6   5   4   3   2

*Library of Congress Cataloging-in-Publication
Data*

Kahn, Paul W., 1952–
  Legitimacy and history : self-
government in American
constitutional theory / Paul W. Kahn.
    p. cm.
  Includes index.
  ISBN 0-300-05499-8 (cloth)
       0-300-06307-5 (pbk.)

  1. United States—Constitutional law—
Philosophy. 2. United
States—Constitutional history—
Philosophy. 3. Political science—
Philosophy. I. Title.
KF4550.K34 1993
342.73'001—dc20
[347.30201]   92-13116

For Suzanne and Hannah

Contents

Preface

Practicing lawyers who read contemporary constitutional theory scarcely recognize in it the legal system in which they work. Traditionally, constitutional theory focused on the institutional arrangements within which power is exercised. Academic writings considered the relations between the branches of federal government and between federal and state authorities, as well as the relation of all these institutions to popular sovereignty and individual rights. Today, leading theorists pursue more esoteric inquiries. They discuss hermeneutics and biblical exegesis instead of the commerce clause. They consider obscure political philosophers rather than judicial precedents. Theorists seem to have lost sight of the realities of political power and the everyday arrangements of public life.

This book began with a simple question: Why has this happened? Why have constitutional theory and constitutional law split apart? Why do the academy and the bar no longer communicate with each other? The answer to this question might be sought in the larger intellectual context that provides the setting for contemporary constitutional theory. Alternatively, the inquiry might turn to contemporary political and social developments that influence the concerns and expectations of theorists. Questions about the nature of contemporary constitutional theory could thus lead to an inquiry into either contemporary philosophy and political theory or contemporary political and social developments.

I reject both approaches. I don't deny that theoretical and sociopolitical influences exist, but I believe a more compelling explanation of contemporary theory can be found in the historical development of constitutional theory itself.

Contemporary theoreticians are writing within a rich discipline. The boundaries of this discipline have not always been clear, because issues of constitutional theory have merged with issues of constitutional law, on the one hand, and issues of political theory, on the other. Nevertheless, at the center of American constitutional discourse has been a focus on the problem of temporality within a system of self-government. The content of the discipline of constitutional theory can be summarized in a single question: How is it possible to understand constitutional government as self-government when those subject to its authority did not participate in its creation? To understand contemporary constitutional theory, we must understand the history of efforts to answer this question.

This book, therefore, is simultaneously intellectual history and constitutional theory. As intellectual history, it traces the broad pattern of constitutional discourse over the past two hundred years. I hope to show that constitutional theory has been a single discipline with a unity of aim and function. That unity has not precluded substantial disagreement. There has been no single understanding of constitutional government, with its dual commitment to self-government and to maintenance of the structure inherited from the founders. Indeed, I focus on the differences among those understandings that characterize each successive period of constitutional thought.

As constitutional theory, this work is an inquiry into the political problem of time. For all but the founders, the state is a historical phenomenon. The structures of authority that characterize the state are the consequences of past political acts in which the current citizens were not participants. My ambition is to explain the conceptual possibility of self-government within the historical state. I give theoretical coherence to the different approaches to constitutional self-government, revealed in the historical inquiry, by showing that not only is each a response to the problem of temporality but together they form a unified series of responses.

I approach the history of constitutional theory as an experimental field in which to discover and test the possible ways of understanding the citizen's relation to political history. I conclude not only that the tension between the ideas of self-government and historical continuity has been the driving force in the development of constitutional theory but also that there is no way to overcome this tension within the constitutional state. The break between contemporary theory and practice is a consequence of the ultimate impossibility of uniting self-government and the historical state. Self-government founders on the shoals of history.

Acknowledgments

Everyone's life is in some ways an exploration of the problem of time. My own life is marked by the self-consciousness with which I have explored it. Philosophy, politics, and family are all aspects of a single effort to understand the temporal character of experience. In all these explorations, I have had a constant companion, Catherine Iino. Whatever I have learned, I have learned with her.

I have been thinking about temporality for twenty years, and in that time my debts have become too numerous to list. Only in the past five years have I come to see that law, too, offers a field within which to explore this problem. Throughout, I have had the support of my colleagues at the Yale Law School, as well as the generous support of that institution. I am grateful for all of this help. I owe special thanks to my two sparring partners, Bruce Ackerman and Owen Fiss. For help in the final preparation of the manuscript I am grateful to Evan Van Hook and Jennifer Mnookin; and I thank Barbara Mianzo for help in producing and keeping track of the many drafts of the manuscript. Earlier versions of some of the materials in chapters 1, 2, and 6 appeared in two articles, "Reason and Will in the Origins of American Constitutionalism," 98 Yale L.J. 449 (1989), and "Community in Contemporary Constitutional Theory," 99 Yale L.J. 1 (1989).

Constitutional History
as Discourse

Contemporary constitutional theory is largely concerned with the concept of community. Community is at the center of the new republicanism so prominent in discussions today. It is also central to the focus on interpretation that characterizes another large part of contemporary theory. The republican and the interpretive approaches share an understanding of community as the locus of discourse. Speaking, not governing, is the main activity of the theorists' constitutional community.

The turn to community is driven by extremely abstract considerations. The new republicans seek to understand how the state can use democratic means of government to advance an objective public good that is more than the aggregation of personal preferences. The interpretivists, in contrast, ask how government can remain democratic if its highest law is found in a historically given text that no one in the current community helped write. Both groups of scholars are dealing with the problem of legitimate constitutional governance. Both understand constitutional governance to require some objective value beyond the immediate desires and interests of constituents. But whatever makes it more than rule by the majority raises problems of justification. Why is it legitimate to displace the expressed desires of a current majority?

To secure this objective value, the new republicans turn to an idea of the public good; the interpretivists turn to a historical text. In both instances, the appeal to an objective norm requires an elaboration of the meaning and character of self-government. The concept of a community of discourse enters contemporary theory at just this point as the vehicle for linking the objective value of a text or of the public good with the citizen who insists that constitutional government is self-government.

Concern with the problem of self-government is not new. Yet the turn to the idea of a discursive community to elaborate the meaning of constitutional self-government is puzzling. The theorists' imagined association of speakers is not the political community of everyday life, with its well-ordered relations of political power. Unlike the actual, legally structured society, the theorists' community is characterized by the equality of its members. They relate to each other as equal participants in an ongoing discussion. This communitarian vision seems to have nothing to do with constitutional law, which creates authoritative institutions operating within an established hierarchy.

Furthermore, the national political community is temporally and geographically stable, whereas a community of discourse is unstable. It appears, disappears, splinters, and changes as debate shifts among discrete groups of speakers. Anarchy is always a possibility when dialogue moves in unexpected directions, challenging old meanings and institutions. Discursive communities are plural, not singular, and they do not obey any principle of order in their relation to each other.

Contemporary theory, then, has turned to an idea that seems to invite equality and anarchy in place of authority and stability as the foundation of the political system. Discursive communities may be morally and socially attractive; a rich life may include membership in a number of such communities. Why, however, would anyone believe that their place is within the structured system of authority by which the state exercises power? Yet isn't that structure what constitutional law is all about?

To one trained in the history of philosophy, this linkage of law and discourse is ironic. The philosopher is likely to place the idea of a community of discourse to the side of revolution rather than the side of constitutional order. The classic model of a discursive community was created by Socrates in his conversations within the community. Those conversations so threatened the state that democratic Athens eliminated their source. Since then, the discursive community has been the philosopher's natural home, not the state's. From that home, philosophy has always represented a challenge to the state—potentially, if not actually.

In seeking to figure out how the discursive community has ended up at the center of the theorists' understanding of constitutional authority, I have not been immune to the communitarian virus sweeping constitutional theory. Instead of looking to community to explain constitutional law, I look to the idea of a discursive community to explain constitutional theory. I propose to consider the two hundred years of constitutional discourse as a single conversation about self-government. A single conversation does not mean a single position with respect to the problems addressed. It does mean that change should be understood as innovation within a larger structure of continuity.

The continuity is expressed substantively in the unity of the underlying theme. The discourse of constitutional theory has in large measure been a conversation about the self of self-government. If the divergence between self and government is too great, then the constitutional system loses its appearance of legitimacy. It would be a mistake, however, to assume that government has been measured against a stable concept of the self. The self-identity of the citizen has been as much the product as the starting point of this conversation.

Methodologically, the idea of conversational continuity suggests that conceptual innovation should be understood from the perspective of a new entrant into the ongoing discursive enterprise. No one entering the debate can avoid using the terms and concepts that he or she finds already deployed. Even more important, the theoretical agenda is established by the problems that appear in the conceptual worldview of those already engaged in this conversation. Progress, in other words, is measured by the capacity to identify weaknesses in the dominant understanding and propose solutions that build on the conceptual possibilities existing within the constitutional discourse. A history of constitutional theory should, therefore, identify stages in the development of this discourse and aim to show the internal logic of their order.

The possibilities of conceptual innovation within this conversation are neither indeterminate nor endless. The structures and limits can be explained in terms of the aims of the discourse and the conceptual means available to it. Innovation within constitutional theory is a process of building a conversation from within. The changing political, social, and economic events that constitute the external world within which constitutional discourse occurs have a role in explaining the pace of change as well as the particular problems focused on at any given time. But those circumstances do not themselves determine the structure of constitutional thought.

Although constitutional government can mean many things, minimally it means that authority is exercised within a set of institutions, operating with defined rules and established limits. To all but the founders' generation, these institutional structures, rules, and limits are an inheritance from political predecessors. The Constitution, by setting forth the structures, marks the state as a single entity, despite the constantly changing composition of its members: one generation of citizens gives way to the next. To participate in constitutional governance is to participate in an intergenerational project.

The need for constitutional theory arises from the difficulty of reconciling this temporal reality with a norm of self-government. If the community had constantly to reconstitute itself on the basis of its own ideas about the best political order, then constitutional theory would be displaced entirely by political theory. An abstract inquiry into the best political order could guide the practical effort at political construction. Similarly, if every community were bound so tightly by its past that political authority could not raise a problem of self-conscious justification, then constitutional theory would be displaced by cultural anthropology. Interest in constitutional systems would be limited to descriptions of other nations' political order. The unique problem of constitutional theory is to explain how self-government is possible under the conditions of temporality within which the state exists. The attempt to answer this question, to explain personal identity within the framework of political history, calls forth conceptual innovation within constitutional discourse. In the simplest terms, self-government cannot mean the same thing to the founders' generation and to those who come later. Even if the different generations speak a common language of self-government, they must bring different understandings to its terms.

I describe the dynamic character of constitutional discourse by appealing to four conceptual models of order. These are the models through which the citizen understands how the historical state can express self-government. The problem of linking the authority of the state, which always appears as a historical phenomenon, to the identity of the self places time at the center of constitutional discourse. Each conceptual model offers a different understanding of how the state maintains—or fails to maintain—an identity through time. These different understandings of the historicity of the state have profound implications for the understanding of individual citizenship—of the self in its relation to the state.

The four models are making, maintenance, growth, and community. In the course of my argument, each model is developed in detail. I discuss its abstract structure, as well as the manner in which it orders constitutional discourse within a specific period of history. History, however, cannot be completely encompassed within an ordered progression among these models. Between the models of growth and community—which characterize, respectively, the beginning and the end of twentieth-century constitutional theory—there was a moment of genuine crisis, when the constitutional enterprise appeared to collapse. The crisis occurred because of a failure to comprehend how self-government could be reconciled with the historical inheritance of a constitution. I describe this crisis in my discussion of modern constitutional theory in chapter 5.

In the conclusion, I consider in a more general fashion the methodological and substantive implications of my focus on conceptual models of order. At this point, I want to introduce the idea of a conceptual model of order by illustrating each of the four models with examples from ordinary experience.

The model of making refers to the classical concept of a *techné*—a practical art informed by an abstract understanding of a particular subject matter. Where the Greeks had arts like pottery and medicine in mind, a good example today would be civil engineering. The civil engineer's art consists of the ability to apply a scientific understanding of abstract principles to particular projects built in time and space. Engineers possess more than personal opinions; they possess knowledge. They deliberately construct physical objects that are in-formed by their abstract knowledge. To understand constitutionalism within the model of making requires identifying one or more political artisans who possess a knowledge of politics that can in-form the construction of the political order of the society.

Opposed to this idea of making is a model that I label organic maintenance. The best example is an organism. To understand the model, however, requires stripping the organism of contemporary associations with evolution and considering it from the perspective of its unique individuality. Unlike the model of making, which requires an artisan to join ideal form and material object, the organism exists only as a combination of form and matter. To be alive is to hold form steady, even though the material elements that embody that form change constantly. The identity of an organism refers to the past of that particular organism, not to an abstract idea. The organism maintains the identity that comes into being at its birth and ends with its death. To understand constitutionalism within this model requires seeing the political order as a self-referential organic whole with the capacity to maintain the formal identity brought forth at its birth through the changing vicissitudes of daily life.

With both the model of making and the model of organic maintenance, theorists have sought to understand temporal experience by locating identities of form within the flow of events. But change can itself be understood as an organizing principle; change can be progress rather than chaos. The model of growth sees change as movement toward an end. Organisms, for example, not only maintain a formal identity across

5

the whole of their lives but also display a pattern of growth. Earlier experiences are linked to later as immature stages to mature stages within a single pattern of development.

The model of growth is exemplified in social institutions, as well as individuals. One can speak of the growth of a church, a political party, a civilization—or a constitutional system. On this model, the Constitution is located neither in the bare text nor in a past moment of birth but in a steadily maturing political order. The Constitution, on this model, grows along with the nation.

The final conceptual model of order is that of community—the community of discourse, in particular. The model of community describes the relation between self and other that emerges in a serious, sustained conversation about values or a proposed course of action. Community members do not enter such a conversation with an unalterable set of commitments or an established agenda. Rather, commitments and agenda are formed in and through the conversation. Self-identity is at issue: who the speakers are depends upon the outcome of the discourse. Discourse is thus an exercise in the simultaneous construction of self and community. These are related to each other as speaker and speech; both exist only in and through the other. To understand constitutionalism on this model requires the specification of the institutional locus of the community of discourse within the organized political order and an analysis of authority as a product of the ongoing conversation.

Each of these conceptual models of order is available to, and informs, ordinary experience. The models characterize not different domains of empirical experience but different understandings of that experience. A church, for example, can be understood as a made object, based perhaps on the divine intuition of its founder. It can also be understood as an object to be maintained in the original form brought forth at its birth or as a growing institution. Finally, a church could be described as a community bound together through the ongoing discourse of its members.

Each model is always available to impose order on phenomena that are the object of understanding, but they do not all enter American constitutionalism at the same time and with the same force. The dominant voice in the constitutional discourse of a particular period tends to develop only one of these models. This is not to say that the others are wholly excluded but that a surprising proportion of the discourse in a period can be organized around a particular model. Tracing the presence and power of these models within U.S. constitutional history will reveal new unities, as well as oppositions.

Properly describing and understanding the movement of constitutional discourse from one conceptual model to another will also disclose a great deal about the general character of, and possibilities for, self-government. The history of U.S. constitutional theory offers the longest sustained inquiry into the possibility of self-government available for study. Possibility here refers to theory, not political events. Self-government is first of all an idea, not a discrete set of political circumstances. A look at the wide variety of regimes that call themselves democratic shows that self-government is always a contested concept. The conceptual models that I describe frame the theoretical possibilities of self-government.

My claim that American constitutionalism demonstrates a coherent pattern of intellectual development will, no doubt, be controversial. Even so, I have a philosophical ambition that goes beyond intellectual history and description: not only can a logic in the history of constitutional discourse be discerned retrospectively, but that logic, I will argue, has shaped the development of constitutional theory. The discourse of U.S. constitutionalism, with its deep conceptual structure, has been driven by intellectual, rather than social or political, necessity. The life of constitutional discourse has been as much logic as experience.

Two caveats are immediately in order. First, conceptual necessity does not carry with it a guarantee of success. Saying that the discourse had to proceed in a certain fashion takes it for granted that it proceeded. For reasons entirely apart from the logic of political discourse, the constitutional enterprise could have ended at any time. I am not, for example, making any claims about the necessity of particular political or military outcomes. The American revolution could have gone the way of the French. I am talking only about the manner in which Americans understand their experience, not the material content of that experience. Necessity refers to the conceptual order they bring to experience, not divine providence in the history of the nation.

Second, conceptual necessity determines the broad stages of development, not the timing of change. It is not a matter of predicting when one conceptual model will be displaced by another—or even of understanding in retrospect why change has to occur at any given moment. My aim, instead, is to understand the manner in which the discourse could advance in light of the problems inherent in the conceptual model dominating the constitutionalism of a particular period. The discourse could, as a theoretical matter, have become stuck at any one place indefinitely, just as the whole enterprise could have been defeated by social, political, or military disaster. The constitutional history of the United States is particularly interesting because constitutional theorists collectively have had long enough to overcome hesitancies and missteps and to advance through the full range of what one might call the logic of self-government within the historical state. That two hundred years has been long enough is not a consequence of theory. I have no idea whether it would be long enough elsewhere or, for that matter, whether the conversation could proceed far more quickly under other political circumstances.

My central concern remains answering the question, How is it possible to have self-government under the conditions of temporality that characterize the state? I look to the development of constitutional theory not to re-present the answers already obtained but to analyze the conceptual conditions that make an answer possible.

My answer is disappointing. Under the conditions of temporality within which any state exists, self-government is not possible. The dialectical course of constitutional theory does lead to a model that envisions the possibility of a community within which the autonomous self and the authoritative voice are identical, but this model cannot support the actual state. Theory and authority break apart. In the idea of a discursive community, theory has turned back upon itself. Theorists have taken their own discursive activity as a model for political authority. Constitutional self-government has merged with the discussion about self-government. Theory has reached its end, but in doing so, it has left the domain of law an actual, operating system of authority.

No one lives in that state of grace in which all government is self-government, in which the voice of authority is nothing other than the voice of the self. People cannot live like that as long as they live within history. To say that the constitutional state cannot support a claim of legitimate self-government is not a counsel of despair; it is not a justification of indifference to the character of political authority or a suggestion that all assertions of authority have the same normative value. Self-government is just one norm by which to measure the state. Justice remains separate and distinct.

The practical lesson in this book, if any, is that we should worry less about democratic legitimacy and more about justice in our thinking about power. Democratically organized states may generally be more just than other states under certain conditions. They may also be less just. We should act accordingly and not be distracted by a search for legitimacy that cannot ultimately be satisfied.

CHAPTER ONE

To Make a Constitution

To refer to the political life of the United States as an experiment in self-government is a commonplace. What it means today is that government policies are subject to trial and error. If a policy does not work, it will be revised or replaced. Government is experimental because it is a process of learning from mistakes and advancing incrementally toward the achievement of specified ends. This understanding of the experimental quality of government is implicit in descriptions of the states as "laboratories for the development of new social, economic and political ideas."[1] Each state learns from the successes and failures of policy innovations in all the other states.

There is, however, another sense in which political life can be considered experimental. Instead of looking to the tentative character of the outcome of an experiment, one can look at the internal structure of an experiment. To act experimentally is not simply to keep open the possibility of future revisions of current plans and activities. An experiment has a conceptual shape from the very beginning. It represents a particular relation between an acting subject and a manipulated object. An experimenter transforms an object by reference to an abstract idea. The idea, which may actually be an entire theory, provides the measure for the experimenter's manipulation of the object.

When the framers of the Constitution referred to the experimental quality of political life, they had this conceptual structure in mind, not the tentative character of their work product. They meant that those who shape the political order must measure their actions by a science of politics. In conceiving of an experiment in *self*-government, the framers envisioned a special relation between the acting subject and the object acted upon. The people would have to be both subject and object of the political experiment. They would have to take themselves as an object for their own transformation. This relation between the people as subject and the people as object had to be mediated by a set of abstract ideas about true or correct government. The people would have to give shape to themselves through their own understanding of the science of politics.

The relation of the subject to each of the other terms of an experiment can be considered separately. In a political experiment, the relation of the acting subject to the abstract idea is one of deliberation. The political experiment begins with deliberation about the correct ends of government and the most appropriate means of reaching those ends. Without adequate deliberation, the experiment will lack direction. The relation of the subject to the object of a political experiment, in contrast, is one of choice. The subject chooses to transform the object based upon deliberation. Without fully articulated choice, the object is likely to slip from the control of the subject. For the subject, therefore, acting experimentally is a process of both deliberation and choice.

If politics is to be experimental, the political life of a nation must be based on deliberation and choice. More specifically, if self-government is to be experimental, then the people themselves must be able to deliberate about the best form of government and choose to act on the basis of that deliberation.

An experimental politics stands in sharp contrast to two other ideas on the basis of political order: nature and accident. The political life of the nation can be approached as if it were a product of nature. It can, in that case, be explained by reference to causal sequences, quite independent of any process of deliberation or act of choice. For example, theories that explain political order as a product of economic relations or geography use such a causal model. Alternatively, the political order can be seen as simply a result of accidents—for example, the idiosyncracies of personal leadership and the chance of battle. Such an explanation again operates independently of considerations of scientific deliberation and choice. These contrasting models of nature, accident, and experiment were just the terms within which the framers conceived of the project of making a constitution. Without an experimental politics of deliberation and choice, the nation would drift between the forces of nature and of accident.

Political independence was linked in the Declaration of Independence and the Constitution to the experimental character of government. The Declaration speaks of the "Right of the People to alter or to abolish [a

form of government], and to institute new Government, laying its foundation on such principles and organizing its powers in such form, as to them
shall seem most likely to effect their Safety and Happiness." A right to alter
or abolish points to the possibility of choice, while the selection of a new
foundation suggests a need for deliberation. Similarly, the Constitution
grandly announces that it, too, is the product of "We the People" acting to
achieve a deliberate end. A written constitution is an explicit statement that
political order is a product of neither nature nor accident. A constitution is
a made object, constructed on the basis of a set of beliefs about how governmental order is most likely to produce safety and happiness.

The assumption in both documents is that the people exist apart
from their political organization—that political organization is an object
to be formed by the people acting as a free subject. In both documents,
subject and object are linked by a set of ideas, which the subject brings
to the object and which are the particular concern of the documents. The
increasing realization that a science was needed to inform those ideas
brought the movement from the principles set forth in the Declaration
of Independence to the articulate structure of government set forth in the
Constitution. The people may have an inherent right to alter or abolish,
but without political science, what "to them shall seem most likely to
effect their Safety and Happiness" is not likely to do so in practice.

In the history of U.S. constitutionalism, the relation between political science and political freedom was most directly the focus of attention
at the moment of the founding. The interaction between these two concepts provides the drama of the foundational text of constitutional law:
The Federalist.[2] The antagonists of this drama can be variously characterized as political science and political legitimacy, reason and will, or truth
and consent. This drama represents an effort to link the modern idea of
self-government to one of the very oldest conceptual models of order: that
of the artisan who makes an object by looking to an abstract idea. Art in
this sense of making refers to a technical practice, not the aesthetic imagination. Artisans, including political artisans, can make objects because
they possess a science, which is more than an opinion and wholly other
than imagination. An experiment in self-government requires an entire
nation of political artisans.

The Federalist: Self-Construction in a Nation of Political Scientists

The political theory of The Federalist has been the topic of considerable debate recently. Two schools of constitutional theory—the repub-

lican and the pluralist—have each claimed to find support in the text.[3] The republican reading emphasizes Publius's concern with deliberation among government representatives. Deliberation is critical, they argue, because Publius believed that the purpose of constitutional governance is discernment of, and action toward, the public good, which stands apart from immediate private interests.

The pluralist reading, in contrast, emphasizes Publius's concern with free expression of the will. The pluralists see no distinction in kind between public and private ends, only a distinction in the process of selection. For pluralists, all ends are a product of will—to be an end is simply to be the object of someone's will. Publius's system of constitutional governance, according to them, was based upon competition and compromise among private interest groups. Publius's achievement was the invention of political institutions that could stabilize and give order to the competition.

Both readings miss the real drama of the work and substitute another one for it: the contemporary conflict between liberalism and the emerging communitarian challenge to liberalism.[4] The liberal reading finds in Publius's theory a concept of individual freedom under which each person determines his or her own ends on the basis of personal values. Politics, for the liberal Publius, is a means of accommodating private interests to maintain public order. The republicans attack the liberals' concept of the self and individual freedom. Their Publius, accordingly, emphasizes the priority of a public good discovered through public deliberation.

These one-sided accounts of Publius's vision misconceive the original project of constitutionalism in the United States. For the framers, reason and will are both required in a well-ordered republic. Without consent, scientific government can claim no legitimate place in political life.[5] Without science, however, popular government will be bad government. What is worse, without science the principle of self-determination will paradoxically lead to a government that violates that very principle. This cycle of political instability was described in classical political thought and that description was obviously present in the mind of Publius.[6]

For Publius, the only way to break out of the cycle was to bring science to popular government. The problem was not to choose between reason and will but to reach a synthesis. Science and legitimacy could achieve a marriage by seizing the unique historical opportunity presented in the postrevolutionary period. The nation had to become a community of political artisans forming itself on the basis of a shared science.

Deliberation and the Unity of Political and Psychological Order

The first page of *The Federalist* contains the following observation: "It has been frequently remarked that it seems to have been reserved to the people of this country, by their conduct and example, to decide the important question, whether societies of men are really capable or not of establishing good government from reflection and choice, or whether they are forever destined to depend for their political constitutions on accident and force." Here, reflection and choice are contrasted with accident and force. An experiment is a choice based on reflection. The immediate end of the constitutional enterprise, of which *The Federalist* is a part, is to make political life experimental: a constitutional order should be chosen on the basis of reflection; it should free itself from accident and force.[7]

The experimental character of the constitutional project reappears at a higher level of generality in Publius's opening remark, when he suggests that the political life of the country will test a larger idea that is independent of the reflection on, and choice of, a particular constitutional order. The introduction of this larger theory is marked by the subtle recharacterization of the audience to whom the argument is addressed. *The Federalist* opens with the following admonition: "After an unequivocal experience of the inefficiency of the subsisting federal government, *you* are called upon to *deliberate* on a new Constitution for the United States of America." The "you" is narrowly the citizens of New York. As the paragraph continues, the "you" becomes "the people of this country." Just as quickly, it expands into all "societies of men." The reader is simultaneously the citizen of New York, this nation, and all nations. At issue in the admonition, therefore, is the "fate of an empire in many respects the most interesting in the world."[8]

Thus, the text is simultaneously a part of a particular political debate and the presentation of a general theory on the nature of political order. The general theory concerns the character of political freedom. If societies cannot make political choices on the basis of reflection, then political freedom will cease to exist.[9] Political history, in that case, would never be other than an account of accident and force. Curiously, the possibility of a space for political freedom depends upon the successful exercise of that freedom. The important question, Publius emphasizes, is whether societies of men can establish a domain of political freedom by choosing a political life on the basis of reflection. Because the possibility of freedom is at stake, the outcome of the experiment is the most interesting in the world.

The two terms introduced in this general theory—*reflection* and *choice*—set the framework for the analysis that follows in *The Federalist*.

Within that framework, reflection precedes choice in two senses. First, political choice must be based on reflection. The successful exercise of free choice depends upon the successful development of a science of politics. In part, the U.S. experience was most interesting because only lately had politics emerged from "the gloomy age of Ignorance and Superstition."[10] Second, reflection must encompass choice as a subject of political theory. That is, a reflection on political order must be self-reflective: it must explain the appropriate relation between choice and reflection in politics. The higher-order theory, of which U.S. constitutionalism should provide experimental verification, was just such a reflection on the relation of reflection to choice in popular self-government. A full analysis of *The Federalist* must place the constitutional experiment of 1787 within the larger context of this higher-order theory.

Popular self-government appears in the first line of the work. "You" are called upon to deliberate because all legitimate political order is self-imposed. Publius writes that "the people are the only legitimate fountain of power."[11] Yet Publius immediately links self-government to deliberation—to reason. "You" are not just called upon to choose but to *deliberate*. Legitimate government will not be "good" government without successful deliberation.

In this opening statement, Publius suggests that political legitimacy and political truth are not identical. The plan of the constitutional convention may be "correct"—a political construction properly derived from true political principles discovered by political science—even if it is rejected by the larger community. Scientific truth may be difficult to grasp, but it is not contingent upon acceptance by the community.[12] Conversely, legitimate government—government based on consent—is not necessarily good government. Majorities can act just as badly as minorities. That political action is freely chosen is no guarantee of its moral worth.

Publius introduces the idea of political deliberation with a warning: "The plan offered to our deliberations affects too many particular interests, innovates upon too many local institutions, not to involve in its discussion a variety of objects foreign to its merits, and of views, passions, and prejudices little favorable to the discovery of truth." He proposes, in response, mutual deliberation upon the nature of government. Deliberation must be freed from the passions and prejudices of the everyday self. Only if that break occurs will deliberation be an exercise in "[t]he science of politics," the end of which is the discovery of truth.[13]

The Federalist initially links political science to freedom in the act of self-denial that is required for successful deliberation. It does so again at the moment of choice. Publius affirms not simply an objective political science but also the possibility of choice based upon that science. The success of the project requires freedom in both dimensions: free thought (reason) and free choice (will). Accordingly, Publius usually links wisdom and virtue, which reflect excellence in both dimensions: "Happy will it be for ourselves, and most honorable for human nature, if we have wisdom and virtue enough to set so glorious an example to mankind!"[14]

This description of Publius's project emphasizes the interrelation of political and psychological phenomena within the argument of *The Federalist*. The political project of discerning and constructing the correct political order rests upon the psychological capacity to transcend "passions, and prejudices little favorable to the discovery of truth." Wisdom and virtue are simultaneously psychological qualities and political capacities. For Publius, the political order necessarily reflects the psychological character of the populace: "But what is government itself but the greatest of all reflections on human nature?" When Publius writes that republican government has a unique need for virtue among its citizens, the statement describes, as well as provides normative support for, republicanism.[15]

The psychological virtue required by republican government is the capacity to deliberate upon and choose a course of action based upon its reasonableness. If people cannot be virtuous in this sense, then there can be no free politics: either reflection or choice will be captured by force and accident. This virtue is required of everyone in the founding act of constitutionalism, of the voters in their periodic deliberations on and choice of representatives, and of representatives in the ordinary course of governing.

The dichotomy of passion and reason—the conflicting bases of choice—has, therefore, a psychological and a political manifestation.[16] As a problem of psychological order, the dichotomy appears as the difference between apparent and true interests. As a problem of political order, it appears as the difference between action in pursuit of private interest, which Publius labels "factious," and action for the public good. The psychological and the political are different perspectives on the same problem. Thus Publius writes: "Happy will it be if our choice should be directed by a judicious estimate of our true interests, unperplexed and unbiased by considerations not connected with the public good." The public good corresponds to the true interests of the individual precisely because both are a function of reason—both are discerned by the wise and chosen by the virtuous. Apparent interests are peculiarly private because they are determined by the individual's passions. Their political manifestation results in a factionalizing of political life. If will is captured by passion, then neither political nor psychological order will be achieved.[17]

To achieve a political order structured by reason and not by private passions requires that the psychological faculties of the citizenry be properly ordered. But their ordering, in turn, depends upon a proper political order. This reciprocity between politics and psychology is captured in Publius's admonition that "it is the reason, alone, of the public, that ought to control and regulate the government. The passions ought to be controlled and regulated by government."[18] A wise and virtuous citizenry will demand republican government, just as republican government demands wise and virtuous citizens. Conversely, a citizenry that lacks wisdom and virtue will have little interest in republican government, nor will the various forms of autocratic government have any interest in wise and virtuous citizens. Progress must occur simultaneously in the psychological and political domains, or it will not occur at all.

Only a revolutionary moment can break the circle of a political and psychological order founded on passion. At such a moment, individual virtue emerges outside the ordinary forms of politics. A political crisis can create the possibility of public deliberation and of choice based upon that deliberation, even in the absence of a government that controls and regulates passions:

[Constitutional] experiments are of too ticklish a nature to be unnecessarily multiplied. We are to recollect that all the existing constitutions [of the states] were formed in the midst of a danger which repressed the passions most unfriendly to order and concord; of an enthusiastic confidence of the people in their patriotic leaders, which stifled the ordinary diversity of opinions on great national questions; of a universal ardor for new and opposite forms, produced by a universal resentment and indignation against the ancient government; and whilst no spirit of party connected with the changes to be made, or the abuses to be reformed, could mingle its leaven in the operation.[19]

The uniqueness of these constitutional occasions is emphasized in Publius's rejection of Thomas Jefferson's suggestion that a new constitution provide for frequent appeals to the people—the only legitimate fountain of power—to correct political errors. Jefferson, according to Publius, has confused legitimacy and truth. The people may be the only legitimate source of power, but they are not ordinarily an appropriate source for the correct resolution of political conflict. Most of the time, the resolution of issues referred to the public "could never be expected to turn on the true merits of the question. ... The *passions* ... not the *reason*, of the public would sit in judgment."[20] Publius's general theory of political freedom, then, requires extraordinary action in the face of ordinary self-interest.

Publius's effort in *The Federalist* is to manage and to sustain an extraordinary political opportunity.

Constitutional politics thus paradigmatically links psychological and political order: in this political form, deliberation can become the basis for effective political choice. The revolutionary moment creates the possibility of a successful, deliberative constitutional politics: "I have had an eye, my fellow citizens, to putting you upon your guard against all attempts, from whatever quarter, to influence your decision in a matter of the utmost moment to your welfare by any impressions other than those which may result from the *evidence of truth*." Through mutual deliberation, truth appeals to reason, not to "[a]mbition, avarice, personal animosity [and] party opposition." Deliberation must become an actual political program if freedom is to be realized in societies of men.[21]

Will and a Nation of Political Artisans

Publius's appreciation of the psychological consequences of the Revolution and of the political possibilities that these created points to a fundamental presumption of the political theory in *The Federalist:* the new science of politics cannot remain in the possession of a few statesmen but must extend to the entire nation. *The Federalist* does not, after all, argue for deference to the Philadelphia Convention because of the scientific credentials of its participants.[22] Rather, Publius immediately integrates the convention and its product into the larger project of *The Federalist,* which is to address "the important question, whether societies of men are really capable or not of establishing good government from reflection and choice." From this perspective, the issue is not the scientific character of the proposed scheme of government but, rather, the capacity of the people to choose that scheme of government because it is a product of science.

Publius thus relocates science from the convention to the larger body politic.[23] The important question concerns the capacity of an entire society to realize political freedom through an act of self-government founded on scientific insight. *The Federalist* centers on the creation of an entire nation of political artisans: Can a nation make itself on the basis of science? The goal is to achieve popular legitimation of an objectively true political order, to found popular choice on popular, though still genuine, wisdom.

The Federalist casts the drama of political construction upon the modern nation-state. The body politic has grown, but more important, the modern nation-state rests upon a particular understanding of political legitimacy. Political legitimacy depends upon the consent of the governed: "The fabric of American empire ought to rest on the solid basis of THE

CONSENT OF THE PEOPLE. The streams of national power ought to flow immediately from that pure, original fountain of all legitimate authority."[24]

Classical thinkers had no distinct concept of the will.[25] Without a separation of the faculties of reason and will, they had no way to formulate the problem of political legitimacy separately from the issue of political truth. The philosopher-king of Plato's *Republic*, for example, is entitled to rule by virtue of his possession of political truth. The discovery of the faculty of will provided a new perspective on, and a new value for, democratic political life, which classical theorists could see only as a model of political order—or disorder—completely devoid of the in-forming art of political science.[26] The challenge of modern popular democracy to classical political science was precisely the question raised by Publius: Can reason and will be brought together in the modern nation-state, or must a choice always be made between good government and legitimate government?

The discovery of will and its implications for popular sovereignty had a profound effect on the character of political deliberation. For classical philosophers, theoretical deliberation required the confined setting of the academy. For Publius, the deliberative community expanded to include the entire body politic. This is the startling difference between the ancient science of politics and the new one.[27] The new science of politics confronts the modern vision of political equality. The social contract must share the original position with the founders' science. Nowhere in the modern idea of the political community is there a place for the founder who stands as an authoritative lawgiver outside the community.[28] Rather, the entire community is to in-form itself through scientific deliberation and free choice. The entire community is simultaneously the artisan and the object of the art of politics.

Optimistic though he was, Publius fully realized the dangers of the project. The opening of *The Federalist No. 10* makes clear that popular government is not necessarily good government. Publius explains that "our governments are too unstable . . . the public good is disregarded in the conflicts of rival parties . . . measures are too often decided, not according to the rules of justice and the rights of the minor party, but by the superior force of an interested and overbearing majority." Majorities are not necessarily virtuous, but popular government is necessarily majoritarian. Democratic disorder, moreover, is not an aberration of politics in the United States. Historically, he says, popular government has not been a successful form of political order.[29]

This historical reflection, together with the politicopsychological analysis that distinguishes reason from will, and political science from political legitimacy, inevitably raises the question of why Publius was committed to the priority of will over reason in political life. If Publius believed that the Philadelphia Convention could reach political truth and that reason and the public good coincide, why subject that objective truth to a national debate that could reject truth and the public good in favor of private interests? Could a truthful end justify an illegitimate means? While Rousseau argues that people can be forced to be free, Publius suggests that a free people cannot be forced to be politically good, even if the cost is their own freedom. Why introduce the possibility of political error through the process of popular ratification?[30]

In one respect, this question represents a category mistake: the new science of politics was a science of republican government, a principle of which is that political order must be subject to popular consent. This answer, however, simply introduces the old conundrum of what to do when the people vote to remove consent from politics or vote to remove any other necessary condition of *good* republican government. Faced with that possibility, the founder could have chosen to apply the principles of political science to achieve a second-best political form—here, a political form that did not rely upon consent.

Practically, Publius believed that a convergence of legitimate and good government was possible at this particular moment in the political life of the country. Accordingly, he presented an argument that would aid in the accomplishment of this end. Even if he had been less confident, Publius did not see much likelihood of achieving the alternative of an illegitimate good government—some variety of aristocratic government— in the postrevolutionary period. American government, Publius wrote, must be "strictly republican" because "no other form would be reconcilable with the genius of the people of America; with the fundamental principles of the Revolution; or with that honorable determination which animates every votary of freedom to rest all our political experiments on the capacity of mankind for self-government."[31] Publius is suggesting that practical options are limited because the war was fought under the legitimating norm of freedom. The experience of the war and its accompanying political crisis created an ethic of political liberty. The commitment to republican government was rooted in the unique historical experience of the nation and the peculiar cultural and political values that accompanied it. This historical material must be shaped by the art of politics. Thus, the nation must find "a republican remedy for the diseases most incident to republican government" or continue to suffer the disorders of popular government.[32] There is no practical alternative.

Apart from the constraints of practical politics in 1787, the best answer to this question was given not by Publius but by James Wilson, who was probably second only to James Madison in his influence and prestige among the framers. Wilson's understanding of constitutionalism generally parallels Publius's. Like Publius, Wilson links the founding to the development of a new science of politics. This allows a politics that is determined by neither force nor accident:

[T]he science even of government itself seems yet to be almost in its state of infancy. Governments, in general, have been the result of force, of fraud, and of accident. After a period of six thousand years has elapsed since the creation, the United States exhibit to the world the first instance ... of a nation, unattacked by external force, unconvulsed by domestick insurrections, assembling voluntarily, deliberating fully, and deciding calmly, concerning that system of government, under which they would wish that they and their posterity should live.[33]

Like Publius, he sees the founding as simultaneously a political phenomenon and a psychological one, in which the common issue is the subordination of individual passion to reason. The problem to be "cured" through the founding is the spread of "licentiousness." The cure can be achieved through "progressive steps in improving the knowledge of government, and [thus] increasing the happiness of society and mankind."[34]

This experiment in popular self-creation through the application of political science to the organization of the political order is for Wilson, as for Publius, an experiment of universal significance: "The great struggle for liberty in this country, should it be unsuccessful, will probably be the last one which she will have for her existence and prosperity, in any part of the globe." Finally, Wilson, too, believes that the exercise of the science of politics is limited by the historically determined character of the populace: "The citizens of the United States, however different in some other respects, are well known to agree in one strongly marked feature of their character—a warm and keen sense of freedom and independence. This sense has been heightened by the glorious result of their late struggle."[35]

Wilson's thought moves in a somewhat different dimension from Publius's, however, when he insists on linking political participation and consent not just to a psychology of order but to moral development as well. Participation is more than a right that may be exercised well or poorly; it is a step in the moral development of the individual. Thus, in the opening of his *Lectures on Law,* Wilson writes that "law and liberty cannot rationally become the objects of our love, unless they first become the objects of our knowledge."[36] The deliberative engagement in the science of politics changes the objects of love and thereby moral character.

Deliberation is linked to virtue not just as the ground of choice but also as the source of character.

Wilson specifically links a founding on "principles of freedom" to "advances in virtue and excellence." Conversely, a "[g]overnment founded on improper principles . . . has a powerful and pernicious bias both upon those who rule, and those who are ruled." Wilson goes on to link direct popular participation in government to the development of the full panoply of moral virtues, including a habit of "liberal investigation and disinterested conduct" and of "governing . . . actions by the result of . . . deliberations." Popular participation will also result in "a lively sensibility to the interests of [the] country," as well as in an effort to satisfy "[t]he love of honest and well-earned fame."[37]

Wilson, then, draws the moral consequences from Publius's identification of psychological and political phenomena. Not only right theory and practical history constrain the act of political self-construction; anything less than self-government would represent a failure to make use of the opportunity for moral development that politics presents. For precisely this reason, Wilson sees government as an expression of the fallen state of humanity and self-government as the manner and method of moral recovery: "Government is, indeed, highly necessary; but it is highly necessary to a fallen state." Here he repeats a Publian theme: "If men were angels, no government would be necessary." For Publius and Wilson, recovery begins with knowledge in both politics and morals.[38]

The Construction of Political Freedom

Reason and will, deliberation and choice, converge in Publius's thought. The convergence is achieved by projecting the model of a scientifically grounded art of political construction onto an active citizenry.[39] Self-conscious realization of freedom of the will is accordingly only a first step in making a new political order. The separation of the political order from the natural, causal order merely opens up the possibility of an art of politics. The goal of this art is to make a political order that is both good and free, both scientifically correct and politically legitimate. Successful self-government requires the entire community to participate in this art, to understand itself as both an acting subject and a made object, linked by the principles of a science.

The science of politics reveals that popular governments are prone to problems of faction: "The friend of popular governments never finds himself so much alarmed for their character and fate as when he contemplates their propensity to this dangerous vice." The answer to this political problem must be found in a "well-constructed Union."[40] The answer lies, in other words, in the art of political construction. Popular governments failed in the past precisely because consent was considered an adequate substitute for reason.[41]

Publius defines democracy as "a society consisting of a small number of citizens, who assemble and administer the government in person." He defines republican government as "a government which derives all its powers directly or indirectly from the great body of the people, and is administered by persons holding their offices during pleasure for a limited period, or during good behavior." Democracy and republicanism are both forms of self-government and are, therefore, equally legitimate political orders. Democracy differs from republicanism in the directness with which the people govern themselves.[42]

The advantages of republicanism over democracy are found in this element of indirectness, which opens a place for the art of political construction. The material upon which this art works is the indirect element of republican self-government. Lacking this material, pure democracy does not allow for the constructive efforts of the political artisan. Democracy is power without form—politically legitimate power to be sure, but without any internal form capable of resisting abuse. Accordingly, it can "admit of no cure for the mischiefs of faction."[43] Political science may begin, but it cannot end, with a theory of consent.

The art of political construction moves in two dimensions. First, the nature of public participation must be molded. Self-government requires that power flow from the people, but the people can be variously organized. They can act directly or indirectly, or as members of larger or smaller groups. Publius's classic argument for a system of representatives elected from large districts reflects this branch of the art. Second, the structure of government itself—the offices of government—must be formed. To say that government must be republican does not say much about the distribution and character of offices within that government. This branch of the art leads to Publius's defense of federalism and the separation of powers.

Only when both the populace and the government operate within a properly constructed order will republican government, which is always legitimate, also be good, correct, and true. Ironically, the threat to popular government comes from those who would keep government close to the people. Direct popular control and decentralization represent unconstructed power, or power without art. A popular political life without art will inevitably succumb to opinion, appetite, and private interests. The antifederalist's fear that centralized authority will be a brake on popular sovereignty is countered by the argument that only a properly constructed, centralized authority can fully realize popular sovereignty.

For Publius, the possibility of eliminating faction rests on the possibility of displacing subjective individual opinions by a science of politics. Publius does not suggest that opinion can be wholly replaced by science: "[A] nation of philosophers is as little to be expected as the philosophical race of kings wished for by Plato."[44] No polity can operate constantly on the basis of assent to scientific knowledge. But the existence of a polity that is both well-constructed and legitimate depends upon a society operating on that basis at the founding moment.[45] If science can *never* displace opinion, then the whole project of *The Federalist* is undermined.

In spite of the constructions of the political art, republican government exists under the threat of passion and opinion at every level and at all times. This is the public, political appearance of the battle between reason and passion in the human soul. Publius summarizes this situation, as well as the presuppositions of republican government, in the following lines: "As there is a degree of depravity in mankind which requires a certain degree of circumspection and distrust, so there are other qualities in human nature which justify a certain portion of esteem and confidence. Republican government presupposes the existence of these qualities in a higher degree than any other form." But the supply of virtue and wisdom is not endless: "Enlightened statesmen will not always be at the helm." Political order cannot always cure the diseases of the soul. A properly structured system of representation and participation cannot guarantee political success. Thus, Publius's argument for an extended republic concludes only that structural innovation makes it "*less probable* that a majority of the whole will have a common motive to invade the rights of other citizens; or if such a common motive exists, it will be *more difficult* for all who feel it to discover their own strength and to act in unison." The populace may elect interested representatives (tyranny of the majority), or the legislature may choose to act in its own self-interest (simple tyranny). In either case, objective reason is displaced by personal opinion, and choice is guided by passion. Political tyranny begins and ends with the corruption of the right order in the soul.[46]

The Invention of Judicial Review

The dual sources of constitutionalism were carried forward in the post-ratification period. Reason and will provided the easy lines along which political debate could polarize yet remain within the boundaries of a common constitutional discourse. Even the key issue of whether the development of constitutional law would be a function of popular movements or expert judicial knowledge expressed this tension.[47] The sharpest and most important expression of Publius's conceptual model of political order as an art founded on a science is in the jurisprudence of Chief Justice John Marshall. He established an institutional structure—judicial review—that reflected an understanding of the founding as the successful convergence of reason and will.

This understanding of constitutionalism was not without challenge in the early history of the Supreme Court. The point of vulnerability was always the place of science in the making of the Constitution. Early on, for example, Justice James Iredell argued that abstract political science can play no useful role in judicial decision making, because there is no such science: "The ideas of natural justice are regulated by no fixed standard: the ablest and the purest men have differed upon the subject; and all that the Court could properly say . . . would be, that the Legislature (possessed of an equal right of opinion) had passed an act which, in the opinion of the judges, was inconsistent with the abstract principles of natural justice."[48] Iredell reduces Publius's claim to science to an opinion, upon which able and pure men may disagree. Publius considered opinion the source of faction; without science, no distinction could be made between the public good and tyranny of the majority. Iredell's denial of science, then, is a denial of the entire project of *The Federalist*. But Marshall, not Iredell, came to dominate the Court.

In *Marbury v. Madison*, Marshall provided the secure foundation for the practice and doctrine of judicial review.[49] Marshall still lived within the unity of the founding moment, when reason and will produced a government that was both correct and legitimate. Even though *Marbury* is still taught as the foundation for judicial review, the understanding of political order that grounded the decision has not survived. The post-*Marbury* generations have inherited the institution of power without the constitutional understanding to which it gave expression. Because of this loss, judicial review has been the troubled object of constitutional theory ever since. In each period in the development of constitutionalism, there has been a struggle to reconcile this institution with the current understanding of the meaning of constitutionalism.

Chief Justice Marshall: Political Science and Judicial Review

Judicial review regularly requires the Supreme Court to measure an assertion of governmental authority against some constitutional limit. Formally, in *Marbury* the Court did just this, considering the constitutionality of section 13 of the Judiciary Act of 1789, which it interpreted to provide original jurisdiction in the Court for a particular form of judicial action called a mandamus. The expansion of jurisdiction was held to be inconsistent with the strict jurisdictional limits that the Court found in the Constitution. This question of the constitutional limits on congressional authority to expand the Court's jurisdiction was only an introduction to the larger issue of the role of the courts in delineating constitutional limits on governmental authority. The real subject of Marshall's inquiry was the constitutional place of such a judicial inquiry.

To make clear that the real issue is the role of judicial inquiry itself, and not the constitutionality of section 13 of the Judiciary Act, Marshall purposely ignores the interpretive difficulties that attach even to the narrow jurisdictional question—difficulties similar to those that characterize virtually all subsequent instances of judicial review. He says section 13 conflicts with "the plain import of the words" of article III. This surely is not true.[50] Denying the interpretive difficulties, however, allows Marshall to focus on judicial review itself; it allows him to shift attention from the Congress to the Court. *Marbury* is an effort at constitutional self-consciousness in which the object of review and the process of review are one and the same.

Marshall starts his discussion of judicial review with an inquiry into abstract political science, wholly independent of the particular written text and its history: "It seems only necessary to recognize certain principles, supposed to have been long and well established." The first of these fundamental principles is "[t]hat the people have an original right to establish, for their future government, such principles as, in their opinion, shall most conduce to their own happiness." From this first principle, which Marshall calls "the basis on which the whole American fabric has been erected," certain propositions follow. Specifically, a hierarchical relation between the Constitution and statutory law can be deduced: "[T]he theory of every such government [which possesses a written constitution] must be, that an act of the legislature, repugnant to the constitution, is void." This is true, he argues, as a matter of logic. Any other view would lead to a logical contradiction: "there is no middle ground" between constitutional supremacy and an approach that would make legislative acts superior to the Constitution. And the latter view would render written constitutions "absurd."[51]

Having deduced this theory of constitutional supremacy from first principles alone, Marshall then turns to the function of the courts: "If an act of the legislature, repugnant to the constitution, is void, does it, notwithstanding its invalidity, bind the courts?" Again, the inquiry relies upon abstract principles of political science. Marshall writes that "[i]t is emphatically the province and duty of the judicial department to say what the law is." This statement is not about the constitutional text or the original intent behind the creation of judicial authority in article III. Rather, it defines the judicial function per se; it explains what it is to be a court. Because he is offering an abstract definition, Marshall accounts for his claim by appealing once again to logical deduction: "Those who apply the rule to particular cases, must of necessity expound and interpret that rule." Necessity here has nothing to do with the positive law; he is referring to the necessities of the republican science of government.[52]

Because the Constitution is law, Marshall argues, the courts will confront conflicts between this law and ordinary legislation. Resolution of such conflicts "is of the very essence of judicial duty." Why? Not because the text says so or because this understanding of the judicial role is supported by the ratification debates. Rather, any other view would "subvert the very foundation of all written constitutions." Any other view would be logically inconsistent with the fundamental principles of political order established by a written constitution. A society that had a written constitution yet denied courts the role of judicial review would be living a contradiction: "It would be giving to the legislature a practical and real omnipotence, with the same breath which professes to restrict their powers within narrow limits."[53]

Marshall has established judicial review from a first principle—the "people have an original right to establish [principles] for their future government"—and a definition of the judicial role. His argument is, so far, simply an exercise in the new science of politics. It speaks to the judicial function in any constitutional republic, not to any unique U.S. constitutional requirements. He has said nothing about either the constitutional text—except that there is one—or the history of that text. He has not spoken of the distribution of powers established by the Constitution, only of certain kinds of institutional authority in the abstract.

At the founding moment, this argument might have been sufficient to explain the constitutional role of the Supreme Court in the proposed scheme of government. In fact, it is largely Publius's argument from *The Federalist*.[54] The task of 1787 was to convince the people that these propositions were elements of a science of politics, which should form the basis of a new constitutional order to be put in place by an act of popular self-government. But 1803 was not 1787. Ratification had been accomplished, and the process of maintaining that which had been made had begun. An argument based upon the science of politics now had to come to terms with the actual founding. This requirement is marked in *Marbury* by the sudden turn from abstract deduction to narrow textualism: "[T]he peculiar expressions of the constitution of the United States furnish additional arguments in favor of its [the doctrine denying judicial review] rejection."[55]

Marshall now looks to specific textual phrases—the "arising under" clause of article III, the oath requirement and the supremacy clause of article VI—as themselves demonstrating an intention that the courts engage in judicial review. In interpreting the text, he speaks in entirely conventional terms of "the intention" of those who gave the courts their powers and of what "the Framers of the constitution contemplated." Not surprisingly, this interpretation of text confirms what has already been deduced scientifically: "Thus, the particular phraseology of the constitution of the United States confirms and strengthens the principle, supposed to be essential to all written constitutions, that a law repugnant to the constitution is void; and that *courts,* as well as other departments, are bound by that instrument." Positive text, the result of an affirmative act of self-government, coincides with abstract science. This coincidence of text and science is the founders' solution to the traditional problems of republican government: a popularly legitimated text lends its legitimacy to a science of politics. Reason and will support each other in constitutional governance.[56]

This pattern of argument—scientific deduction linked to, and thus legitimated by, an exposition of positive text—is characteristic of Marshall's greatest work. In particular, it is at the heart of *McCulloch v. Maryland.* There Marshall uses this methodology to determine the power of Congress to create a national bank and the power of a state to tax that bank—questions that Marshall describes as concerning the "constitution of our country, in its most interesting and vital parts."[57]

The *McCulloch* opinion is divided into two large sections corresponding to these major issues. Each section begins with a discourse in pure political science and then makes an explicit turn away from abstract political theory to textual interpretation. The break in the first section is marked by the proposition that "the constitution of the United States has not left the right of Congress to employ the necessary means, for the execution of the powers conferred on the government, to *general reasoning.*" The break in the second section is marked by a similar proposition: "We find, then, on *just theory,* a total failure of this original right to tax the means employed by the government of the Union. . . . But, waiving this *theory* for the present, let us resume the inquiry, whether this power can be exercised by the respective States, consistently with a *fair construction* of the constitution?"[58]

The breadth of theoretical discourse in each section is remarkable.

With respect to congressional authority to create a bank, for example, Marshall's inquiry encompasses a theory of popular sovereignty and its delegation, a theory of conflicts of law, a theory of constitutional form—distinguishing a constitution from a legal code—and a theory of implied governmental powers.[59] The argument on state power to tax begins with "[t]his great principle ... that the constitution and the laws made in pursuance thereof are supreme." Marshall continues: "From this [principle], which may be almost termed an axiom, other propositions are deduced as corollaries. ... These propositions, as abstract truths, would, perhaps, never be converted." Application of these abstract truths to the question before the Court allows Marshall to develop a theory of taxation in a way that results in an "intelligible standard" by which to measure "the power of taxation residing in a State." This exercise in political science is wholly independent of any legitimating act of popular self-government in the creation of the Constitution. General reasoning, or just theory, exists as objectively true, regardless of the actions—the expressions of the will—of any particular political community in incorporating such truths into their system of government.[60]

Marshall, then, is explicit in his belief that arguments from the abstract science of politics are essential to constitutional inquiry. The Constitution embodies the principles of republican government, which are deducible as a matter of science. The abstract inquiry into republican principles, however, does not displace text; the text will normally be read to confirm what scientific deduction has already established.

The text itself includes more than the individual clauses that grant or constrain authority. Whereas the theoretical deduction of federal authority to establish the bank in the first part of the opinion is legitimated by an interpretation of the necessary and proper clause of article I, section 8, the just theory of taxation of the second section of the opinion is legitimated not by a specific textual provision but by the general character of the written document: "If we apply the principle for which the state of Maryland contends, to the constitution generally, we shall find it capable of changing totally the character of that instrument." The overall character of the document demonstrates that "the American people ... did not design to make their government dependent on the States." The institutions of government are ordered through a positive act of self-government. That institutional arrangement can therefore confirm the deductive results of the abstract science of politics.[61]

In *McCulloch*, the twofold character of constitutional argument extends even into the subsections. For example, squarely within the scientific argument on the character of the delegation of sovereign authority to the federal government is the following appeal to the twofold scheme:

If any one proposition could command the universal assent of mankind, we might expect it would be this—that the government of the Union, though limited in its powers, is supreme within its sphere of action. This would seem to result necessarily from its nature. . . . But this question is not left to *mere reason:* the people have, in *express terms,* decided it, by saying, "this constitution, and the laws of the United States, which shall be made in pursuance thereof, shall be the supreme law of the land."[62]

Thus, at each stage of the argument there is a reciprocal relation between text and science. Science renders the text intelligible, but the text renders the science legitimate. This reciprocity structures the broad outlines of the constitutional inquiry, as well as the details of the argument.

Marshall's faith in the success of the founding moment, in the integration of science and positive law, explains this manner of argument. Even though Marshall, like Publius before him, acknowledges the priority of consent over science—"[i]f . . . such be the mandate of the Constitution [limiting Congress to an inadequate choice of means], we have only to obey"—he operates with the founders' faith that a conflict between political legitimacy and political science will not emerge.[63] The Constitution is an artifact, constructed on the principles of political science. Therefore, constitutional interpretation can confidently employ, and, indeed, must employ, the principles and the techniques of the abstract science of government.

The Changing Locus of a Science of Politics

Judicial review carried forward the founders' understanding of the success of the founding moment: the achievement of an integration of political science and popular legitimacy. The idea of a successful integration, so prominent in *Marbury* and *McCulloch,* nevertheless represented a subtle change in the relation between science and the political community. In *The Federalist,* the political scientist still stands outside, or apart from, the community.[64] Publius was speaking to the community but had no authority to impose order upon it. He could draw upon his science to imagine a new model of political order, but that model still had to be impressed upon a living community through an act of self-government. For Publius, the role of science was to inform an art of politics that could then be applied in the political life of the nation. His aim was to create a nation of political artisans.

Marshall tells us that Publius succeeded. Precisely because of the success of Publius, Marshall claims the right to regulate the constitutional order by virtue of his access to the principles of political science. Unlike Publius, Marshall does not stand outside the community holding forth an ideal model; he stands squarely within it. To stand within this particular community, however, does not require a disavowal of abstract science in favor of positive law. The integrity of the founding moment, the legitimation of republican science, allows Marshall to speak simultaneously as political scientist and as representative of the community itself. He is the quintessential artisan in a community of political artisans.

Marshall speaks in the same manner as Publius but with a new authority. The relocation of the political scientist into the community corresponds to the relocation of the will of the community into the text. Only because the public will has been frozen in the text can judicial scientists claim popular legitimacy for their role. Marshall claims this legitimacy despite his rejection of legislation that would ordinarily appear to express the will of the community.

Marshall stood too close to the founders and their belief in the necessity of a science of politics to see the difference, but the role of science in the political life of the nation was being reconceptualized even as Marshall appealed to science to establish judicial review. The Constitution was no longer understood as an experiment, testing whether a community could make its government according to abstract principles of republican government. Emerging was a view of the Constitution as the internal source of order of a historical community.[65] Self-government still depended upon understanding the founders' science, but that science was no longer simply an external source upon which a political artisan could draw in order to impose ideal form upon a recalcitrant social matter. Science was now the source of self-regulation in a community that had begun to maintain a political identity through time. Because constitutional order was identified with the product of science, the distinction between an external scientific perspective and an internal perspective on the political order of the community remained hidden. But the problem of relocating the science of political order from the abstract and universal to the constitutional text and so to the concrete community itself was evident to Marshall's intellectual successor on the Court, Joseph Story. For Story, the science of law separated from the science of politics. Legal science, which the Court was meant to apply, became a science of interpretation of texts.

The proposition that political science can serve as a source of constitutional order remained true only as long as the founders' faith that the political order is the product of science could be sustained. In U.S. constitutional history that was not very long. The founders' faith in science was soon lost, just as Iredell foreshadowed. Without a belief in science, the idea that the Constitution is the product of an art of political construction could not survive, nor could the Constitution appear any longer as an experiment in self-government. The task of the next generation was no longer that of making, but that of maintaining, the Constitution. The conceptual model of making, which shaped the founding generation's understanding of their relation to the Constitution, had to give way to a new conceptual model of order.

CHAPTER TWO

Maintenance and the Organism of the State

The founders' generation had a unique relation to the project of constitutional self-government: only this generation could give the law to itself. Every subsequent generation has had to reconcile the historical givenness of the Constitution with the idea of self-government. The conceptual model of making, within which the founders understood their own relation to the Constitution, cannot comprehend this new relation to time. A new model is required to deal with the emerging historicity of the constitutional order.

The Rise of Political Religion

Abraham Lincoln's Lyceum speech of 1838 is one of the most self-conscious elaborations of the political and psychological issues raised by the passing of the first generation.[1] His topic is "the perpetuation of our political institutions," or what I shall call maintenance. The speech illustrates the dimensions of the problem of changing from a constitutionalism of making to one of maintenance.

Lincoln addresses a new generation of Americans, who, "mounting the stage of existence" in the nineteenth century, find themselves the inheritors of a completed political order. Of this generation, he says, "We toiled not in the acquirement or establishment of [constitutional provisions]—they are a legacy bequeathed us, by a *once* hardy, brave, and patriotic, but *now* lamented and departed race of ancestors." He defines the political task of the current generation by a threefold orientation in time:

"[t]his task of gratitude to our fathers, justice to ourselves [and] duty to posterity." The task is to "transmit . . . undecayed by the lapse of time and untorn by usurpation, to the latest generation" the "political edifice of liberty and equal rights" made by the fathers. Maintenance of the constitutional edifice will simultaneously honor the fathers, provide for posterity, and accomplish justice among contemporaries. This is the political role of his generation and of every post-founding generation.

Lincoln's central concern is the political psychology of maintenance. What sort of citizens can understand themselves as serving the past and the future in their political lives? In his threefold characterization, Lincoln suggests an answer: citizens who identify the inherited law with justice. The maintenance of the state requires citizens who seek justice, but more important, they must believe that the laws of the state provide access to justice—that law and justice coincide. "In any case that arises, as for instance, the promulgation of abolitionism, one of two positions is necessarily true; that is, the thing is right within itself, and therefore deserves the protection of all law and all good citizens; or, it is wrong, and therefore proper to be prohibited by legal enactments." The need for this belief leads Lincoln to present a series of psychological vignettes in which he describes the impact various character types have on politics.

For Lincoln, as for Publius, the threat to law comes from passion. He complains of "the growing disposition to substitute the wild and furious passions, in lieu of the sober judgement of Courts." Passion may be a quality of the one or the many. His first vignette describes the passion of the many, which leads to the politics of the "savage mob" in which "the lawless in spirit . . . become lawless in practice." His second vignette describes the passion of the single individual who is "possessed of the loftiest genius, coupled with ambition sufficient to push it to its utmost stretch." Such a person will not find an adequate field for passion merely "in supporting and maintaining an edifice that has been erected by others" but only in "pulling down" the political edifice, "whether at the expense of emancipating slaves, or enslaving freemen."

The danger of passion to politics may, therefore, come from an individual or from a group. In each case, passion is the enemy of law, and law is the ground of constitutional maintenance. In response to the threat of passion, Lincoln preaches each individual's obligation to participate in a new "political religion" founded on reverence for the laws: "Let reverence for the laws, be breathed by every American mother, to the lisping babe, that prattles on her lap—let it be taught in schools, in seminaries, and in colleges; let it be written in Primers, spelling books, and in Almanacs;—let it be preached from the pulpit, proclaimed in legislative halls, and enforced in courts of justice." Only a political religion will enable the many to resist the passion of the great-souled individual: "[W]hen such a one does [arise], it will require the people to be united with each other, attached to the government and laws, and generally intelligent, to successfully frustrate his designs."

The political problem of maintenance, then, arises from the psychology of passion. Passion, as Lincoln describes it, is the assertion of individual identity and the subordination of all social and political structures to that identity. The founders could naturally enlist passion in support of their political function, because the "success of that experiment" promised "celebrity and fame." For the new generation, passion is only destructive of political order. "Passion has helped us; but can do so no more." The new generation can rely on reason alone: "Reason, cold, calculating, unimpassioned reason, must furnish all the materials for our future support and defense."

Only the founders' generation had the good fortune to be capable of passion and law. According to Lincoln, even the bodies of those members of that generation who still survive testify to the complete interpenetration of their private and political lives. Their bodies are a "history bearing the indubitable testimonies of [the founding's] own authenticity, in the limbs mangled, in the scars of wounds received, in the midst of the very scenes related." Only the fathers could find in their political role an affirmation of the whole self. To maintain, rather than build, the state, the citizen must be less than whole.

Lincoln is acutely aware of the problem created by the passing of the founding generation. Those men and women were the anchor of the past in the present. They were "*a living history* . . . found in every family . . . [b]ut *those* histories are gone." Their deaths break the personal, familial link with the past. Without them to mold the personal identity of the new generation, the possibility of a new outbreak of private passion arises. To avoid this threat requires the reconstruction of the psychological basis of the political order, of the individual's understanding of the relation between the self and the Constitution.

Lincoln's answer to the problem is a political religion of reverence for law. That religion requires the suppression of a part of the self. Reverence is not passion tamed; it is the opposite of passion. Unlike passion, which seeks to subordinate the state to the individual, reverence starts from the community and subordinates personal identity to it. The bounds of community, according to Lincoln, are law, and law is the object of reason, not passion. Thus, Lincoln's political religion relies on reason to produce a "united" and "intelligent" community. Reason here is not the abstract science of Publius. Reason, says Lincoln, must be "moulded into *general intelligence, sound morality,* and, in particular, a *reverence for the constitution and laws.*" But reason is foreign to the passionate urge for self-expression. Lincoln's model for this subordination of the self is religion. His idea of reason refers neither to logic nor to science but to reasonable people who are directed by their reverence—both political and religious. The role of a political religion is to create this new model citizen, to create a sense of personal identity that is no larger than the political role of maintenance requires. The new generation must have a political identity built upon a kind of distancing from certain aspects of the self.

The Constitution was no longer a technical product of an applied science. Reasonable though it might be, it was fundamentally an object of reverence. The constitutional struggle of Lincoln's generation was over the character of this political religion. All agreed that the constitutional role of their generation was to maintain the edifice made by the founders. Theorists as far apart substantively as Joseph Story and John Calhoun agreed that if maintenance failed, the contemporary generation no longer had the capacity to remake a constitution.[2] The question that divided the nation was, What is the character of the founders' creation? This question went directly to personal identity. Everyone agreed that they were the children of the founding fathers, but they did not agree on the meaning of the familial obligation. The furor and violence of this debate rested directly on this linkage of politics and personhood.

The End of Marshall's Constitutionalism

Lincoln's discussion of the need for a political religion marked a change in constitutional thought. This new perspective was also implicit in his identification of the founders' passion as a critical element of their relation to the Constitution. The founders did not conceive of their own project in these terms. For their generation, the Constitution was above all the product of political science. For succeeding generations to hold to the same republican science that informed the artisanship of the founders was possible but unlikely. When that scientific understanding faltered, the political order became a historical artifact. Lincoln's focus on passion—both the founders' and the current generation's—corresponded to the new awareness of the historicity of the constitutional order.

In U.S. constitutionalism, the move away from the founders' conceptual model of order was intertwined with the legal controversy over race and slavery. A constitutionalism centered on a republican science of government was not adequate to the problem of slavery. At Philadelphia, James Madison had already commented: "We have seen the mere distinction of colour made in the most enlightened period of time, a ground of the most oppressive dominion ever exercised by man over man."[3] Chief Justice Marshall continued this theme when he spoke of the slave trade as "contrary to the law of nature."[4]

Publius had been clear in *The Federalist* that the treatment of slavery in the proposed constitution did not rest on the science of republican government. In this respect, the Constitution was only a political compromise.[5] For this reason, rather than speaking for himself, Publius put the arguments in favor of the proposed treatment of slavery in the mouth of a southerner. Though complaining of the logic of the argument, Publius nevertheless accepted it: "Such is the reasoning which an advocate for the Southern interests might employ on this subject; and although it may appear to be a little strained in some points, yet on the whole . . . it fully reconciles me to the scale of representation which the convention ha[s] established."[6] That Publius attributed this argument to southern *interests* identifies its theoretical status. Publius consistently identified interests as the enemy of reason, deliberation, and science.[7] These particular southern interests proved too strong, too hard formed, to be molded by political science. On the issue of slavery, the Constitution rested on will alone, without any support from reason.

The new Constitution had been ratified in 1787 at the political cost of protecting the institution of slavery. This political reality tested the constitutional worldview of the founders' generation, challenging the claim that the founding had successfully integrated reason and will. To maintain that view, slavery had to be understood as an exception to the general scheme of the constitutional project. Story captured this idea of exceptionality when he introduced a discussion of the treatment of slavery in the Constitution with a warning: "Before . . . we proceed to the points more immediately before us, it may be well—in order to clear the case of difficulty—to say, that in the exposition of this part of the Constitution [the fugitive slave clause], we shall limit ourselves to those considerations which appropriately and exclusively belong to it, without laying down any rules of interpretation of a more general nature."[8] When the issue of slavery became critical to the life of the nation, this idea of exceptionality was threatened. As the nation confronted constitutionally legitimated inequality, the scientific foundation of the whole constitutional edifice came under tremendous stress.[9] The claims of science were denied to support the existing constitutional order.

The emergence of political inequality as the central fact of constitutional life was not the only factor leading to a shift in the conceptual model by which constitutional authority was understood. The shift also reflected the peculiar theoretical difficulties of republican political science in the first half of the nineteenth century. Opposed to the nationalism of Marshall and Story was a republican science based on decentralization and states' rights. As early as the Virginia and Kentucky resolutions, two competing first principles of American political structure, and thus two competing sciences of politics, were present.[10]

This great theoretical battle rages throughout the constitutional arguments of the period, from Marshall's opinion in *McCulloch*, to Story's *Commentaries*, to Calhoun's *Discourse on the Constitution*.[11] Marshall and Story argued that the Constitution was the work of the people of the entire nation acting in their unified, sovereign capacity. Opposing theorists argued that the Constitution was the product of a compact among sovereign states. Instead of emphasizing the opening words of the document—We the People—these theorists emphasized the process of state ratification and the careful preservation of state authority. In this view, the science of constitutional law generally resembled that of international law, because both involved the interaction of distinct, sovereign entities. The most important of the principles that the states' rights theorists took from international law was a rule of narrow construction: the Constitution had to be construed narrowly to protect the sovereignty of each of the parties.[12]

In addition to its enormous practical significance, the conflict between theories of nationalism and states' rights had important theoretical consequences for the role of science in constitutional theory. The conflict over the first principles of the republican science of politics challenged the authority of science per se as a source of constitutional law. Science could not be determinative if there were competing sciences, particularly when those sciences led to opposite conclusions on the major constitutional issues of the day, including congressional power, state nullification, and secession.

The conflict between republican political science and slavery and the conflict between competing sciences of politics inevitably undermined Marshall's constitutionalism. An opinion about the Constitution could no longer rest on abstract political science. A new methodology was required for a new generation. Beyond these political developments, the generational change itself called for a new, positive understanding of what the Constitution had constituted. Lincoln spoke at the Lyceum of the need to create a political religion to explain the relation of the new generation to an inherited Constitution. If constitutional governance was to continue to be understood as self-government, a new understanding of the self was required—one that could make sense of the historical givenness of the Constitution.

Story and Calhoun: Membership in the Corporate Community

All of these tensions are evident in the great constitutional controversy that engaged the generation that came immediately after the founders. Story and Calhoun were key figures in this debate. Their constitutionalism displays the shifting status of political science, the linkage of political and personal identity, and the emergence of history as a domain of meaning.

Both men were children of the revolution. Story was born in 1779; Calhoun, in 1782. Both grew up within that familial atmosphere that Lincoln described as bearing living witness to the founding. Both put maintenance of the constitutional order at the center of their work. For both, the threat to constitutional maintenance was made clear by the move of South Carolina toward secession in response to the 1828 tariff. Each, however, perceived the views of the other as the source of the threat to constitutional maintenance. Even though history played an important role in both of their approaches to the Constitution, they looked to different kinds of history: Story relied on a history of political culture; Calhoun, on a history of governmental authority. Each approach was a reasonable means of anchoring the present in the past. Each was likely to suggest itself to a generation that could still remember the relevant history, if not as participants, then as children of participants. Each approach rested upon an unproblematic, personal identification with the history of a community, although each man identified with a different community.

Although Story often joined in and defended the decisions of Chief Justice Marshall, there was a fundamental difference between them. For Marshall, the science of law coincided with the science of politics. A member of the founders' generation, Marshall understood the work of the Court as continuous with the founding: judicial decisions would give effect to republican political science. For Story, the work of the Court was not making, but maintenance. Maintenance required a science of law.

Story's most vitriolic criticisms were directed at those who approached the Constitution with "mere theory," or abstract concepts of political science. Story didn't doubt that the founders were driven by a theoretical vision, but he thought that vision did not fully inform their construction. "[F]or the system was human, and the result of compromise and conciliation, in which something of the correctness of theory was yielded to the interests or prejudices of particular states, and something of inequality of benefit borne for the common good."[13] Because the Constitution was not a product of pure political theory, its interpretation could not rely on theory alone. Although the place for the science of politics in constitutional interpretation was limited, Story saw no such limits on the science of law.

Story's understanding of constitutional maintenance can best be approached by examining three propositions central to his thought: first, the Constitution is the product of a single, national political community; second, the Supreme Court is the ultimate interpreter of the Constitution; third, the Court makes its determinations by applying a legal science.

Whether the Constitution is the self-ordering of a single community or a compact among states is, Story tells us, a question of "practical importance," not merely of "theoretical speculation." Maintenance of the whole depends upon the correct answer to this question because "a pure confederation, is a mere treaty or league between independent states, and binds no longer, than during the good pleasure of each. . . . [E]ach is, or may be the supreme judge of its own rights and duties."[14] Story's rejection of the idea of a compact provides a model of the application of legal science and, therefore, provides a good measure of the strength of his vision of maintenance.

Story turns immediately to the text: "There is nowhere found upon the face of the Constitution any clause, intimating it to be a compact, or in anywise providing for its interpretation, as such." Instead of using the language of states contracting, the text speaks of "the people" creating. The implications of the text are confirmed by an easy access to historical context: "If it had been the design of the framers of the Constitution or of the people, who ratified it, to consider it a mere confederation . . . it is difficult to conceive, that the appropriate terms should not have been found in it." History matters, not because original intent is authoritative, but because context may illuminate text.[15]

Story summarizes this view when he writes that "the constitution . . . was submitted to the whole upon a just survey of its provisions, as they stood in the text itself. . . . Nothing but the text itself was adopted by the people."[16] In his inquiry into the communal character of the Constitution, his measure of a just survey is provided by a review "of the nature and objects of the instrument," "the known history [of objections to the proposed Constitution], and the acts of ratification," and "the debates of the various conventions called to examine and ratify the constitution." All of these inquiries aim to establish the reasonable inferences that the language itself supports—in this case, the self-ordering of a single, national political community. This "careful survey of the language of the constitution itself," which does not mean mere textualism, is contrasted with "artificial reasoning founded upon theory."[17]

An important consequence of the compact theory was to deny the authoritative character of the Supreme Court. Story's argument again illustrates the methodology of legal science, and again he starts with the text. Joining the supremacy clause of article VI to the jurisdictional provisions of article III, he concludes, "[W]e have express, and determinate provisions upon the very subject. Nothing is imperfect, and nothing is left to implication." Recognizing, however, that the text may not be enough for skeptics, Story turns once more to broad historical characterizations. He locates the function of the Supreme Court within the popular understanding of courts, arguing that judicial review by the Supreme Court is consistent with prior practice: "It would seem impossible . . . to presume, if the people intended to introduce a new rule in respect to the decisions of the Supreme Court, and to limit the nature and operations of their judgments in a manner wholly unknown to the common law, and to our existing jurisprudence, that some indication of that intention should not be apparent on the face of the constitution." The meaning of text is confirmed by context. Here, the institutional history of the courts provides the context.[18]

Story's belief that it is text, not history or theory, that is authoritative is evident in his turn to post-ratification history to support his interpretation. The Supreme Court, he argues, has occupied the role of supreme interpreter for forty years and "three fourths of all the states composing the Union have expressly assented to, or silently approved, this construction." This, he writes, "affords as satisfactory a testimony in favor of the just and safe operation of the system as can well be imagined; and, as a commentary upon the constitution itself, it is as absolutely conclusive, as any ever can be." Story asks, "Who . . . is at liberty to reason down [from mere theory] the terms of the Constitution, so as to exclude their natural force and operation?" The natural force is often best found in the actual force and operation of the words.[19]

To determine the natural force and operation of the words, then, one must look to the expectations of those who acted upon them and who still act upon them. Past and present are linked as expressions of a single community. Temporality is unproblematic; indeed, it constitutes a virtue: "Time, and long and steady operation are indispensable to the perfection of all social institutions."[20] History is no longer the imperfect medium for the embodiment of abstract ideas. Abstract ideas—at least in political science—can only be partial. They are embryonic, requiring history to display their meaning fully. Story's view of history stands between the classical view of the framers and the evolutionary views that came to dominate later nineteenth-century thought. Unlike the framers, he does not believe that history inevitably corrupts the true but abstract ideas of political order. Unlike the evolutionists, he does not believe that ideas are transformed through a process of historical development. Rather, history is for him the medium for the full exhibition of what an idea really is. For example, people cannot fully understand the idea of separation of powers as an abstraction but must look to its expression in the actual history of the nation.

History, for Story, can be compared to a book. The book presents what started as an abstract idea of the author. Without its elaboration in the book, the idea would have a thinness. For any particular reader to grasp the author's idea requires that he or she read the book. History constitutes the medium for the display of legal order, but not its substance.

Constitutional interpretation must begin with the text as an expression of popular consent, but it cannot end with the text. The text will often not be self-explanatory. The necessity for interpretation creates the possibility of judicial arbitrariness. To combat judicial arbitrariness, a science of law is required. Story, therefore, sets out the "true rules of interpretation applicable to the constitution; so that we may have some fixed standard."[21]

These rules are an effort to systematize and summarize the interpretive approach already illustrated in the arguments concerning communal character and institutional authority. In contrast to the historical approach of many of those arguments, the rules emphasize the need for openness to change in constitutional interpretation. If the ends of the Constitution are to be attained, the means available must be responsive to the changing "manners, habits, and institutions of society, which are never stationary." Unless the Constitution permits change, the whole of society will be "revolutionized at every critical period, and remodeled in every generation." Maintenance thus requires a science of law that can distinguish the permanent from the transitory. Maintenance will fail if it allows too much permanence or too much change. Law exists in this middle realm, assimilating change to permanence and permanence to change.[22]

The science of law forms the core of Story's vision of constitutionalism. Law gives objective, historical continuity to the single national community. This is expressed institutionally in the vision of the Supreme Court interpreting the Constitution as law. Without science, there would be no reason to believe that the decisions of the Court could withstand the competing interests of other institutional actors, including the states.

The Court might be final, but it would be arbitrary. Arbitrariness would lead to discord.

But can this science of law sustain the enterprise of maintenance? A corporation maintains its identity in and through law, but can the political community be understood on this model? Put differently, the science of law must distinguish the permanent from the changing, but what binds the present generation to the legal vision of permanence? What justifies Story's belief that citizens will rely on law to maintain the work of the founders and suppress the urge to revolutionize and remodel society in each critical period? Story has no good answer. He recognizes the need to move beyond reason to the "affections" and concludes the work with a remark similar to Lincoln's discussion of a political religion: "If these Commentaries shall but inspire the rising generation with a more ardent love of their country, an unquenchable thirst for liberty, and a profound reverence for the Constitution and the Union, then they will have accomplished all, that their author ought to desire."[23] Yet the grounds for this reverence fail to emerge.

Indeed, those aspects of political order that might seem most important to the individual—peace and economic prosperity—must be most open to change, according to Story.[24] Affection must attach instead to institutional structure and legal process. These remain the same while the material attributes of government change. This argument seems far too thin to ground an understanding of the self as a "keeper" of the Constitution.[25] Only to those who already understand themselves as part of the national community will this task of maintenance appear compelling. Story's work, in other words, assumes the critical link between the individual and the national community. It is unlikely to convince nonbelievers. Calhoun did not believe.

Calhoun is viewed too often in the light of events that followed his death in 1850: secession and civil war. He is better understood as a constitutional conservative: "I am a conservative in its broadest fullest sense and such I shall ever remain, unless, indeed, the Government shall become so corrupt and disordered, that nothing short of revolution can reform it."[26] His goal was to develop a constitutionalism capable of resisting the forces of dissolution that threatened the maintenance of the founders' work.

According to Calhoun, the threat to the constitutional order comes from the conjunction of the forces of democracy and centralism.[27] The national government, he says, has been captured by a single section of the country. Although this section represents a majority of the population—and of the states—the founders never intended centralized majoritarianism. The coalescence of a majority of the population, a majority of the states, and the national government has destroyed the intended balance among diverse local, regional, and national interests. He predicts the imbalance will lead to sectional conflict, which will result in the disaster of either national absolutism or secession.

Conflict can be averted and the union maintained, according to Calhoun, only by a constitutional interpretation that allows the development of alternative institutions to maintain the balance of state and national interests. There must be a return to the original design of a "complex and refined [system] calculated to express the sense of the whole (in the only mode by which this can be fully and truly done—to wit, by ascertaining the sense of all its parts)." Calhoun attempts to ground a balance of the parts in the doctrine of interposition, under which every state can declare national policy within its jurisdiction unconstitutional: "Nothing short of this can possibly preserve this important division of power, on which rests the equilibrium of the entire system."[28]

Calhoun agrees with Story that the character of the constitutional community is "by far the most important [issue]." He moves beyond Story in recognizing explicitly what is only implicit in Story's work. At issue is not simply the practical character of the institutions of government but also the nature of individual identity. The question raises the problem "of the allegiance of the citizen; or, in other words, the question to whom allegiance and obedience are ultimately due." Are the citizens of the nation united "socially" "into one great community," or are they just "politically connected through their respective States?" Calhoun answers that the great community does not exist, that citizens are members of state communities.[29]

Calhoun and Story are both writing about political identity in the post-foundation world. They simply have different views of what community constitutes political identity. Calhoun concludes that "[t]here is . . . no such community, *politically* speaking, as the people of the United States, regarded in the light of, and as constituting one people or nation. There never has been any such, in any stage of their existence; and, of course, they neither could, nor ever can exercise any agency,—or have any participation, in the formation of our system of government, or its administration."[30] He supports this claim by offering an interpretation of the founding.

Unlike Story, who focuses on the text, Calhoun focuses on the actors who had authority to establish the Constitution. He proposes that constitutional interpreters proceed by looking to the authority of those who created it. Because no one can legitimately act beyond the bounds of his or her authority, the constitutional order created cannot exceed the limits of the state law that authorized the founders' actions.

Calhoun starts his analysis with George Washington's letter transmitting the work of the Philadelphia Convention to the Congress. Washington speaks as the "organ" of the convention, which had the "high authority" to frame the document. Calhoun's aim is to understand the meaning the convention "intended to attach to the expression,— 'the United States.'" The intent of an authoritative organ can then be used to counter what might otherwise be a reasonable inference from the text: "[I]t could not have been intended, by the expression in the preamble,—'to form a more perfect union,'—to declare, that the old was abolished, and a new and more perfect union established in its place: for we have the authority of the convention which formed the constitution, to prove that their object was to continue the then existing union."[31]

By far the most authoritative source for understanding the Constitution, Calhoun says, is the history of state ratification, to which he promptly turns. Looking to the instruments of ratification, he writes, "we are not left to conjecture, as to what was meant by the ratification of the constitution, or its effects." Again, Calhoun uses authority to displace text and, implicitly, to respond to Story:

Nothing more is necessary, in order to show . . . who are meant by,—"We, the people of the United States;" . . . To this there can be but one answer:—it meant the people who ratified the instrument; for it was the act of ratification which ordained and established it. . . . The process preparatory to ratification, and the acts by which it was done, prove, beyond the possibility of a doubt, that . . . "We, the people of the United States,"—mean,—We, the people of the several States of the Union.[32]

Story understands constitutional maintenance to rest on the application of a science of law. Calhoun, though less explicit, is just as much the legal technician in his understanding of maintenance. His constitutionalism flows directly from his first principle of state corporatism in American political identity. If the citizen understands political identity in and through state citizenship, then the relation of the individual to the nation is mediated through actions of the state as a corporate entity. The model of such corporate action is contract. Indeed, the state corporatism of Calhoun provides an easy answer to the transtemporal problem of constitutionalism. Just as a corporation has a single identity across generations, so does the state. The state is bound by its prior contractual undertaking—but no further—in ratifying the Constitution. To honor the fathers is to comply with their contracts. To understand those contracts requires looking to the intent of those with the authority to act.

In spite of the radical differences in their claims about political identity, Story and Calhoun share a great deal. Both are conservative, understanding the current generation's task as maintenance of the work of the founders. Both theories rest on the ability to recall easily the political identity of the fathers, who they were and what they thought they were doing. Thus, for both theorists, the issue of personal identity is inseparable from an understanding of history. To answer the question of identity, both turn to their legal methodology. But in each case, the assumptions about identity explain the methodology—not vice versa. Indeed, to the degree that Story's law-centered nationalism is too thin to resist the claims of competing communities to constitute individual political identity, one expects, and indeed finds, the rise of a constitutionalism of state contract.

The differences in the theories of Story and Calhoun derive from the differences in their premises about political identity. Story asks of the text, What did We the People understand? Calhoun asks, What did We the State authorize? They are translating their assumptions about who Americans are into legal arguments about the character of the Constitution. Nevertheless, they agree that constitutional maintenance depends upon law and that the continuity of law expresses the underlying continuity of a single corporate entity within which political identity is formed and manifested. Individual attachment to this corporate entity is more a matter of affection and reverence than reason and law. The problem of early constitutional history is that the Constitution permitted competing answers to this fundamental question of political identity.

The constitutionalism of Story and Calhoun takes the form that one would expect during a period in which identification with the past of a particular community remains unproblematic. Accordingly, the problem of history for Story and Calhoun was limited to their conflicting interpretations of a single set of past events. As the distance from the founding increased, the easy identification with the past failed. Constitutionalism had to constitute directly this linkage of past and present. Disputes about history moved from conflicts over the meaning of events to conflicts over the meaning of history itself for the constitutional enterprise. How is the individual linked to the political actions of the founding generation? Addressing this problem required a new mode of constitutionalism, one that appeared with startling clarity in *Dred Scott*, the first case after *Marbury* to hold a federal statute unconstitutional.

Dred Scott: Popular Sovereignty without Science

In the history of constitutional law, *Dred Scott v. Sandford*[33] is at least as infamous as *Marbury* is famous. In *Dred Scott,* the Court held that a free black person could not become a citizen of the United States and that the Missouri Compromise was unconstitutional. Neither disagreement with its holding nor an understanding of its political consequences should prevent a clear appraisal of its theoretical significance.

Dred Scott demonstrated a fundamental shift in the framework of constitutional theory. Republican science was left no role in the new constitutional jurisprudence. It was replaced by inquiry into the intent of the founders. This shift survived the demise of *Dred Scott;* it continues within a substantial segment of the bench and academy today.[34]

Dred Scott is an appropriate place to look for a self-conscious expression of the nature of constitutional authority, because of the Court's belief that proper performance of the judicial role is critical to the preservation of national order in the face of a mounting political crisis.[35] The case represents the translation of the political crisis over slavery, sectionalism, and national authority into a legal question. Remarkably, the Court believed it could invoke law to settle these political controversies.

Chief Justice Roger Taney's opinion has been criticized on many fronts, for misrepresenting the history of the treatment and status of freed slaves, for needlessly addressing constitutional issues, and for reading the Constitution in an implausibly strained way. My interest is not in renewing this critique of Taney's judicial craftsmanship.[36] Rather, my concern is the ground of authority claimed for the argument that he does offer. Instead of asking whether Taney adequately supported the particular propositions of his argument, I focus on what he thought he had to prove, or perhaps discover, in order to decide the constitutional issues. This focus reveals a rich constitutional worldview that is otherwise lost in the details of a negative critique.

Originalism and the Inherited Constitution

If Marshall's opinions are marked by a confidence in the coincidence of the science of politics and the constitutional text, Taney's *Dred Scott* opinion is marked by the frank acknowledgment of a gap between political science and the Constitution. Taney starts his analysis of the possibility of black citizenship by anchoring the judicial role in positive law, as opposed to political theory:

It is not the province of the court to decide upon the justice or injustice, the policy or impolicy, of these laws. The decision of that question belonged to the political or law-making power; to those who formed the sovereignty and framed the Constitution. The duty of the court is, to interpret the instrument they have framed, with the best lights we can obtain on the subject, and to administer it as we find it, according to its true intent and meaning when it was adopted.[37]

Publius uses the priority of the principle of self-government to argue for the necessity of national deliberation upon a correct, scientific order of government. Taney, in contrast, uses the same principle to justify a rejection of scientific deliberation. Interpretation of the Constitution, he says, has nothing to do with an abstract theory of justice or an analysis of right policy. Judicial interpretation is nothing more than the articulation of historical intent. The Court must stabilize the present and preserve the future of constitutional order by carrying forward the past. The Court's function is not to do justice but simply to maintain the law as it finds it. Justice is a concern of the sovereign, not of the instrumentalities of the law. Justice may have been a concern in the past, and it may be a concern in the future, but it is not a concern in the present.

The tension between present and past and the understanding of the Court's role as one of looking backward is the central theme of Taney's argument.[38] Marshall's Court existed in the present—the expanded present of the founding. Marshall's opinions are continuous with Publius's arguments in setting forth the scientific character of the constitutional construction. Story, too, understood the community as still living within the expanded present of the founding. He could, therefore, look to the post-ratification history of constitutional practice as a source of interpretation just as valid as the original understanding.

By contrast, Taney sees the Court as exclusively oriented toward the past. It no longer lives within the presence of the founding generation. For example, of the assertion of universal equality in the Declaration of Independence, Taney writes: "The general words . . . would seem to embrace the whole human family, and *if they were used in a similar instrument at this day* would be so understood. But it is too clear for dispute, that the enslaved African race were not intended to be included."[39] Constitutional documents are now seen as the finished products of history. They are not vehicles for the expression of contemporary meanings.

The justices, as the guardians of this founded order, possess an esoteric knowledge. This knowledge is no longer a universally accessible political science; rather, it is a body of highly particularistic, historical facts. Without rational form and deductive inference, constitutional interpretation can be the product only of a special training in the origins of political order.

Taney may have been reading into his account of the historical treatment of blacks nothing more than a reflection of his own prejudices.[40] To know that, however, requires a knowledge of history, not political science. The issue, from Taney's perspective, is a matter of fact. Rediscovery of past meaning may be a difficult task—one in which Taney may fall into error—but rediscovery defines the judicial role: "It is difficult at this day to realize the state of public opinion in relation to that unfortunate race, which prevailed in the civilized and enlightened portions of the world . . . when the Constitution . . . was framed and adopted." Having discovered that opinion, the Court is bound by it: "No one, we presume, supposes that any change in public opinion or feeling, in relation to this unfortunate race, in the civilized nations of Europe or in this country, should induce the court to give to the words of the Constitution a more liberal construction in their favor than they were intended to bear when the instrument was framed and adopted. Such an argument would be altogether inadmissible in any tribunal called on to interpret it." The appropriate role of the Court in interpreting and applying the Constitution requires, therefore, a complete separation of present from past opinion.[41]

Historical inquiry exhausts constitutional interpretation, but Taney does not have a narrow view of the relevant materials with which that interpretation is to be constructed. He aims to determine the broad context of beliefs within which the public would have understood the constitutional text. For example, speaking of the drafters of the Declaration of Independence, he says: "They spoke and acted according to the then established doctrines and principles, and in the ordinary language of the day, and no one misunderstood them." This ordinary language is given meaning by the "state of public opinion."[42] Judicial interpretation must strive to understand that public opinion, because it defined the content of the act of popular sovereignty in 1787. The public can will only what it believes.

The Constitution, according to Taney, is not a technical document, addressing a specialized audience. It uses "general terms" without offering any explicit definitions: "It uses them as terms so well understood, that no further description or definition was necessary." Interpretation must reconstruct that general understanding. Thus, speaking of federal regulation of slavery in the territories, Taney writes: "The powers of the Government, and the rights of the citizen under it, are positive and practical regulations plainly written down. . . . [The] reasoning of statesmen or jurists upon the relations of master and slave, can [not] enlarge the powers of the Government, or take from the citizens the rights they have reserved." What is plainly written down is what is ordinarily understood. That ordinary understanding, not the reasoning of jurists, is the object of constitutional interpretation.[43]

The character of Taney's methodology is illustrated by his treatment of the question of citizenship for freed slaves. Taney inquires into the treatment of blacks in state legislation contemporaneous with the founding. He concludes that "it is hardly consistent with the respect due to these States, to suppose that they regarded at the time, as fellow-citizens and members of the sovereignty, a class of beings whom they had thus stigmatized." The idea that simultaneous actions in the domain of state legislation and national constitutionalism must be coherent is immediately joined with a similar coherence approach to the intent of the framers: "It is impossible . . . to believe that the great men of the slaveholding States [who owned slaves], who took so large a share in framing the Constitution . . . could have [intended black citizenship]." The understanding of institutional (state) and personal intent that emerges from this inquiry is confirmed by an examination of the history of the actual drafting of the text, the treatment of blacks in specific clauses of the Constitution, and the actions of the first Congress. All reveal the general state of popular belief, and so of popular intent, at the founding.[44]

For Taney, then, the Constitution is not the product of a science. It is written in ordinary language addressed to the common understanding. The Court can interpret the ordinary language of the Constitution either by reference to public opinion at the time of its writing or by reference to contemporary opinion. The latter, however, would abrogate the judicial character of the Court, which would become "the mere reflex of the popular opinion or passion of the day." Taney concludes that "[t]his Court was not created by the Constitution for such purposes. Higher and graver trusts have been confided to it."[45] This notion of a trustee, preserving the constitutional principal for future generations, is an apt image for Taney's idea of the judiciary. The Court should preserve what the founders brought forth. The pattern and meaning of the state were set at the moment of its birth.

The constitutional order may be remade to correspond to contemporary notions of justice or contemporary ideas of republican political science, but reconstruction is not the responsibility of the Court:

If any of [the Constitution's] provisions are deemed unjust, there is a mode prescribed in the instrument itself by which it may be amended; but while it remains unaltered, it must be construed now as it was understood at the time of its adoption. . . . [A]s long as it continues to exist in its present form, it speaks not only in the same words, but with the same meaning and intent with which it spoke when it came from the hands of its framers, and was voted on and adopted.[46]

The roles of political science and of a political art based upon that science are thereby cast into the future. Application of political science is not the role of the Court in the present.[47] The place of science in the Court's self-understanding is replaced by originalism, the belief that the meaning of the Constitution can be discovered through an inquiry into its true intent and meaning when it was adopted. The Court's new role is that of historian, not political scientist.[48]

Originalism and Political Identity

The sweeping methodological change represented by the constitutionalism of *Dred Scott* expressed a dramatic substantive reorientation of the character of political identity. The question Lincoln raised in his Lyceum speech remained: How must the citizen conceive of the self if maintenance is to succeed? Originalism is the methodology of maintenance, but what is the political psychology that will find originalism a convincing form of argument? By re-presenting the origins to the contemporary generation, the Court hoped to save the nation from the dissolving consequences of change. Its approach presupposed a citizenry that could see itself in those origins.

The political psychology of originalism is apparent in Taney's response to the question of black citizenship. His answer contains a striking reliance upon family. His interest in the political nature of the family goes well beyond the common appeal to familial order as an analogue of the political community. Taney is interested in the family as a biological phenomenon and in the connection between political and biological order. Family provides Taney with the framework for understanding membership in a historical community, just as religion provided the framework for Lincoln's Lyceum speech. Politics and blood merge in Taney's argument. The Constitution established an intergenerational political family bound by blood, not by a shared capacity to deliberate on an abstract idea of political order.

Taney runs together ideas of race, blood, marriage, children, and political community. He suggests over and over again that the most significant evidence of membership in the political community is the attitude of the law toward racial intermarriage. He collapses biological and racial identity, on the one hand, and political identity, on the other. The political community is attested in the blood of its members.

Taney is not making a category mistake, confusing the public and the private domains. Talking of popular sovereignty is, according to Taney, another way of talking about the community created by the Constitution. If the community constitutes personal identity, then to understand the community requires turning to those relationships that most fully portray the sense of the self. Cultural and biological identity—which are expressed most strongly in the family—say a great deal about political identity.

Taney, consequently, rejects the idea that one can move from the fact that some states may have allowed blacks to vote to the proposition that they are members of the national political community. Blacks, he argues, have never been treated as members of the community that defines American political identity. Difference, what he calls "a stigma," has always marked the relationship between blacks and whites.[49] The stigmatic character of black identity is not merely a formal legal quality; rather, the stigma lies in the refusal to mix bloodlines. Those with whom individuals are not permitted marriage cannot be considered members of the same community. This is a powerful thought. It echoes the relationship of parents to children. In their children, parents see themselves. Those with whom one cannot have children cannot contribute to one's sense of identity except by exclusion and opposition. Taney suggests that the community that is constitutive of political identity be understood as an extension of the community that is constitutive of familial identity. In neither case is identity an object of deliberation or choice. In both cases, identity is determined by a past that the individual does not control. The hold of the past on the present is given a visible presence in the physical being of the individual. The body is literally the link between past and present.

This collapse of the public and the private is at the heart of Taney's rejection of black citizenship. The elimination of a separate domain of the public was already implicit in his separation of a public value of justice from law. Law falls back on the popular sovereign, but the popular sovereign can speak only through public opinion, which is driven by private values, not public order. Taney is making real what Publius feared as the disappearance of the public if political science were replaced by opinion.

To accuse Taney of failing to see a similarity between the legal rights of women and children, on the one hand, and blacks, on the other, misunderstands his project. Had he seen this similarity, it is argued, he could have recognized that citizenship extends across differences in legal rights.[50] But Taney wanted to make the opposite point—that women and children are members of the political community because relationships with them are, according to Taney, elements of personal identity. Even though they do not exercise the full range of legal and political rights, they are part of the community that defines the self. Even if blacks exercised rights similar to those of white males, they would still not be members of the political community unless relationships with them were seen as constitutive of the personal identities of community members.

Taney melds politics with the physical body in his other example of the unbridgeable gap between the two races: the militia.[51] Blacks, he argues, are not allowed to die for the political community. Again, Taney suggests a deep connection between the body and political identity. By denying blacks the right to serve in the militia, the community denies them the right to connect their bodies to the community.[52] At best, the loss of black lives is like the loss of property. Members of the community cannot see these deaths as an affirmation of the historical identity of the community. Blacks, Taney suggests, cannot defend the political order, because their deaths cannot mark the historical existence and continuity of the community.

Taney argues that the historical identity of the political community must be affirmed in the individual's body. The state appropriates the individual's body, but the state is only an idea; it has no powers of appropriation outside the attractiveness of the idea to the individual citizen. The idea of the state offers the individual a way to transcend individual finitude. Through a politics of personal identity, transcendence of the limits that attach to the individual body becomes possible. What appears from one perspective to be an appropriation is, from another perspective, an affirmation of personal identity in the state. To be as a part of the state is to assume the temporal dimensions of the state. If citizens' bodies are appropriated by the state, the citizens themselves are the appropriating agents.

Lincoln grasped this idea in his Lyceum speech when he linked the bodies of the founders' generation "bearing the indubitable testimonies of its own authenticity" to the "celebrity and fame" they had personally achieved through their act of political construction. Lincoln's problem in 1838 was to find an alternative form of submersion in the state for the new generation. Taney suggested, twenty years later, that in this respect every generation stands to the state just as the founders did: they must bear the state in their own bodies. Lincoln taught the same lesson five years later at Gettysburg.

Taney wrote the myth of the American body politic. The myth

collapses the distinction between the present and the past by collapsing the distinction between self and community. It appropriates the body of the individual to embody the state. The Constitution is an idea that must be given a physical presence; it must be given a body. That body is the individual citizen's body. The citizen affirms the continuity and identity of the state in his or her own blood. Only then does the state become more than an idea; it becomes a historical actor. When the idea loses this power to embody, the historical continuity of the state is threatened.

Lincoln's Moral Myth

To describe *Dred Scott* as a myth about the appropriation of the individual's body by the state in order to maintain the Constitution is to find within it a substantive message parallel to that explicitly set forth in what is probably the greatest speech in U.S. history: Lincoln's Gettysburg Address. The whole of the address is an effort to give meaning to the sacrifice of the individual's body on the battlefield by answering two questions simultaneously: how the state can motivate individuals to make the sacrifice and how society can perceive value in the slaughter. Lincoln's answer is to locate the individual's death within the expanse of time that political history makes possible: they "gave their lives that [the] nation might live."[53] The individual transcends the temporal boundaries of the self by merging with the state.

Taney's myth makes this same point. Nevertheless, they offer quite different accounts of the political meaning each individual is to embody. Lincoln locates the value of the nation in the moral values of liberty and equality; Taney locates its value in the familial link of blood. Lincoln is giving voice to the political religion of reason, which he described years before in the Lyceum speech.

The power of the address comes largely from its use of ironic reversals. Lincoln announces his purpose to be the dedication of "a portion of that [battle]field, as a final resting place," but quickly inverts the place of actor and subject. "[W]e cannot dedicate—we cannot consecrate—we cannot hallow—this ground. The brave men . . . who struggled here, have consecrated it." Rather than our dedicating it to them, they have dedicated it to us. "It is for us the living . . . to be dedicated here to the unfinished work which they who fought here have thus far so nobly advanced." The living are linked to the state through the dead, who have subordinated their bodies to the community.

The reversals continue in Lincoln's denial of the significance of his own words. "The world will little note, nor long remember what we say here, but it can never forget what they did here." Yet the memory of what they did is wholly dependent upon its being carried forward in the speech of the living. Their deaths have no significance until they are recounted in a story. That story is the history of the nation. But if the memory of the dead depends on the living, the living depend upon the dead as well. Victory will come, if at all, from their deaths. If the war is lost, the words and the memory will be lost. Thus, memory and the language that will carry that memory depend upon the capacity of the living to "resolve that these dead shall not have died in vain."

Memory depends upon the future. In yet another reversal, however, Lincoln promises for the future only the rebirth of the past: "It is rather for us to be here dedicated to the great task remaining before us . . . that this nation, under God, shall have a new birth of freedom." This clause, appearing in the last sentence of the address, refers the listener or reader back to the first sentence, with its description of "our fathers" who "brought forth . . . a new nation, conceived in Liberty, and dedicated to the proposition that all men are created equal." The structure of the speech ties the end to the beginning, just as the substance of the speech portrays a repetition of the work of the fathers as the meaning of the present generation's political life.

More pointedly, the address moves uneasily between metaphor and reality in moving from the past to the present. The fathers are described metaphorically as engaging in an act of birth. Their bodies are appropriated by the metaphor of birth: they conceived and brought forth. But the Civil War tests this political metaphor in the living flesh of the present generation. "Now we are engaged in a great civil war, testing whether that nation, or any nation so conceived and so dedicated, can long endure." It can endure only if individuals understand their own identity as so linked to that of the nation that a war to maintain the Constitution is perceived as an act of self-affirmation. Thus, Lincoln ends by collapsing the distinction between self and nation: "[G]overnment of the people, by the people, for the people, shall not perish from the earth." The bodies of the founders are linked to those of the present generation as aspects of a single subject: the people.

The Gettysburg Address is an eloquent affirmation of the myth of the state. It simultaneously locates individual identity in the political community and embodies the idea of the state in the physical body of the individual. It affirms the transtemporal character of political identity, identifying the past, present, and future. The people are no longer linked through the aggregation of individual acts of will; rather, the people constitute the organism of the state. That organism had a distinct birth. The task for the present generation is to maintain—that is, to be—what was brought forth at that birth. Thus, Lincoln describes the great political conflict, with its call upon the individual's body, as an act of rebirth; it is a re-presentation of the origin. The aim of the myth is to link present to past by appropriating the bodies of the present generation to maintain the creation of the founders. The myth thereby makes citizens one with the founders.

Henry Jaffa has noted that "in the Gettysburg Address, what was called a self-evident truth by Jefferson becomes in Lincoln's rhetoric an inheritance from 'our fathers.'"[54] The power of these truths no longer lies in their impact upon reason—upon the deliberative capacities of individuals. Rather, their power lies in the maintenance of communal identity over time. Lincoln describes this power elsewhere, in terms as dramatic as those of the Gettysburg Address:

We hold this annual celebration [July 4th] to remind ourselves of all the good done in this process of time, of how it was done and who did it, and how we are historically connected with it; and we go from these meetings in better humor with ourselves— we feel more attached the one to the other, and more firmly bound to the country we inhabit. . . . We have besides these men—descended by blood from our ancestors—among us perhaps half of our people who are not descendents at all of these men, they are men who have come from Europe . . . or whose ancestors have come hither and settled here, finding themselves our equals in all things. If they look back through this history to trace their connection with those days by blood, they find they have none, they cannot carry themselves back into that glorious epoch and make themselves feel that they are part of us, but when they look through that old Declaration of Independence, they find that those old men say that "We hold these truths to be self-evident, that all men are created equal," and then they feel that that moral sentiment taught in that day evidences their relation to those men, that it is the father of all moral principle in them, and that they have a right to claim it as though they were blood of the blood, and flesh of the flesh, of the men who wrote the Declaration, and so they are.[55]

Morality becomes blood, and truth becomes history in Lincoln's myth.

Lincoln is confronting the racial communitarianism of Taney with a moral communitarianism of his own. He is developing the political religion that he spoke of twenty years earlier at the Lyceum. In his myth of the state, the morality of the Declaration of Independence replaces the bloodline of the family. This morality creates a link between individual and community that is just as strong as the link of blood. Indeed, it, too, demands that the individual body become an expression of the idea of the state. The dynamic of maintenance is the same for Lincoln as it was for Taney. In spite of their substantive conflicts over who Americans are, they share a common conceptual model of order.

Although moral truth may give special value to this community, Lincoln understands the primacy of the historical givenness of the community. Even to him, union is more important than truth.[56] It would not be enough, for example, for the seceding states to affirm the same true principles at their foundation. Full vindication of the moral truths of equality and liberty would not justify a failure to maintain the community. Truth can be a first principle only when the problem of constitutionalism is making a state, not when it is maintaining one.[57] For this reason, Lincoln's most sustained explanation of his views, in the 1858 debates with Stephen Douglas, are filled with mutual allegations of patricide. Each man claims to be the faithful son of the founding fathers; each accuses the other of killing them.[58] Each uses the claim of filial piety to define the political identity of the community. Lincoln attempts to make moral truth relevant to the community by identifying it with the fathers: "[W]hen I say that I desire to see the further spread of [slavery] arrested, I only say I desire to see that done which the fathers have first done."[59]

This theme of filial piety is behind Lincoln's famous use of the "house divided" metaphor. The political role of his generation is to maintain the house. When he argues that the union "cannot endure, permanently half slave and half free," he does not claim to be expressing a new insight or a new political truth. Repeatedly, he claims that his position represents only a return to the moral foundation established by the fathers: "All I have asked or desired any where is that [slavery] should be placed back again upon the basis that the fathers of our Government originally placed it upon."[60]

According to Lincoln, the founding fathers recognized the contradiction that slavery posed to democratic self-government, but they could do no better than put slavery "on a course of ultimate extinction."[61] But the fathers failed to anticipate the development of the cotton gin, which has provided a new economic foundation for slavery. For this reason, Lincoln says, extinction has not occurred. Nevertheless, slavery remains a moral contradiction at the foundation of a democratic house. A government that supports slavery uses the coercive power of the state to destroy the grounds of a democratic, self-governing political order. A popular government that supports slavery is ultimately a tyrannical government.[62] Slavery must be ended to redeem the political freedom of both master and slave. With this argument, Lincoln is not trying to correct the work of the fathers by making a new appeal to the abstract truths of political and moral science. He is instead recovering the fathers' own meaning.

Douglas is no less concerned with maintaining the fathers' house: "Why can it not exist divided into free and slave States? Washington, Jefferson, Franklin, Madison, Hamilton, Jay, and the great men of that day, made this Government divided into free States and slave States and left each State perfectly free to do as it pleased on the subject of slavery. Why can it not exist on the same principles on which our fathers made it?" The fathers, according to Douglas, saw that maintenance of the union is possible only within a divided house, so they established the house on the principle of local community self-determination. Lincoln's effort to introduce the morality of slavery into the national debate—and to displace the principle of popular sovereignty—is, for Douglas, a "revolutionary" effort to recast the foundation of the constitutional order. Even if morally correct, it is an act of patricide that will result in division, disunion, and war. [63]

The Lincoln-Douglas debate is one of the most interesting in the history of U.S. politics, because it deals directly with the identity of the community constituted by the Constitution. Lincoln and Douglas perceive a common problem of maintenance. No less than Taney, they both believe that maintenance requires a reaffirmation of origins. Like Taney, they understand the deep linkage of familial identity and political identity. Each claims to speak as the faithful son of the fathers; each claims to be the representative of the house of the fathers. Yet they have fundamentally different answers to the question of political and personal identity. For Lincoln, the community must affirm its moral character and work to cleanse itself of the sin of slavery. Douglas, following Taney, understands the Constitution to constitute a community defined by blood and popular will channeled into legal process. [64]

The constitutional contest at mid-century was, as all maintenance is, about self-identification. Only this claim of the state to be the individual and of the individual to be the state can account for the willingness to accept the carnage of the Civil War. The war was not a use of violent means to accomplish some separate political end. The violence was itself a form of maintenance; it was the affirmation of the state in the bodies of the new generation. Lincoln, in his Second Inaugural Address, presents the war as the moral penance this generation must pay for the sins of the nation. In an assertion of intertemporal identity, he describes "this terrible war, as the woe due to those by whom the offence [slavery] came." [65] What amazes the modern mind is not so much Lincoln's rhetoric as the fact that it could move those countless individuals who owned no slaves and had no personal connection to that past but who nevertheless gave their bodies to affirm the state.

Douglas tried to reduce the moral intensity of constitutional politics by suggesting a constitutionalism based on legal process and personal self-interest. Douglas's political fate suggests that these rather modern ideas are not enough to satisfy the twofold needs of maintenance: first, the need of the individual to find in the temporal dimension of the state a means of overcoming the finitude of the body and, second, the need of the state to appropriate the body of the citizen to secure its own historical continuity. The nation polarized between the competing myths of Lincoln and Taney.

From Science to Myth

In introducing his Lectures on Law in 1790, James Wilson speaks of the need to "teach our children those principles, upon which we ourselves have thought and acted." Such principles can be taught because "[t]he foundations of political truth have been laid." The first principle of this "genuine science of government," which informed the founders' actions as well as their political creation, is what Wilson calls the revolution principle: "[A] revolution principle certainly is, and certainly should be taught as a principle of the constitution of the United States, and of every State in the Union." Wilson goes on to describe the principle and its consequences: "This revolution principle—that, the sovereign power residing in the people, they may change their constitution and government whenever they please—is not a principle of discord, rancour, or war: it is a principle of melioration, contentment, and peace."[66] Sixty years later, the project of constitutionalism had become reverence, not revolution. The founders had become the fathers to whom filial piety was owed, not political artisans modeling a government on the basis of political science. Thus, Daniel Webster ends a famous speech, given in 1848, with a reminder of "the sacred trust, attaching to the rich inheritance which we have received from our fathers" and with the cry "Thank God, I—I also— AM AN AMERICAN."[67]

In this sixty-year period, the conceptual model of order within which constitutionalism was understood changed dramatically. Methodologically, this change was marked by the emergence of originalism. Substantively, it was marked by the linking of individual identity to the historical state. Both changes are elements of what I will call an organic model of maintenance. The critical elements of the organic model are these: the organism is born, not made; it maintains the formal identity that emerges at its birth throughout its life; and each constituent element of its body gains its identity as a part of the larger whole.

The account I have given of the early development of constitutional theory describes the character of the American experience of this shift in political self-understanding from making to maintaining. The constitutional project is no longer that of making something new but that of maintaining what has been made. For the founder, political time is a future to be shaped; for the maintainer, political time is a past to be preserved. In the remainder of this chapter, I want to elaborate the difference between the models of making and maintenance and, in so doing, explain the mythical character of originalism in U.S. constitutionalism.

Myth is the state of belief that supports an organic model of politics, just as science supports the model of making. Political myths display two characteristic attitudes toward the political order.[68] First, myth denies the artifactual character of the political order, representing political life instead as a part of nature. Myth knows no place for the freedom of a political art. Second, myth understands the present life of the citizen to be a representation of the past.[69] Myth makes an assertion of intertemporal identity. In sum, myth works by putting nature in the place of art, and the past in the place of the present. Originalism shares both of these characteristics. It does not explicitly hold them forth, but both are operative within it, and they account for the continuing power and attraction of originalism. Originalism, accordingly, is the supporting myth of an organic model of constitutional order.

Originalism and a Natural Constitution

The conceptual model of making organizes political experience around the concept of a founder who mediates between an abstract idea and historical experience. The founder's end is to construct political order in the image of the timeless pattern revealed by science. Time is, in this model, a force of disorder to be overcome by measuring the existing social order against an ideal pattern. The measure of the founder's art remains outside the product of that art, which is the political order of the actual community.

This model of a scientifically informed political art dominated the argument of *The Federalist*. The uniqueness of Publius's argument inhered not in his use of this model to explain the making of the Constitution but in his effort to combine the model with a theory of political legitimacy based on consent. Doing so required the creation of an entire nation of political artisans who could order their political institutions on the basis of political science.

The organic model, in contrast, denies the separation of the ideal and the real, of timeless form and temporal matter. Without an ideal or abstract form, there is no place for the maker. The organism is itself both form and matter. For it, form exists only as temporally embodied. To be organic—to be alive—is to maintain identity in difference through a constant synthesis. The perceived alternative to organic maintenance is not an ideal form of abstract meaning but disintegration and the meaninglessness of death.

The dissolution of organic form brings meaning itself to an end. This is true of an individual's personal history and, even more vividly, of the life of a community, which understands itself as having both a past and a future. When self-perpetuation stops, history stops, and the organic community simply dissolves. Time becomes chaos again. The problem of an organic constitutionalism, therefore, is to maintain the constitutional order as it was established at the birth of the nation. Because constitutional order is self-instantiating, history, not science, is its measure. Failure to maintain the past order will result in the death of the body politic.

Both models—art and organism—make historical communal life possible, though neither is a necessary condition of historical experience. An alternative, for example, would be an idea of history as developing or moving toward an end. Both models understand history as moving away from a founding moment, which makes history possible by giving form to what would otherwise be chaotic change. But history has a different meaning in each. In the model of art, history represents the intrusion of a recalcitrant, disorganized social life into the instantiated scientific idea achieved by the political artisan. For Publius, the problem of history is the introduction of interests and passions into the scientifically constructed political order. The lesson that the republican political scientist learns from the study of past political experience is that time threatens every political order with decay.

In the organic model, history is the only domain of meaning; it is not a force in competition with meaning. There is no abstract ideal of political order against which history might be measured. There is just the self-expression of a historical community. The community maintains its identity by continually reaffirming its historically legitimated order.[70] Its concept of political legitimacy is exhausted in the communal expression of self-identity. Time can still bring disorder, but the life of a community does not inevitably represent a gap between ideal meaning and historical reality.

The organic state is, therefore, self-referential: nothing outside its own history in-forms the social order. Taney gives voice to this idea when he rejects justice as a measure of law, looking instead to original intent. On this model, the appropriate attitude toward the past is reverence. For just this reason, the debate among Lincoln, Taney, and Douglas is not over correct principles but over filial piety. Each claims to be the good son of the founding fathers; each claims to re-present the origins of the community. The turn toward reverence does not suggest that they believe that no moral judgments can be made apart from the historical state. The separation of morality from politics is a common legacy of Western culture. Yet each is careful to limit the relevance of such external judgments to the constitutional struggle in which they are engaged. Each affirms the autonomy of the political domain, and each believes that the raging political controversies of the period can be settled by renewing contact with the historical origins of the political order. Renewal, not reconsideration, is their goal. Each, one suspects, would have liked to believe that filial piety corresponds with moral obligation, that the fathers brought forth a just order. But ultimately, each places piety and reverence at the center of their arguments, not morality.

The organic model of maintenance is distinctly historical, then, in a way that the model of making is not. Art and the science upon which it is based are timeless. They are always present for those who would remake political order. The problem of order within the organic model, in contrast, is to perpetuate the meaning of the political community established at the birth of the nation. The centrifugal forces of disorder that emerge in the temporal life of the community are overcome by holding steady the historical identity of the nation.

The organic model always looks to political origins, but it is likely to deny that the founding was itself a product of art. This reconceptualization of the founding is implicit in the shift from making to maintenance. To recognize a place for political art would undermine the self-perpetuation of public order. That which has been made by individual artisans can be remade. Art suggests freedom. It suggests that public order can be measured against ideal form and that it can, therefore, be made better and made anew. To suggest that history can be started over is to deny the foundation of the organic model.

In U.S. history, the shift from art to organism is marked by the change in attitude toward the early political leaders: they become the founding fathers and assume an almost sacred status. They are seen, by the mid–1800s, not simply as political scientists with a favorable opportunity to exercise their art but as figures that are larger than life. Webster, for example, speaks of John Adams and Thomas Jefferson as extraordinary: "No two men now live . . . perhaps it may be doubted whether any two men have ever lived in one age, who, more than those we now commemorate, have impressed on mankind their own sentiments in regard to politics and government."[71]

Originalism expresses this self-authentication and self-legitimation of the constitutional order. More than that, it expresses the unchanging character of the state, its character as already determined. The naturalness of the modern myth of originalism does not inhere in a literal continuity between political and natural phenomena—though even this is present—but in the denial of the relevance of a political art. Like the mythical assertion of the natural origins of political order, originalism suggests an inevitability in the outcome of political controversies. The political order cannot be other than it is. It presents itself to the citizen as no less an objective fact of life than the natural order. In asserting that the past determines the present, originalism extends the temporal character of a pre-Darwinian nature to political life. For both nature and politics, the past contains the determinative categories or forms of life. Temporal experience is merely the continuing manifestation, the maintenance, of a set order.

Originalism, Individuality, and Popular Sovereignty

Implicit in every model of political order is an understanding of the character of the individuals who constitute that order. The model of making relies upon an idea of individual subjects as political scientists able to achieve a critical distance from their political role. To give shape to political life through art requires the ability to take that life as an object of deliberation and choice. Creating this distance was the goal of Publius's call to the citizens to deliberate together and thereby remove themselves from their everyday opinions and interests. The organic model denies the separability of subject and object in political life.

Within the organic model, individuals do not stand apart from the political community in which they find themselves. Rather, individual identity is understood as only a part of a larger public order, which is itself determined by a unique history.[72] Individual identity exists prior to, and apart from, any deliberative act. Identity is no longer a function of the capacity to deliberate; it is carried in the blood and borne by the body. The state, on the organic understanding, takes on the body of the individual citizen.

One can see this change in self-understanding as another expression of the natural character of the organic state. The mixing of blood, family, and politics is a vivid aspect of mid-nineteenth-century constitutionalism. The natural character of the political order is analogous to the natural character of the family: both represent a social order grounded in blood. Conceiving of political life on the model of family again suggests that the political order is predetermined: children don't choose their parents. The analogy of the family also makes clear that the natural and the normative are not distinct domains. Familial order may not be chosen, but it defines a set of social relationships of enormous normative significance to the individual.

The meaning of this merger of the individual body with the body of the state is not, however, exhausted in the idea of nature. The political cannot be reduced to the natural without misrepresenting the self-conscious character of the individuals who make up the political order. The state does not appropriate each citizen's body as though it were a natural organism engaged in mortal combat. The coercive powers of the state may be deployed in any individual case, but ultimately the state has no existence outside the imagination of some set of individuals. Only a positive act of self-identification makes possible and sustains the organic state. The individual body is appropriated because the act of appropriation is simultaneously an act of individual self-expression. This is Webster's jubilant claim that he is an American.

To understand this positive act of self-identification with the state, one must understand what the organic state promises the individual. Most simply, it offers the expanded temporality of political history. As a part of the state, the individual is not just the inheritor of a past but is con-stituted in those past acts. By supporting the total appropriation—body and soul—of the individual by the state, the myth transforms the tem-poral dimensions of human existence. It is no accident that Lincoln calls for a political religion: politics, too, must take as its subject the human need to overcome finitude.

For this reason, the American myth of originalism is linked to a particular idea of popular sovereignty. The methodology of originalism is legitimate because it reveals the authentic actions of the popular sovereign, not because the past has some normative priority over the present. Taney, for example, says that if the popular sovereign acted again, the normative claim of the past would disappear. The popular sovereign is the dramatic actor in the myth of originalism. The popular sovereign suggests identity across time and space, not just linking the entire nation at the moment of birth but linking subsequent generations back to the moment of birth.[73] Present and past citizens share a common identity as aspects of a single popular sovereign.

Originalism denies individual freedom in the present by asserting participation in the popular sovereign. "Popular sovereignty" asserts that "we"—the current generation of U.S. citizens—are them. The "them" is all those who came before plus all those who will come after. Problems of individual differentiation are submerged in the affirmation of this vague political entity. Differences in belief, in history, in political participation, and even in biology are submerged in this mythical entity.[74]

Through this assertion of intertemporal identity, the organic model of political order comes to terms with the idea of popular self-government. The popular sovereign is the political self, just as the individual body is the physical self, and the soul is the moral self. The understanding of popular sovereignty that emerges in the mid-nineteenth century is linked neither to universal reason nor to individual expressions of consent. Instead, it is completely national and hence completely historical. This mythical concept of popular sovereignty asserts that Americans are their history.

Members of the present generation are not the descendants of that popular sovereign. The idea of a descendant is challenged by the myth of popular sovereignty. Popular sovereignty suggests identity—we are them—and not just genealogy, even though what the popular sovereign intended must be excavated through esoteric historical research. Contemporary citizens do not know themselves; yet they are that intent, even before they know its content. The constitutional model of both Taney and Lincoln is founded on this idea: history can resolve public political disorder because it tells us who we are.

The myth of popular sovereignty suggests that constitutional order is not the work of political artisans but rather the expression of a particular national identity. Just as the traditional myth expressed the belief that individuals are part of nature in their public lives, so the myth of popular sovereignty expresses the belief that citizens are part of a historical past in their political lives. As long as that belief is maintained, the artifactual character of political rule is denied and the political order is maintained.[75] When the myth fails, history will require a new foundation, and politics will again become a field for making.

Myth is required to support an organic model of political order. By turning to that model, constitutional life turned away from the revolutionary moment of political founding. Until the break is made with the model of making, a state lives simultaneously at the end and beginning of history but never within it. To live within history requires a reconceptualization of constitutionalism. By mid-century this reconceptualization had occurred in American thought.

CHAPTER THREE

The Evolving Unwritten Constitution

In *A Covenant with Death*, Phillip Paludan describes how the ideology of a war to save the union brought in its wake a conservative constitutional law. The war, he argues, inspired constitutional innovation only to the degree required to justify wartime necessities. The more fundamental need was to link the idea of the rule of law to the military effort. This entailed a commitment to the existing constitutional order as a goal and as a limit to the meaning of the union victory: "The Civil War was a struggle for the familiar federal Union, a fight for a constitutional system under which Americans had achieved unparalleled prosperity and liberty. Although prospects existed for vast constitutional change, they might be undone by a respect for constitutional traditions so powerful that men would die for them."[1] For Paludan, the consequence of this wartime ideological necessity was the postwar failure of constitutional law to free itself of traditional understandings of federalism and state's rights. This failure, in turn, limited the capacity of the federal government to protect the newly achieved civil and political rights of the former slaves.

At a more abstract level, a similar conservativism informed postwar conceptions of constitutionalism. Patterns of organic maintenance continued to dominate constitutional thinking. For example, much of the debate over the Fourteenth Amendment—in retrospect, the most striking constitutional innovation brought about by the war—was framed in terms of maintenance. The amendment was seen not as a revolutionary remaking of the constitutional order but as a return to the founders' vision.[2]

Many in Congress understood the amendment as continuous with the war effort: both were attempts to clarify and to enforce what the founders had created. Congressman John A. Bingham, who drafted the initial version of the amendment, described it as "simply a proposition to arm the Congress of the United States, by the consent of the people of the United States, with the power to enforce the bill of rights, as it ' ands in the Constitution today." Another congressman stated that the proposal would "only have the effect to give vitality and life to portions of the Constitution that probably were intended from the beginning to have life and vitality, but which have received such a construction that they have been entirely ignored and have become as dead matter in that instrument." Another spoke of the proposed amendment "as more valuable for clearing away bad interpretations and bad uses of the Constitution as it is than for any positive grant of new power which it contains."[3]

The Fourteenth Amendment was seen not as an innovation on the work of the founders but as a recovery mandated by the mistakes of *Dred Scott* and, before that, *Barron v. Baltimore*.[4] Although a constitutionalism of maintenance could produce the amendment, it simultaneously produced a Supreme Court that could substantially diminish the power and breadth of the new text by agreeing formally with the amendment's supporters that it was not intended to change the prewar constitutional order: "[W]hen in fact [an interpretation of the amendment] radically changes the whole theory of the relations of the State and Federal governments to each other and of both ... to the people; the argument [against that interpretation] has a force that is irresistible."[5]

The conservativism of postwar constitutional thought was in tension with the actual innovations wrought by the war. The war fought to save the union could not help but change the national political order. The struggle between sameness and difference ultimately overwhelmed the model of maintenance. In its place was put a new conceptual model of growth, or evolution—to use the word that came to dominate late nineteenth-century thought.

Under the new model, the present is understood to be different from, and better than, the past. Nevertheless, it is bound to the past: there is no way to achieve *this* present without going through *that* past. History is no longer simply the maintenance of a form established at a moment of birth; it is the means by which growth occurs. A mature society, like a mature individual, is better than an immature one; yet maturity is the result of a historical process for which there is no alternative. One cannot get to the end without starting at the beginning.

Under this conceptual model, the life of the state in history is understood as the working out of the normative identity of the community. In the highly rationalistic, scientific culture of the United States in the second half of the nineteenth century, history was seen as the working out of reason itself. The rationality of the state could no longer be found in an abstract idea apart from history. Neither, however, could it be found full blown at the beginning of history. Instead, as a historical product, it had to be found in the development of the state through time.

To accomplish this change in conceptual models of order, constitutional theory seized upon certain obvious resources: the common law and the idea of growth. These resources were given a new force and theoretical context in the intersection of three different intellectual traditions: the tradition of British conservative thought represented by Edmund Burke and Frederick Pollock; the modern, scientific theory of evolution represented by Charles Darwin and Herbert Spencer; and a surprisingly strong influence of Continental thought, represented by Friedrich Karl von Savigny and Rudolf von Jhering.[6] These intellectual movements did not cause the shift in constitutionalism; rather, they provided the context within which to make sense of an all-but-inevitable development in the constitutional dialogue.

The inevitability of this change was rooted in the weakness of the organic model of maintenance as a model of self-government and in the mythical attitude required to sustain it. As I described in chapter 2, a belief in self-government under the organic model requires a mythical identification of the present generation with the founders. If the belief in this intertemporal identity fails, then maintenance appears not as self-government but as government by the dead hand of the past. The ideology of self-government thus contains within itself all of the conceptual apparatus needed to overturn the organic model of the state and its particular conception of the obligation of maintenance. Not surprisingly, postwar developments of constitutional theory were marked by just that patricidal attitude toward the founding fathers that antebellum figures fought to avoid.

The founders were now reduced from semidivine fathers to naive children, operating without an understanding of political science. They were particularly naive to believe that they could reduce the Constitution to a permanent, written document. What had previously been seen as the greatest contribution of the founders' republican political science—a written constitution—became an accident, an aberration in a longer history of constitutional development. The latter part of the nineteenth century was the age of the "unwritten constitution." The Constitution lost its support from a myth of the fathers and became instead a moment in the evolution of the Anglo-American race.

This shift in constitutionalism took some time. It emerged first in theory; later it came to dominate judicial thinking. Even within theory, the new model had to struggle with old ideas of maintenance. The war was at once a source of and a constraint on innovation in constitutional theory. These contradictory effects are well illustrated by comparing the work of John Pomeroy and that of Sidney George Fisher.

Conceptual Innovation and the Civil War

John Pomeroy, dean of the Law School at New York University, published *An Introduction to the Constitutional Law of the United States* in 1868. This was the first treatise on federal constitutional law published after the war. Pomeroy already had a substantial reputation because of a book on municipal government, written during the war, which attacked the constitutional arguments for state sovereignty.[7] His new work was widely read and extremely influential, not least with members of the Supreme Court.[8]

For Pomeroy, the key question of constitutional law remained what it was before the war: to determine "the essential character of the Constitution itself, and of the United States as a body-politic."[9] His account of this dispute followed the familiar prewar pattern. There are, he writes, three contending schools: the first sees "[the] Constitution as the organic, fundamental law of ... the collective People of the United States as a political unit"; the second sees it "as a compact ... between the separate, independent, sovereign states"; and the third "occupies a middle ground [understanding] the states as originally independent, sovereign commonwealths, but as having surrendered to the United States a portion of their sovereignty."[10] His resolution in favor of the first view contained little that was new. It repeated much that Story had said some thirty years earlier, looking to constitutional text and history. But Pomeroy gave this old argument a new purpose by tying it to the war. "The important lesson in which the public mind now demands to be instructed, is that of our own inherent nationality. It cannot be denied that an attachment, a devotion to the Union, pervades the great mass of citizens. The blood which has been poured out, the treasure which has been expanded ... abundantly attest this fact. But this has been rather the result of sentiment, than of an enlightened conviction." Sentiment must be displaced by "deliberate opinion," which requires a renewal of "the teachings of our fathers."[11] Sentiment sustained the war, but only the fathers' teachings can sustain its outcome.

This constitutionalism of maintenance produces a tremendous sense of unreality in Pomeroy's work. For example, comparing the present to the pre-ratification period, Pomeroy writes: "But now this Constitution is fixed; no one thinks of substituting in its place any new or different form of government; no one suggests any fundamental, or even important, change in its detail. . . . Such as it is, it must continue to be our organic law." Speaking of the conflict between nationalism and federalism, Pomeroy writes, "Our fathers, by an almost divine prescience, struck the golden mean, and devised a scheme in which these opposing forces meet, not to neutralize and destroy, but to support and strengthen each other." At the time he was writing, a substantial argument could surely have been made that these forces, let loose by the fathers, tended to neutralize and destroy each other.[12]

Pomeroy sensed some of the sources for a new model of constitutionalism, but he was too wedded to the task of maintenance to seize hold of them. He saw, for example, the need for progress within constitutional law and suggested that progress comes from the development of the constitutional understanding of the people. Accordingly, his defense of judicial review denied any truth to the claim that judges are "unyielding to the demands of the people's progressive development." Rather, "[c]ourts do yield to the pressure of the popular will, do move with the popular progress, slower perhaps than legislatures and Presidents, but as certainly and efficiently." He also saw that constitutional checks and balances would not be sufficient to restrain the development of a sovereign legislature: "The Constitution is well so far as it goes; the design was good; the checks and balances were carefully and skilfully arranged; but no mere organic law can place a lasting barrier to the advance of a popular legislature." For Pomeroy, this advance nonetheless remained a danger: "Unless our forefathers were wholly wrong, unless the organic law is framed upon an entire misconception of the needs of a free people . . . the three departments . . . must be kept separate, independent, co-ordinate."[13]

To Pomeroy, these ideas about progress, popular understanding, and institutional authority all suggested a parallel between the British common-law system of parliamentary sovereignty and the U.S. constitutional system. Even though embracing the similarity would give rise to theoretical innovation in U.S. constitutionalism, Pomeroy rejected it. He held to a strong doctrine of American exceptionalism: "The Constitution of the United States is peculiar in that it is all written; that it has nothing of tradition. The government and the people go to the instrument itself as the embodiment of all granted functions." A common-law model of constitutional interpretation is, therefore, inappropriate: "[T]his instrument must be read, interpreted, expounded, in the same manner, by the same means and methods, which are appropriate to all other legislative acts." In a line that indicates the continuity of his thought with prewar constitutional maintenance, he says, "[T]he writing remaining unaltered, the various departments of the government can ever be held to these plain utterances of the people's will."[14]

Yet the tension in his thought remained. Immediately after calling "the habit of thought of the lawyer necessary to correct understanding of the Constitution," he called as well for a role for the statesman who concerns himself with "great principles, with considerations of high expediency, with far-reaching national results." How these two approaches could be integrated in practice remains less than clear, though the reason for moving beyond simple maintenance is clear: "Combine the two [the techniques of the lawyer and the statesman], and . . . the national development may go on uninterrupted by arbitrary restraints, and unbroken by sudden shocks."[15]

Pomeroy, in short, was a constitutionalist of the old school, struggling with the problem of growth. He saw the war as a symbol of maintenance while implicitly recognizing that it was more than this. The constitutionalism of maintenance was soon swept away by a new generation of constitutional theorists, who saw the war not as the affirmation of the old order but as a symbol of the defective character of the founders' Constitution. This new generation emerged with a loud voice in the writings of Sidney George Fisher in the midst of the war.

In 1862, Fisher published *The Trial of the Constitution*. Fisher was a well-connected Philadelphia lawyer-farmer who churned out a steady stream of books and articles on legal issues. In his 1862 book, he sought to justify the wartime powers claimed by the Lincoln administration, which included the following:

[Lincoln] called out troops, he enlarged the army and navy, he arrested and confined persons suspected of treasonable acts or designs. . . . The freedom of the press was suspended, members of a State Legislature were imprisoned on the eve of its meeting; over the whole country was stretched the arm of a discretionary power, paramount to the Constitution. . . . Congress has entertained and is now debating plans which greatly exceed the powers granted by the Constitution, plans for a general emancipation of all the slaves in the South, for the confiscation without trial of the property of rebels, for reducing the rebellious States to the condition of Territories.[16]

Although Fisher was not alone in offering constitutional justifications for the political and military expediencies of the Civil War, he was distinguished by the boldness of his thought and his willingness to abandon prewar ideas of constitutionalism.[17]

For Fisher, the war revealed the imperfections of the founders' Constitution: "The Constitution has failed to protect us from the calamity of a bloody Civil War. ... [I]ts defects must be corrected. What they are and what is the remedy are the problems presented by the war."[18] These defects, he says, encompass most of the structural presumptions of the original Constitution, including the doctrines of the reserved power of the people, judicial review, and separation of powers. These errors all arose because of a failure to understand the reality of power in a system of popular government. That reality makes a popularly supported legislature omnipotent. According to Fisher, this is as true of the United States Congress as of the British Parliament.

Fisher rejects a constitutionalism of maintenance: "The Constitution belongs to the people,—to the people of 1862, not to those of 1787." Rule by the dead hand of the past is inconsistent with popular government. "A fixed, unchangeable government, for a changeable, advancing people, is impossible, and were it not so, would be a sad spectacle." The institutional structure of an originalist constitution must fall to the practical reality of popular government: "If the Constitution be immutable, what was law in 1787, must be law as long as the Constitution lasts. To maintain it, therefore, the Judiciary must be stronger than the people, stronger than the representatives of the people. In a popular government this is impossible."[19]

Fisher's positive theory starts from the premise that the Constitution must reflect the will of the contemporary community. It must, therefore, be capable of continuous change. The formal amendment process of article V, which requires cumbersome state and federal procedures as well as supermajorities, cannot embody such changes. Indeed, article V has proved to be unworkable: "[I]n democratic America, innovation is guarded against with such jealous care, that it is doubtful whether the means provided by law for making needed changes can ever be employed."[20] The framers put too tight a constraint upon the possibility of future constitutional development.

Fisher responds to this formal constraint by offering a theoretical account of law that denigrates written constitutions and recognizes constitutional change—that is, constitutional amendment—outside the formalities of article V. He contends that law is custom: "[I]t is philosophically true that all law, in the long run, is and can be nothing but custom."[21] The real Constitution, therefore, is whatever has emerged through the interaction of governmental decision making and popular response over a long period of time. Aspects of the written Constitution that fail to make the transition from text to custom—such as the original plan for indirect election of the president—are not law at all.

The mechanism of real constitutional change exists within, not outside, the ordinary apparatus of representative government. The people express their attitude toward constitutional innovation in the same manner that they respond to any other governmental act: at the ballot box. The foundation of the Constitution, therefore, is not the written document or the work of the founders but the intelligence of the people: "If that fail, the Constitution will fail. If the people prove unfit for freedom, they cannot maintain free government, for its essence consists in the exercise of power by the people."[22]

Thus, Fisher is anti-originalist in his methodology and not bound to the past in his understanding of political self-identity. In place of a myth of origins, Fisher turns to custom, which he understands as a progressive force that leads out of the past and into the future. By identifying law with custom, Fisher places a mechanism for intelligent growth within the law itself. He quotes Lord Coke's proposition that the law "is the perfection of reason" and explains that "[t]he meaning of this is . . . that the reason of the people is always employed in perfecting [law] to suit the demands which are made by time, so that the law grows with the mental growth of the nation, and fits its shape and stature always."[23]

Custom is not simply well-established habit; it represents rational growth through experience. Indeed, Fisher emphasizes contemporary innovations that establish new customs, rather than inherited practices. Custom, and so law, is the evolving pattern of reason in the self-ordering of a community. Much though one might respect the framers, "they were men, and no match for the centuries. They were an assembly called from the fleeting present, and not so wise as the generations of the past."[24] The later in time is superior to the past. It would be irrational to respect the founders' constitution over contemporary custom.

Fisher's rejection of originalism links a number of critical ideas. First, he says, the Constitution was neither made nor born at a particular moment in the past. It is in a continuous process of development. Second, that process is necessary if the Constitution is to derive its legitimacy from popular consent. Third, that process is the working out of reason in the form of law. Custom, Fisher says, links the reasoning, innovative aspect of the state—Congress—with popular will. Fourth, U.S. exceptionalism is unfounded. The reality of power in a popular government places ultimate power in the elected representatives. The effort to structure a constitutional order radically different from that of the British, therefore, had to fail.

Fisher offered a broad theoretical account of the nature of constitutionalism that suggested a radically different future. Thomas Cooley, in 1868, began to do the hard work necessary to connect Fisher's theoretical innovations to actual doctrine in constitutional law. In doing so, he radically changed the political direction in which Fisher's theory had pointed.[25] Fisher took a Burkean appreciation of custom and fitted it to a democratic government, one in which Congress provides intelligent leadership that is always subject to a popular check. Cooley turned away from Congress and toward the courts.

Constitutionalism and the Common Law

In 1868, Cooley, a law professor at the University of Michigan and a justice on the state supreme court, published *A Treatise on the Constitutional Limitations Which Rest upon the Legislative Power of the States of the American Union*. This is generally recognized as the single most influential work in constitutional law in the latter part of the nineteenth century.

Much that is innovative in Cooley's theory is suggested in the broad sweep of the project. The subject is state constitutions, not the federal Constitution. His focus on the states was not, however, an invitation to contemplate the diversity of state constitutional history or law. Cooley aimed to elaborate the single character of constitutional governance, despite the apparent diversity among the state systems. Just as the common law of torts in different jurisdictions converges on a single set of principles, so, according to Cooley, does constitutional case law. The organization of Cooley's book emphasizes this convergence: it is a treatise with sections on individual rights and state powers, rather than on the law of diverse jurisdictions. Cooley hopes to state "clearly and with reasonable conciseness the principles to be deduced from the judicial decisions."[26] The case law of diverse jurisdictions is the subject matter for a scientific study that will produce a unified, systematic set of principles that are the true basis of constitutional order.[27]

In announcing his subject, Cooley breaks with the originalism of the prewar period.[28] Although he remains interested in history, he writes about the history of the common law and the constitutional case law, not the history of the founders' intent. On his view, the single character of constitutional governance, if such exists, cannot be rooted in the diverse histories of state constitutions. Nor does he suggest that the unitary constitutionalism of the diverse state systems is located in their common effort to embody a single abstract political science. Cooley instead combines history and science by identifying constitutional law with the common law. Cooley writes of "the grand old common law, of which American constitutional principles formed a part."[29]

Cooley defines constitutional government as government in which the "fundamental rules or maxims not only locate the sovereign power in individuals or bodies . . . but also define the limits of its exercise so as to protect individual rights and shield them against the exercise of arbitrary power."[30] He links the common law to each of these aspects of constitutional government: the definition of grants of political authority and the establishment of individual rights.

With respect to the definition of political authority, Cooley argues that one can understand the nature of constitutional delegations of authority to the various organs of government only against the common-law background. "The maxims of Magna Charta and the common law are the interpreters of constitutional grants of power."[31] To understand, for example, what was entailed in the grant of "legislative power," it is necessary to know what the appropriate objects and limits of legislative power were at common law. There is no shortcut to obtaining this information; it can come only from a study of the cases.

This function of the common law in defining the scope of delegated authority is evident in the nearly identical language Cooley uses to describe the constitutional police power of the state and the common law. He defines the former as the "system of internal regulation, by which it is sought not only to preserve the public order and prevent offences against the State, but also to establish for the intercourse of citizen with citizen those rules of good manners and good neighborhood which are calculated to prevent a conflict of rights, and to insure to each the uninterrupted enjoyment of his own, so far as is reasonably consistent with a like enjoyment of rights by others." The common law consists in "those maxims of freedom, order, enterprise, and thrift which had prevailed in the conduct of public affairs, the management of private business, the regulation of domestic relations, and the acquisition, control and transfer of property from time immemorial." Both describe a system of public order and private interaction. The sources of both are the same: not abstract reason but the pattern of regulation embodied in the case law.[32]

A scientific inquiry into the police power of the state, therefore, cannot usefully be an articulation of general principles alone. To the degree that there are general principles, they are too broad and abstract to be of much use in the actual work of the law.[33] The real scholarly work must be done among the cases, giving a detailed topography of the legitimate range of state authority. One reason for the wide influence of the treatise was that it moved beyond abstraction to deal with the regulation of railroads, liquor, license fees, quarantines, inspection laws, and many other details of the social and economic order of the nineteenth century.

The common law operates in Cooley's system as the background against which grants of state authority must be understood and, more decisively, as a limit on state authority. His most significant doctrinal contribution was to reemphasize a threefold identification of "due process," the "law of the land," and the common law.[34] This put the due process clause at the center of the constitutional doctrine of individual rights.

Due process, Cooley writes, does not refer to "mere form" alone. The law of the land does not mean "everything which may pass under the form of an enactment." Rather, both due process and the law of the land refer to those limits on the "exertion of the powers of government as the settled maxims of law sanction, and under such safeguards for the protection of individual rights as those maxims prescribe." The primary limit on governmental authority is that "vested rights must not be disturbed." Vested rights, however, are not defined by their formal character. Those rights are vested "which it is equitable the government should recognize, and of which the individual cannot be deprived without injustice."[35]

To know the constitutional limits on government requires knowing what is just in the relations between citizen and state and among citizens themselves.[36] To know this requires falling back on that history of order and regulation embodied in the common law:

While every man has a right to require that his own controversies shall be judged by the same rules which settle those of his neighbors, the whole community is also entitled at all times to demand the protection of the ancient principles which shield private rights against arbitrary interference, even though such interference may be under a rule impartial in its applications. It is not the partial character of the rule, so much as its arbitrary and unusual nature, which condemns it as unknown to the law of the land.[37]

If "arbitrary" means "usual," recourse to an abstract science of reason is not possible. The common law is the sole record of reasonable, that is, nonarbitrary, action.

As with the police power, only the case law shows the system of justice that exists within the political order of society. Accordingly, Cooley writes of the character of vested rights with respect to inheritances, marriage relations, judicial remedies, statutes of limitation, rules of evidence, and a wide variety of other interests and legal structures. In each area, there is a reasonable and just way for the state to act, which is embodied in the common law. The common law is "the best of all laws," because "[c]ustom, when voluntary, is the conclusive proof of the final and settled conviction of the people as to what the rule of right and conduct should be on the subject to which it relates."[38] Or as he puts it elsewhere, "The reason of law . . . is in its fundamentals the reason of religious morality; and no one can think the thoughts of law with its reasons, unless he is in sympathy with the morality and truth which underlie it."[39] The proof of the truth of the law rests in the fact of belief in the law. The common law has no abstract natural law behind it but comes to be seen as natural itself.

Cooley's analysis of the common-law sources of government powers and individual rights substantially undermines the significance of a written constitution. Government action must be evaluated against a standard of regularity; the principles of constitutional law, which are largely the principles of common law, establish the measure of arbitrary action. To declare a statute unconstitutional, a court need not "be able to find in the constitution some specific inhibition which has been disregarded, or some express command which has been disobeyed." Again, "constitutions are to be construed in light of the common law. . . . [I]n judging what [a constitution] means, we are to keep in mind that it is not the beginning of law for the State, but that it assumes the existence of a well-understood system."[40]

Cooley's own text replaces the constitutional text and original history as the handbook for judicial decision: he offers the common-law gloss on constitutional government. Cooley shares with Sidney George Fisher a desire to reject the old models of making and maintenance. Both reject abstract science and originalist inquiries. Yet both deny that constitutional law represents merely an assertion of contemporary will. Each thinks constitutionalism must be an expression of reasonableness, and each links reason to popular government through a model of growth. For both, the pattern of legal growth is the development of reason in an institutional form that receives support from the contemporary community.

This conceptual model of growth, like the earlier models of making and maintenance, did not determine the content of any particular theory. Cooley's turn to common law was distinctly more conservative than Fisher's turn to custom. For Fisher, custom was a way of liberating constitutional law from the dead hand of the past, of legitimating the extraordinary changes in the wartime Constitution. Fisher used the new model of evolving reason to legitimate an omnipotent Congress. Cooley used the same model to point constitutional law backward, not to the work of the founders, but to the historical development of the legal culture. His constitutionalism empowered the courts, not Congress. This battle over the meaning, source, and locus of evolution in constitutional law, whether driven by a common-law model or a political-legislative model, continued for the next fifty years.

The Evolving Unwritten Constitution

After Cooley, perhaps the most influential constitutional theorist of the latter part of the nineteenth century was Christopher Tiedeman.[41] In 1886 he published a treatise on the limitations of police power, aimed at linking constitutionalism and laissez-faire doctrine.[42] Like Cooley's earlier work, Tiedeman's *Treatise* was a systematic review of the case law, which purported to demonstrate the narrow limits within which state assertions of police power must operate. Four years later, Tiedeman wrote a shorter work that set forth the basic substantive and methodological principles of his constitutionalism.[43] Just as his treatise typifies a good deal of substantive constitutional doctrine in the late nineteenth century, the short work typifies the dominant conceptual model of order of that time. Tiedeman shared much with Cooley, but he also added a specifically Continental perspective to the common-law model of an evolving Constitution.[44]

A startling aspect of Tiedeman's book is its direct attack on "the national habit ... to look upon the members of the convention of 1787 as demigods, giant heroes, far surpassing the foremost men of to-day." He rejects the idea that the Constitution was the product of an exercise in political science. It was, instead, the result of political compromises among people who disagreed radically. These compromises left much unclear and undefined. For example, of the problems of reconciling state and national citizenship, Tiedeman says: "Like every other question which was raised before, and which divided, the constitutional convention, this was laid aside with a compromise, which constituted a partial and unsatisfactory recognition of the claims of both parties, the final settlement and adjustment of those claims being left to the future." The framers, in short, dealt in expediency, leaving principled resolution to future development.[45]

Tiedeman's patricide is part of a larger attack on both models of conceptual order that characterized earlier constitutional theory. He argues, first, that the Constitution is not the technical product of political artisans applying the principles of an abstract science. The founders were poor political scientists, and in any case, constitutions are not made: "[T]he fundamental principles which form the constitution of the state cannot be created by any governmental or popular edict." Second, the Constitution was not born in a past act of will on the part of the popular sovereign. No social contract ever existed: "[I]t is not true that the power [of government] is derived from the consent of all the governed." More important, even if such a social contract had existed, "[a]ll governmental authority rests upon the commands, not of a dead generation, but of a living generation. . . . The binding authority of law, therefore, does not rest upon any edict of the people in the past; it rests upon the present will of those who possess the political power." He puts this same point more colorfully later: "No people are ruled by dead men, or by the utterances of dead men."[46]

In place of these models of making and maintaining, Tiedeman substitutes a new conceptual structure based on the idea of evolution. "[C]onstitutions," he writes, "are not made, they grow." The evolving constitution is the "unwritten constitution," which is the real or living constitution.[47]

Understanding the character of the real constitution also answers "[t]he fundamental query of political philosophy [which] is, By what right do those in authority command your and my obedience?" This collapse of the descriptive and the normative is clear in Tiedeman's summary of his work: "I believe I have succeeded in showing the same social forces which create and develop the ethics of a nation create and develop its law; that the substantive law is essentially nothing more than the moral rules." If legal rules are moral rules, no separate question of a moral duty to obey the law can arise.[48]

Tiedeman writes that the moral rules "[do] not remain stationary"; their "growth and evolution [follow] an easily recognized law of development." The law, including constitutional law, must follow this same course of evolution. The success of the Constitution, therefore, does not rest on the written document produced at the end of the eighteenth century but on that mass of judicial precedent, governmental practice, and popular opinion that determines the changing political practice of the nation. "The great body of American constitutional law cannot be found in the written instruments, which we call our constitutions; it is unwritten, in the constitutional and legal acceptation of the term, and is to be found in the decisions of the courts and the acts of the National and State legislatures, constantly changing with the demands of popular will." This living law supports his conclusion that the excellence of the Constitution lies in "the complete harmony of its principles with the political evolution of the nation . . . and not [in] the political acumen of the conventions which promulgated it."[49]

The changing circumstances to which the law must respond are primarily changes in the "prevalent sense of right." When there is too great a divergence between that sense of right and the formal law, whether statutory or constitutional, the law becomes nothing but "dead letters." This link of law to popular morality is not a claim about the subjective character of constitutional law. Rather, the prevalent sense of right has a determinate, evolving shape that can be scientifically appraised. To understand the true character of constitutional law, one must understand the true shape of the evolution of public morality. To do so requires a decision maker, in particular a court, to distinguish popular whim from the popular will: "If one professes any faith at all in popular government, he must confess to a desire that the popular will shall prevail, and that the danger to the commonwealth lies not in the people's will but in their whims and ill-considered wishes." Tiedeman is hardly a populist.[50]

The courts, not popular movements, are the producers of the raw material of constitutional evolution—the case law. They are also the scientific interpreters of the true meaning of that evolutionary process. That true meaning is the expression of reason in and through history and constitutes the true popular will. Thus, the evolution of constitutionalism is not just the subject matter of a scientific inquiry but produces a pattern of scientific or reasonable governance. For example, speaking of a range of possible interpretations of the written text of the Constitution, Tiedeman writes: "[T]hat interpretation becomes the only possible one, when it may be shown by the experience of a century, that the alternative construction, which reflects the intentions of the original enactors of the written word, is pernicious to the stability of the government, and in violation of the soundest principles of political science."[51] Sound principles of political science are embedded in, and accessible only through, the history of the nation.

Tiedeman does not, in *The Unwritten Constitution*, fully describe the evolution of public morality and constitutional law. That project would require a study of the development of the case law, the sort that he provided in his earlier treatise. Nevertheless, several propositions are clear.

First, the shape of the evolution of the popular will is revealed only through scientific inquiry, not by the measurement of popular opinion. Writing of John Austin's positivism, Tiedeman says, "I cannot believe that he was unconscious of the natural sequential development of the law, operated upon by all the social forces, out of which civilization is in general evolved. But the reader of his work . . . will have no very clear conception of this scientific development if he has not obtained the idea elsewhere."[52] The same can be said of the reader of Tiedeman's work.

Second, the scientific understanding of the development of constitutional law appeals to a model of social evolution. Like Herbert Spencer, Tiedeman sees evolutionary movement resulting from a clash between forces of integration and disintegration: "[I]t is necessary, as elsewhere, to take cognizance of the existence and effect of the two opposing social forces, which are present everywhere in bodies-politic . . . the force of consolidation or centralization, and the force of disintegration."[53] The forces will meet violently, not smoothly and gradually. The examples Tiedeman has in mind include the American Revolution and the Civil War—political crises that do not represent new constitutional foundations but moments in a continuous development. American constitutional law is a particular strain of the much longer evolution of Anglo-American law.

Third, and perhaps most important in the immediate use to which Tiedeman's work was put by lawyers and courts, some statements about the end point of this evolutionary process can be made. Again, the substance is Spencerian: "With the general growth and spread of popular government, there appeared a political philosophy whose central thought and fundamental maxim was, that society, collectively and individually, can attain, its highest development by being left free from governmental control, as far as this is possible." A link between constitutional self-government and laissez-faire doctrine is necessary—not from the perspective of abstract logic but from that of a scientific account of social evolution. The link, however, is not apparent to popular opinion, which remains uninformed and nonscientific. Tiedeman complains of the rising challenge to "*laissez-faire* philosophy" made by "Socialists and Communists" and writes that "the conservative classes stand in constant fear of the advent of an absolutism more tyrannical and more unreasoning than any before experienced by man,—the absolutism of a democratic majority."[54]

The voice of popular opinion need not be respected, because it is "unreasoning." The Constitution is the embodiment of reason in the order of the state. Accordingly, Tiedeman, who has just argued that there is "no such thing . . . as an absolute, inalienable, natural right," praises "the disposition of the courts to seize hold of these general declarations of rights [in the Fourteenth Amendment] as an authority for them to lay their interdict upon all legislative acts which interfere with the individual's natural rights, even though these acts do not violate any specific or special provision of the Constitution."[55] The task of courts, as well as constitutional theorists, is to distinguish the path of reason in the evolution of social phenomena. The language of natural rights is a politically convenient means of accomplishing this end, even if natural rights do not exist as a matter of theory.

Tiedeman has tied together many of the elements typical of late nineteenth-century constitutional theory. The theory purported to be scientific, which meant to these theorists that there had to be an observable mass of data—here, the cases—from which general principles could be derived. The conceptual framework by which these data were organized depended upon an evolutionary model. Within this evolutionary framework, the U.S. Constitution was an epiphenomenon in the historical development of the political and legal life of the Anglo-American race.[56] The theorists simultaneously spoke of the evolution of the modes of popular self-government and displayed a serious mistrust of popular government.[57] Self-government was understood as the particular trust and product of the courts, which were to apply a scientific jurisprudence. Finally, the end of jurisprudential science was to identify and empower reason as it showed itself in history.

If Tiedeman's little book on the unwritten constitution reads like a popular essay, Francis Wharton's *Commentaries on Law*, which preceded Tiedeman's work by six years, reads like a scholarly tome.[58] They nonetheless share a common model of an evolving unwritten constitution. Like Tiedeman, Wharton was a prolific writer of legal texts, including works on criminal law, international law, negligence, evidence, and contracts. Again like Tiedeman, he had spent time in Germany, and the Continental influence on his thought is manifest.

Wharton, too, begins with a rejection of earlier ideas about the source of law. He puts this bluntly on the opening page: "The laws which are really operative ... [are] not the creatures either of *a priori* political speculation or of arbitrary sovereign decree." In the models of making and maintenance, the Constitution is conceived to be a product of a discrete historical act—although each model characterizes that act differently. Wharton denies this conception: the real laws are "emanations rather than efforts," even in the United States, which purports to be a self-governing democracy, "the law which obtains ... is not a scheme invented by statesmen at a particular crisis, but is the silent and spontaneous evolution of the nation, past as well as present, adapting itself to the conditions in which in each epoch it is placed." Laws "are the instinctive and unconscious outgrowth of the nation." They "are the products and not the moulders of custom."[59]

Wharton's appeal to the nation as the subject of custom puts a new gloss on the idea of the popular sovereign. The nation "comprises that people as wrought up in one continuous body with those who preceded it as part of a common race." Unlike the prewar idea of popular sovereignty, which suggested a transtemporal identity of the present generation with the first, Wharton's conception of the nation is that of a single subject displaying temporal development. By linking race and nation, Wharton expands the relevant temporal and geographic domain of the growth of law: "[T]he people of the United States, as primary law-makers, form one with the people of England."[60]

Wharton, who is a far more articulate legal philosopher than Tiedeman, reflects on the relation of this evolutionary theory of law to larger theoretical developments. Although the model appears Darwinian, Wharton argues that it has deeper roots. He places himself in the "historical" school of jurisprudence, in particular the "progressive" branch of that school. He traces this school back to the works of Burke and Savigny, both of whom located the origin of law in custom and understood custom to evolve in response to the changing "conscience and need" of the nation. Wharton approvingly quotes Pollock's description of the relation of the historical school to Darwin:

The historical method is not the peculiar property of jurisprudence. . . . The doctrine of evolution is nothing else than the historical method applied to the facts of nature; the historical method is nothing else than the doctrine of evolution applied to human societies and institutions. . . . Savigny, whom we do not yet know or honor enough, and even our own Burke, whom we know and honor, but cannot honor too much, were Darwinians before Darwin.[61]

Wharton also shares Tiedeman's enthusiasm for Herbert Spencer: "[Spencer] has advocated the main contention of the historical school— that of the evolution of law from the past and its inevitable and necessary evolution in the future." In U.S. constitutional law, the evolutionary tendency has been toward laissez-faire limits on the authority of government. Wharton sees the fulfillment of this idea in the Fourteenth Amendment, which like all real law, declares rules already established by custom. The effect of the Fourteenth Amendment is to give constitutional stature to common-law limitations on the scope of state police power:

Where a statute . . . makes a business penal which was not penal at common law as a nuisance, such statute is unconstitutional, if not as impairing the obligation of contracts, at least as taking away rights without due process of law. And by the fourteenth amendment . . . the states are now prohibited from passing statutes which would have the effect of unjustly impairing private rights.[62]

Wharton is not just concerned with placing constitutional evolution in a larger intellectual context. He also offers a detailed analysis of the mechanism of legal evolution through custom. He writes that "the source of law is reason combined with national conscience and need." The needs of the community and the prevailing sense of right will generate a course of action or a pattern of behavior: "[T]o be judicious and effective, [law] must come from the people and conform itself to their sense of right and to their national needs, as moulded by their past training, as well as their present environments." Yet reason must measure this communal response. Convictions as to right "are to be modified by reason, and [the] materials on which reason is to act are to be enumerated national aptitudes and tastes, national resources, national traditions." Reason has "a co-ordinate rank" with the sense of right and need in the evolution of law. Ultimately, reason gives form to the whole process.[63]

The result of this evolution of custom is a historicized reason. The system of law is moving toward a comprehensive rationality—not the abstract rationality of a speculative system but its opposite. Wharton writes that "the logic of facts," and not "the logic of textual criticism," provides a model of reason in constitutional law. The logic of facts allows for the combination of seemingly inconsistent principles, which would be incomprehensible to the speculative philosopher: "[T]here is nothing strange in the position that a political constitution should combine contradictory opposites, logically irreconcilable, yet practically correlative. It is so in the kindred sciences of theology and metaphysics." This logic of facts has forced the modification and elimination of constitutional provisions "which practically jar with the general spirit of the instrument, however theoretically consistent they may be." For example, the logic of facts has revised the meaning and function of the electoral college, as well as the meaning of "advice" in the "advice and consent" clause.[64]

This understanding of law as the evolving expression of a concrete, communal reason produced in Wharton the same attitude toward the role of popular majorities in a popular government that was found in Tiedeman. Both favored courts as the vehicle for development of law: "Undoubtedly from the legislature must come revolutionary changes in the law, such as make a catastrophic transition from one era to another. But, when the change is one of logical evolution, it is likely to be done far more accurately by the judiciary." The responsibility of the courts is that of "evolving from [the law] rules which should properly govern present issues, and winnowing from it limitations which are withered and dead."[65]

If reason is embedded in history and law is the expression of that reason, then there is little place for the making of new law, either statutory or constitutional. Rather, Wharton says, "[t]he law should be allowed to grow by itself; the reason being that the unconscious tendencies of a Christian nation . . . are more wise and healthy than the conscious policy of its legislators or rulers, or even of its own component members meeting for popular deliberation."[66] Of course, law does not grow by itself, unaided by human effort. Wharton's real point is that the appropriate aid comes from the courts. The courts read the character of national reason as it has evolved in and through the growth of the customs of the community.

The Political Branches in an Evolving Constitution

Tiedeman and Wharton followed Cooley, not Fisher, in placing the Court at the center of constitutional evolution. The role of the Court was to distinguish the true public opinion from the public whim, to differentiate the reasonable order of the state from the irrational interests of the multitude. The evolutionary model of constitutionalism is not necessarily linked, however, to this focus on the Court.[67] James Thayer and Woodrow Wilson, two of the leading constitutional theorists at the end of the century, demonstrate the power of the evolutionary model even when loosened from this institutional contraint.[68]

James Thayer is usually seen as a forerunner of the legal realist movement that developed at the beginning of the twentieth century. There is good reason for this. Thayer was a friend and professional colleague of Oliver Wendell Holmes, first in law practice and then at Harvard, where Thayer taught for thirty years.[69] Louis Brandeis was a student of Thayer's, and Felix Frankfurter, who just missed Thayer at Harvard, acknowledged Thayer's substantial influence.[70] Of Thayer's most famous essay in constitutional law, "The Origin and Scope of the American Doctrine of Constitutional Law," Holmes wrote, "I agree with it heartily and it makes explicit the point of view from which implicitly I have approached the constitutional questions upon which I have differed from some other judges."[71] To read Thayer wholly from this backward-looking perspective is nevertheless a mistake. Indeed, it would be surprising if Thayer could write contemporaneously with Tiedeman, in a period dominated by Cooley—whom Thayer frequently cites—and within a law school committed to a scientific approach to the common law yet be uninfluenced by his environment. Looked at from the perspective of the evolutionary model, Thayer appears to share a good deal with his contemporaries.

Thayer's classic essay on the American doctrine of constitutional law begins with a historical explanation of the judicial role. The practice of judicial review was not a logical consequence of adopting a written constitution, as Marshall argued in *Marbury*. Rather, Thayer says, it resulted from the colonial history of the United States. Because legal authority in the colonies derived from delegations of power by an external sovereign— the Crown—courts had regularly to review colonial legislation to assure that it remained within the boundaries of the delegations. This judical practice, according to Thayer, was continued, more out of habit than design, under the radically different circumstances of the postindependence period. Judicial review originated in nothing more than historical accident, which is why it serves no systematic function in the making of law: "The judiciary may well reflect that if they had been regarded by the people as the chief protection against legislative violation of the constitution, they would not have been allowed merely this incidental and postponed control."[72]

Thayer does not believe that the Court can speak in the name of the people: "The sovereign himself, having written these expressions of his will, had retired into the clouds; in any regular course of events he had no organ to enforce his will, except those to whom his orders were addressed in these documents."[73] The Court has no privileged access to the popular sovereign. Both courts and legislatures are ordinary organs of governance, separated from the sovereign in any regular course of events.

Although Thayer argues for a relocation of authority to Congress and away from the courts, he does not confuse Congress and the people. Indeed, Thayer describes the reality of Congress in harsh words: "[T]he question is not merely what persons may rationally do who are such as we often see, in point of fact, in our legislative bodies, persons untaught it may be, indocile, thoughtless, reckless, incompetent."[74] The justification for judicial deference toward Congress cannot be grounded in institutional competence nor in representational capacity. Thayer instead relies on an instrumentalism aimed at the moral development of the larger community. The people must struggle with the practical requirements of government from the perspective of morality, not law. Law should be a product of the moral growth of the people. Too much court-made law will undermine popular moral growth. This focus on moral growth puts Thayer far closer to Tiedeman and his colleagues than his modern readers might ordinarily suspect.

Thayer typifies late nineteenth-century thought in accepting the idea of popular moral evolution. He shared the common objective of producing a constitutional doctrine that would further the moral progress of the people. Thayer expresses these larger views in an essay on the government of the territorial acquisitions—"Our New Possessions"—resulting from the Spanish-American War. One benefit of these new possessions is, he thinks, the "reflex effect of colonial administration upon the home government, and its people and public men." He goes on to write:

These new duties will tend to enlarge men's ideas of government and the ends of government. . . . [T]he childish literalness which has crept into our notions of the principles of government, as if all men, however savage and however unfit to govern themselves, were oppressed when other people governed them; as if self-government were not often a curse; and as if a great nation does not often owe to its people, or some part of them, as its chief duty, that of governing them from the outside, instead of giving them immediate control of themselves—these things are taking their proper place in the wholesome education of the discussions that are now going forward.[75]

Thayer differs from scholars like Cooley and Tiedeman in his failure to comprehend how judicial review advances growth in popular morality. He describes judicial review as "always attended with a serious evil, namely, that the correction of legislative mistakes comes from the outside, and the people thus lose the political experience, and the moral education and stimulus that come from fighting the question out in the ordinary way, and correcting their own errors."[76] Here he explicitly describes intervention by the Court in the political process as external. This characterization is critical. For Tiedeman and Wharton, the Court speaks for the people. The Court can tell the people who they really are, because it speaks in the name of the popular sovereign when it locates the shape of reason in history. Thayer rejects this when he describes the Court as an external source of rule. He discounts the Court's claim to represent the popular sovereign to virtually nothing at all. Judicial intervention does not further popular sovereignty—it undermines it. Although external rule may be appropriate for "our new possessions," it is not appropriate for a people at the stage of moral development found in the United States.

Thayer's problem with judicial review, then, must not be confused with the modern assertion that representative institutions have a claim, stronger than that of the courts, to legitimacy in a democratic polity. He does not believe that the legislature, any more than the Court, speaks in the name of the popular sovereign. Indeed, the real legislature, of which

Thayer has a very low opinion, is displaced in theory by a fictional legislature that is the "majestic representative of the people . . . a coordinate department of the government, charged with the greatest functions, and invested, in contemplation of law, with whatsoever wisdom, virtue, and knowledge the exercise of such functions requires." If courts indulge in this fiction, a space will open for popular moral growth. A restrained Court "will help, as nothing else can, to fix the spot where responsibility lies, and to bring down on that precise locality the thunderbolt of popular condemnation."[77]

Thayer perceives judicial review as weakening the responsible exercise of popular sovereignty. If the legislature cannot decide constitutional issues for itself, it will think only of satisfying the demands of the external sovereign—the Court. It will look to the Court instead of the people: "No doubt our doctrine of constitutional law has had a tendency to drive out questions of justice and right, and to fill the mind of legislators with thoughts of mere legality, of what the constitution allows. And moreover, even in the matter of legality, they have felt little responsibility; if we are wrong, they say, the courts will correct it." Judicial review has this subversive effect not only on the legislature but also on the people: "[N]ot being thrown back on themselves, on the responsible exercise of their own prudence, moral sense, and honor, [they] lose much of what is best in the political experience of any nation." In short, the more the Court tries to represent the people, the more the people cease to function as the popular sovereign.[78]

Thayer illustrates both his institutional and substantive concerns in a discussion of the *Granger* cases, which upheld regulatory legislation arising from populist political movements.[79] He writes that had the Court decided these cases the other way, "we should have been saved some trouble and some harm." Nevertheless, he defends these decisions because of "the good which came to the country and its people from the vigorous thinking that had to be done in the political debates that followed, from the infiltration through every part of the population of sound ideas and sentiments, from the rousing into activity of opposite elements, the enlargement of ideas, the strengthening of moral fibre, and the growth of political experience that came out of it all."[80] That good, however, is hardly the continuation of the popular political agenda out of which the specific regulatory actions emerged. Thayer's argument for judicial deference does not suggest approval of social welfare legislation. He attacks contemporary legislation that does not respect "private rights."[81] When he praises these decisions, his concern is institutional and instrumental; he is not agreeing with their content.

Thayer's institutional analysis results in a new standard for judicial review: "[T]he ultimate question [for a court] is not what is the true meaning of the constitution, but whether legislation is sustainable or not." In exercising judicial review "it is never ... merely the dry question of what the judges themselves may think that the Constitution means." "This way of putting it," Thayer writes, "easily results in the wrong kind of disregard of legislative considerations; ... [i]nstead of taking them into account and allowing for them as furnishing possible grounds of legislative action, there takes place a pedantic and academic treatment of the texts of the constitution and the laws."[82]

Thayer argues instead that the Constitution can have a variety of meanings. Where its meaning is ambiguous, authority is a function of institutional role. He writes that "the constitution often admits of different interpretations; ... there is often a range of choice and judgment; ... the constitution does not impose upon the legislature any one specific opinion, but leaves open this range of choice." This idea of a range of choice is Thayer's substitute for a doctrine of informal amendment, so prominent in his predecessors' thought. It makes growth possible outside the formal amendment process. The only role for the Court is to set the outside boundaries of reason: it must ask whether an alleged inconsistency with the Constitution is "so clear that it is not open to rational question." The legislature, however, is not likely to act in such ways; constitutional disputes usually involve controversy, not contrariness.[83]

Thayer's appeal to the political and moral evolution of the community as a framework for understanding the proper limits of judicial review is similar in tone and substance to the views of Justice Holmes. Holmes admitted as much.[84] Holmes's famous dissent in *Lochner v. New York* also argues for a broad view of legislative choice under the Constitution: "[The Constitution] is made for people of fundamentally differing views, and the accident of our finding certain opinions natural and familiar or novel and even shocking ought not to conclude our judgment upon the question whether statutes embodying them conflict with the Constitution of the United States." Like Thayer, Holmes links this "accidental" quality of the Court's involvement to a deferential standard of reasonableness: Would a "rational and fair man necessarily ... admit that the statute proposed would infringe fundamental principles?"[85] Again, this institutional vision does not oppose, but rests upon, a broader understanding of an evolving constitution: "[Constitutional provisions] are not mathematical formulas having their essence in their form; they are organic living institutions transplanted from English soil. Their significance is vital not formal; it is to be gathered not simply by taking the words and a dictionary, but by considering their origin and the line of their growth."[86] Finally, just as Thayer's institutional analysis should not be mistaken for a substantive attitude favoring populist and progressive legislation, neither should Holmes's. Holmes, in his own view, remained "an unrepentant Spencerian Darwinist," extremely skeptical of the modern growth of government regulation.[87]

For both Holmes and Thayer, the disagreement with competing theorists was over institutional role, not the conceptual model of constitutionalism. All the participants in this debate have adopted an evolutionary model of constitutionalism. The dissension was over the locus of evolution, not over the fact of constitutional growth. This institutional conflict figures deeply within the thought of Woodrow Wilson.

Wilson wrote two works on constitutional governance: *Congressional Government,* in 1885, and *Constitutional Government in the United States,* in 1908. To a reader today, the earlier work seems distinctly more modern. By 1908, Wilson, too, was thoroughly committed to the evolutionary model, abandoning the critical, comparative approach that characterized the earlier work.

Both of Wilson's works are centrally concerned with the problem of time and its effects upon any established system of political order. But the two works represent fundamentally different attitudes toward change. In the earlier work, Wilson sees time as a liberation from the past; in the later work, he sees it as the evolutionary development of patterns of governance. In the earlier work, he sees temporality as inviting a constitutional remaking, based upon political science; in the latter, he sees temporality as growth.

The liberating consequences of time are seen in *Congressional Government* in the constrast between the Constitution in theory and the Constitution in fact. In the first chapter, Wilson offers a "rapid outline sketch of the two pictures, of the theory and of the actual practices of the Constitution . . . to show the most marked points of difference between the two." His aim is "to escape from theories and attach himself to facts, not allowing himself to be confused by a knowledge of what that government was intended to be . . . but striving . . . to photograph the delicate organism . . . exactly as it is today."[88] The possibility of taking this critical attitude toward the past is itself a function of time. Such a theoretical attitude was not conceivable earlier: "[O]pposition to the Constitution as a constitution, and even hostile criticism of its provisions, ceased almost immediately upon its adoption; and not only ceased, but gave place to an undiscriminating and almost blind worship of its principles." This period of "formal deference to the worshipful fundamental law" ended—or rather was shattered—with the Civil War. The "rude shock of the war" has created a new generation no longer bound to the past: "[W]e of the present generation are . . . the first Americans to hear our own country-men ask whether the Constitution is still adapted to serve the purposes for which it was intended; the first to entertain any serious doubts about the superiority of our own institutions . . . the first to think of remodel-ing the [federal] administrative machinery." For Wilson, the war repre-sents the failure of maintenance and the opportunity for a new begin-ning.[89]

When Wilson speaks of growth in this early work, he does not mean a natural process of political development. Rather, growth serves only to separate the present from the past and thus to allow a critical reevaluation of the founders' political order: "[W]e are really living under a constitution essentially different from that which we have been so long worshiping as our own peculiar and incomparable possession. In short, this model gov-ernment is no longer conformable with its own original pattern. While we have been shielding it from criticism it has slipped away from us." Wilson concludes that "we are farther than most of us realize from the times and the policy of the framers of the Constitution." This movement away from origins is unavoidable. It is "another illustration of [a] universal principle of institutional change." Constitutional maintenance cannot last forever.[90]

The image of change dominates that of growth in *Congressional Government.* Change allows a critical distance on the past and justifies a comparative approach to constitutional criticism. According to Wilson, the new generation of critics has a historical awareness that breaks the tie between present and past, freeing them from the task of maintenance. The overwhelming message of *Congressional Government* is that mainte-nance of the founders' ideal form of political order has hindered the de-velopment of a rational constitutional order. It has created burdens that the critic can identify and seek to remove. Wilson concludes, "It is . . . manifestly a radical defect in our federal system that it parcels out power and confuses responsibility as it does. The main purpose of the Conven-tion of 1787 seems to have been to accomplish this grievous mistake."[91] So much for republican political science and its doctrine of separation of powers.

Wilson's study of facts convinces him that congressional government is inevitable in any modern democracy: "The natural, the inevitable ten-dency of every system of self-government like our own and the British is to exalt the representative body . . . to a position of absolute supremacy." The founders' effort to prevent this through institutional checks and bal-ances has resulted in "simply an unpleasant, wearing friction which, with other adjustments, more felicitous and equally safe, might readily be avoided." In a final irony, Wilson calls on the founders to testify to their own irrelevance to the critical, reconstructive mission of the new generation: "It is quite safe to say that were it possible to call together again the members of that wonderful Convention to view the work of their hands in the light of the century that has tested it, they would be the first to admit that the only fruit of dividing power had been to make it irresponsible."[92]

Constitutional Government, written twenty years later, purports to continue the contrast of theory and fact, past and present. Wilson introduces the new work with the following sentence: "My object in the following lectures is to examine the government of the United States as a constitutional system as simply and directly as possible, with an eye to practice, not to theory."[93] By 1908, however, Wilson is so thoroughly imbued with theory that the contrast between fact and theory now means nothing other than a contrast between theories. Facts are simply the products of the "correct" theory.

The correct theory speaks to the evolutionary character of constitutional governance: "The government of the United States was constructed upon the Whig theory of political dynamics, which was a sort of unconscious copy of the Newtonian theory of the universe. In our own day, whenever we discuss the structure or development of anything . . . we consciously or unconsciously follow Mr. Darwin; but before Mr. Darwin, they followed Newton." Wilson rejects the founders' theory because of its failure to recognize growth: "The trouble with the theory is that government is not a machine, but a living thing. It falls, not under the theory of the universe, but under the theory of organic life. It is accountable to Darwin, not to Newton." A Newtonian constitution would have been a static machine; it would have no history. "The government of the United States," by contrast, "has had a vital and normal organic growth." Growth has required cooperation among the institutions of government, not the opposition envisioned by the earlier theorists. The new book is designed to show the nature of this cooperation, which accounts for the pattern of growth of constitutional governance.[94]

This elaborate appeal to Darwin and the contrast of theoretical accounts notwithstanding, Wilson writes that institutional cooperation and growth "is not theory, but fact, and displays its force as fact, whatever theories may be thrown across its track. Living political constitutions must be Darwinian in structure and practice." To stick to the facts no longer suggests a release from history and the application of a critical, comparative approach. Rather, the facts have become imbued with a normative, theoretical principle. Constitutional governance is not something to be remade or even made at all; it is, instead, the result of a natural developmental process. For example, writing of the new U.S. colony, the Philippines, Wilson states: "[W]e cannot give them self-government. Self-government is not a thing that can be 'given' to any people, because it is a form of character and not a form of constitution. No people can be 'given' the self-control of maturity." The idea of maturity links evolution among political forms to the life cycle of the individual, with the same normative assessment of the value of later stages of development. The depth of Wilson's commitment to the evolutionary model and his repudiation of his earlier embrace of remaking is evident in his conclusion: "Having ourselves gained self-government by a definite process *which can have no substitute,* let us put the peoples dependent upon us in the right way to gain it also."[95]

Wilson develops this evolutionary model in two directions. First, he offers a world-historical account, tracing the character of constitutional government through four stages of growth of human society. Not surprisingly, U.S. constitutional development occurs wholly within the final stage of world history.[96] Second, he retails the evolution of the U.S. Constitution into a system that he now characterizes as one of presidential, not congressional, leadership. The most interesting aspect of the book is the underlying tension that develops between these two accounts of constitutionalism. Implicit in Wilson's thought is exactly that conflict over the locus of evolution in constitutional structure that informs the larger constitutional debate of this period and that will ultimately topple this model of order.

Wilson starts *Constitutional Government* with a definition: "A constitutional government is one whose powers have been adapted to the interests of its people and to the maintenance of individual liberty." Although the dual focus on interests and rights goes all the way back to Madison, the idea of adaptation is distinctly new and links constitutionalism to evolutionary thought. Wilson initially illustrates this idea of constitutional government with the model of contract: "the ideal of a government conducted upon the basis of a definite understanding, if need be of a formal pact, between those who are to submit to it and those who are to conduct it, with a view to making government an instrument of the general welfare." Yet it rapidly becomes clear that contract is not adequate to the idea of adaptation. Contract freezes a particular conception of liberty, but "political liberty is the right of those who are governed to adjust government to their own needs and interests. . . . The ideals of liberty cannot be fixed from generation to generation."[97]

In place of contract, Wilson develops a model of constitutional government as a process of constant adjustment between public opinion and the institutions of political authority: "The object of constitutional government is to bring the active, planning will of each part of the government into accord with the prevailing popular thought and need, and thus make it an impartial instrument of symmetrical national development."[98] Wilson, however, cannot settle on the institutional structure of this process of adaptation.

He places a new emphasis on the presidency. Conceiving of public opinion as the articulated view of a national community, Wilson argues that the president is in the best institutional situation to understand and respond to that expression. Although the framers intended the president to be subordinate to Congress—an executor of the laws—in his position as the sole representative of the "people as a whole," he has evolved into the leader of the nation, as well as of a political party. His leadership is the inevitable result of his power to give voice to public opinion:

The nation as a whole has chosen him, and is conscious that it has no other political spokesman. His is the only national voice in affairs. Let him once win the admiration and confidence of the country, and no other single force can withstand him, no combination of forces will easily overpower him. His position takes the imagination of the country. He is the representative of no constituency, but of the whole people. When he speaks in his true character, he speaks for no special interest. If he rightly interpret the national thought and boldly insist upon it, he is irresistible.[99]

His earlier views on congressional government have been abandoned. Wilson now sees a Congress that has "greatly weakened itself as an organ of public opinion" and thus as an organ of governance: "[T]he greatest power lies with that part of the government which is in most direct communication with the nation itself."[100]

But just as Tiedeman was not satisfied with a formal account of the relation between public opinion and the evolution of constitutional order, so Wilson is committed to a substantive understanding of the meaning of liberty and the end of constitutional development. Public opinion is not indeterminate but is moving toward a determinate content: "[V]ague talk and ineffectual theory though there be, the individual is indisputably the original, the first fact of liberty. . . . A man is not free through representative assemblies, he is free in his own action, in his own dealings with the person and powers about him, or he is not free at all. . . . Liberty belongs to the individual, or it does not exist." This understanding of the end point of the evolution of liberty compels Wilson to shift his attention from the political to the judicial institutions of government: "So far as the individual is concerned, a constitutional government is as good as its courts. . . . Indeed, there is a sense in which it may be said that the whole efficacy and reality of constitutional government resides in its courts." But just as Wilson's first turn to contract yielded to a more complex understanding of interaction between the community and the institutions of government, so the turn to the courts as the enforcers of rights against government yields to a more complex understanding of the individual's relation to constitutional government through the courts.[101]

The courts are uniquely related to Wilson's conception of the meaning and role of individual citizenship in the final stage of constitutional government. In spite of what he says about the communal character of public opinion perceived through the institution of the presidency, Wilson presents a notably individualistic picture of the "dignity [of] citizenship among a free people": "Every man's thought is part of the vital substance of its institutions. . . . That is what constitutes citizenship so responsible and solemn a thing. Every man in a free country is, as it were, put upon his honor to be the kind of man such a polity supposes its citizens to be." This idea of the dignity of individual citizenship is then linked to the institutional structure of the courts as the forum within which each individual, as an individual, participates in constitutional governance. "Constitutional government exists in its completeness and full reality only when the individual . . . is regarded as a partner of the government in the conduct of the nation's life. The citizen is not individually represented in any assembly or in any regularly constituted part of the government itself. . . . It is only in the courts that men are individuals in respect of their rights."[102]

The courts, then, integrate the individual and the political order. A little later Wilson summarizes this institutional role of the courts: "The individual citizen among us can apply the checks of law to the government upon his own initiative, and they will respond to his touch as readily as to the touch of the greatest political officer of the system." At this point the contract model has completely collapsed: individual and government are one in the courts. In the courts the individual becomes an instrument of constitutional governance, and through the courts the government evolves into a system that fully respects the individual. "The courts are meant to be the people's forum."[103]

This conclusion forces a reconsideration of institutional priority within the constitutional system, and now, instead of recognizing presidential leadership, Wilson writes that "[t]he whole balance of our federal system . . . lies in the federal courts. It is inevitable that it should be so." Political actors are subordinated to the courts, which exercise "the statesmanship of control." "[E]ach generation of statesmen looks to the Supreme Court to supply the interpretation [of the Constitution] which will serve the needs of the day. It is a process necessary but full of peril."[104]

Wilson's focus on the courts in *Constitutional Government* is even more remarkable than his shift of attention from Congress to the presidency. In *Congressional Government* he at least criticized Congress for its failure to institutionalize a mechanism for responding to and informing public opinion. But he completely failed to deal with the function and status of the courts in the early book. It is not surprising that the reinvigorated presidency of the latter part of the century alerted Wilson to the possibilities of presidential leadership. But this development cannot account for his turn to the courts. The explanation lies in the need to claim that constitutional governance is evolving toward a system of increased rationality. Wilson stands with other nineteenth-century theorists in seeing evolution not as pure process but as the vehicle by which the state becomes the expression of reason. This conception requires some judgment about what reason requires. For Wilson, as for the others, a market model of individual liberty expresses the requirements of reason. Wilson ends his explication of the relation between the courts and evolving public opinion with a warning that echoes that of Tiedeman:

The atmosphere of opinion cannot be shut out of their court rooms. Its influence penetrates everywhere in every self-governed nation. What we should ask of our judges is that they prove themselves such men as can discriminate between the opinion of the moment and the opinion of the age, between the opinion which springs, a legitimate essence, from the enlightened judgment of men of thought and good conscience, and the opinion of desire, of self-interest, of impulse and impatience.[105]

Politics, public opinion, and custom may be the sources of law, but constitutional evolution, according to Wilson, still requires an institution that can separate the true from the false in public opinion, the way of reason from the way of interest. Constitutional governance requires evolution, but evolution is not process alone; it is the development of reason in the state. No purely political institution can be trusted with this function.

Evolution as Synthesis

By the turn of the century, constitutional theory was completely dominated by an evolutionary model of order. This was true for legal and political theorists and for much of the theoretically inclined practicing bar as well.[106] The model of growth had displaced earlier models of making and maintenance. The Constitution was now a moving object that corresponded to the moral and political development of the nation. Development, however, did not simply mean change. It meant the increasing rationalization of the order of the state. From the earlier model of making, the new model of order carried forward the claim for the comprehensive rationality of constitutional order, although the new model relocated rationality from the starting point to the end point of history. Individual resistance to the Constitution remained irrational. Equally, the evolutionary model carried forward from the earlier model of maintenance the understanding of the individual as part of a historically continuous community. However, it took a distinctly longer view of history, substantially eliminating the special claim of the founding as a defining act. Similarly, it took a broader view of the subject that expresses itself in law. The new theorists were less likely to speak of a unique popular sovereign and were more likely to talk about the Anglo-American race.

Though distinctly different from the prior models of order, the evolutionary model can be understood as a synthesis of its predecessors. Instead of contrasting making and maintenance, the evolutionary model suggests that no hard line can be drawn between maintenance and making. It suggests that maintenance of the constitutional order requires a continuous remaking. That which cannot be continuously made anew to respond to changing circumstances cannot be maintained. It cannot be maintained because without change, the Constitution would lapse into irrationality. The source of rational governance must, therefore, be located in the historically developing state itself.

While there was widespread agreement on this basic model of constitutionalism, similar agreement on the institutional implications of the model did not obtain. The disagreement focused on the institutional location of the source of reason within the historically evolving state: Was it in the courts or the political branches? The tension in the movement from the abstract conceptual model to the analysis of institutional role ultimately exploded within the constitutional jurisprudence of the Supreme Court.

CHAPTER FOUR

The Forum of Science in the Constitutional Order

In U.S. constitutional theory, the period from the Civil War to the turn of the century was marked by a transition in conceptual models: a static model of organic maintenance gave way to a model of growth. This transformation entailed changes in attitudes toward time and in modes of understanding. The idea of progress displaced the idea of origins, and science displaced myth. Instead of presenting a mythical account of origins to link the contemporary community to an idea of self-governance under the Constitution, the new model envisioned a historically progressing constitutionalism that represented the growth of reasonable governance.

The theoretical developments in the second half of the nineteenth century cohered around the idea of an evolving unwritten constitution. The constitutionalism of the Supreme Court of this period lacked a similar coherence, however. The new model entered the Court's jurisprudence soon after the war, but it did not become dominant until the early part of the twentieth century. The difference in the pace of development of constitutional theory and practice probably reflects the emergence of the professional legal academic. Theory could now take shape independently of the practical constraints of governance. Adjudication, though influenced by academic theory, did not take the working-out of constitutional theory as its primary objective. Theory had a role in practice, but it did not displace the ordinary workings of a common-law court. Most important, it did not displace precedent in judicial practice.

Because the Court does not operate under a norm of theoretical consistency, alternative—and even incompatible—conceptual models can survive alongside each other. No formal mechanism exists for removing older conceptual models from the corpus of precedents. Nothing that might prove useful ever wholly disappears. A prior opinion can always be used to support a present outcome. The judicial enterprise, therefore, can become increasingly incoherent in terms of theory. A cross section of the Court's product at a particular moment is likely to appear disordered. Nevertheless, it is possible to describe what is new in the Court's understanding of constitutionalism and to see a surprising coherence in those developments. By the beginning of this century, the Court was an enthusiastic supporter of the model of an evolving unwritten constitution. Understanding this conceptual model will provide a new perspective on the constitutional crisis of the New Deal.

Currently, there are two competing accounts of that crisis. The first understands it as a confrontation between a popularly supported political program and a judiciary committed to a substantive set of natural rights. The resolution of the crisis, on this view, represents a return to the democratic, majoritarian grounds of the constitutional order—grounds that entail substantial judicial deference to political decision makers. The second understands the resolution of the crisis as a genuinely creative moment in the history of constitutionalism—in effect, a constitutional amendment legitimating the modern welfare state.[1]

Both readings fail to portray the terms within which the constitutional debate occurred and within which it was resolved. In fact, the resolution of the crisis called for very little change in the operative conceptual model; there was no conceptual revolution at all. Nor was the crisis understood as a confrontation between a substantive theory of rights and a theory of popular democratic constitutionalism. Instead, the dispute was over the locus of the science of politics, which remained—both before and after the New Deal crisis—the basis for understanding the evolving unwritten constitution.

Conceptual Confusion in the Court

Lawyers trained before the Civil War could appeal to two different conceptual models of constitutionalism, each with radically different methodological implications. The first understood the Constitution as a practical application of an abstract science of politics. Constitutional controversy, on this view, could be resolved by a renewed appeal to first principles. The second understood the Constitution as a historically unique expression of the will of the popular sovereign. On this view, controversy called for a renewed contact with the origins of the Constitution in the work of the founding fathers. Not surprisingly, despite the innovations in constitutional theory that began to appear during the Civil War and multiplied after its conclusion, the Court remained conceptually conservative, though it moved easily back and forth between these two early models.

Typical of how the postwar Court treated the relation between the national and state governments is *Collector v. Day*, involving a federal effort to tax the salary of state judicial officers.[2] The Court sees here exactly the same situation as that presented in *McCulloch v. Maryland*, which it now views as a case about the place of taxation in the relation between independent sovereigns, not about federal supremacy.[3] The opinion proceeds in a formal deductive fashion from the proposition "The general government, and the States ... are separate and distinct sovereignties, acting separately and independently of each other, within their respective spheres." Because a judiciary is necessary for republican government, the federal government cannot possess any power destructive of the state judiciary. *McCulloch* established that the power to tax is the power to destroy. The exemption of state judicial officers from a federal tax is, accordingly, supported by "principles and reasons as cogent as those" that exempt federal officers from state taxes.[4]

The Court's respect for state sovereignty, just six years after the war, is politically remarkable. My concern, however, is not with the substance of the decision but with the character of the Court's constitutionalism. The opinion is written in an explicitly Marshallian fashion. There is the same assumption that the Constitution embodies an abstract system of political science. Thus, the exemption from federal tax "rests upon necessary implication, and is upheld by the great law of self-preservation; as any government, whose means employed in conducting its operations, if subject to the control of another and distinct government, can exist only at the mercy of that government." The argument relies upon "principles and reasons."[5] There is also the same casual approach to a supporting text. Here, it is the sparse language of the Tenth Amendment. Little turns on text. Everything depends upon the Court's abstract understanding of republican political organization: "Without this power [to appoint and maintain judicial officers], and the exercise of it, we risk nothing in saying that no one of the States under the form of government guaranteed by the Constitution could long preserve its existence."[6]

The appeal to the abstract logic of republican political science is typical of a number of the most important constitutional decisions of this period. For example, in *Tarble's Case*, this style of reasoning is used to support the proposition that state habeas actions cannot extend to individuals held under federal authority. And, in *Crandall v. Nevada*, which strikes down a state tax on all those leaving the state, the Court specifically declines to rely upon either of two proffered textual grounds, relying instead upon the broad principles outlined in *McCulloch*.[7]

Similarly, in *Loan Association v. Topeka*, in which the Court declares void the use of municipal bonds to finance a private manufacturing operation, no specific text or history is cited. The Court rests its decision on pure theory: "The theory of our governments, State and National, is opposed to the deposit of unlimited power anywhere. . . . There are limitations on [governmental] power which grow out of the essential nature of all free governments." One such limitation is the principle that government may not use its powers to transfer property from one citizen to another "to aid private enterprises and build up private fortunes." The controverted bond issue fails because it rests upon just such a transfer of assets from one private party to another. And, "[a] government which recognized no such rights, which held the lives, the liberty, and the property of its citizens subject at all times to the absolute disposition and unlimited control of even the most democratic depository of power, is after all but a despotism."[8]

These appeals to an abstract science of politics notwithstanding, the Court did not have a strong commitment to this conceptual model. In two of the most important postwar cases, the Court turned to an originalist conception of constitutional adjudication. In *Hepburn v. Griswold*, which declares unconstitutional the legal tender issued during the war, the Court explicitly rejects those sources of constitutional change upon which Sidney George Fisher relied in building his new model of constitutionalism: "It is not surprising that amid the tumult of the late civil war, and under the influence of apprehensions for the safety of the Republic almost universal, different views, never before entertained by American statesmen or jurists, were adopted by many. The time was not favorable to considerate reflection upon the constitutional limits of legislative or executive authority." The Court then returns to "what was intended . . . in the minds of the people who ordained" the Constitution. This is "happily, not a matter of disputation. It is not left to inference or conjecture."[9] The Court appeals to the founders to justify its conclusion that the war fought to vindicate the Constitution was itself supported in an unconstitutional manner.

In perhaps the single most important constitutional controversy of the postwar period, the *Slaughter-House Cases*, the Court again appeals to the conceptual apparatus, not of Marshall, but of Taney. The cases involved the application of the Thirteenth and Fourteenth amendments to a state-granted monopoly to pursue the slaughterhouse business in and around New Orleans. This was the first opportunity for the Court to interpret these amendments, whose "history is fresh within the memory of us all, and . . . free from doubt." The necessity of appealing to history to understand their meaning follows from the fact that the Constitution rests not upon reason but upon the expression of the will of the popular sovereign: "Nor can such doubts [about the amendments] . . . be safely and rationally solved without a reference to that history; for in it is found the occasion and the necessity for recurring again to the great source of power in this country, the people of the States, for additional guarantees of human rights; additional powers to the Federal government; additional restraints upon those of the States."[10] The abstract republicanism of *Loan Association v. Topeka*, which was written by the same Justice Samuel Miller who writes the majority opinion in *Slaughter-House*, simply has no place here.[11]

This understanding of the meaning of the Constitution imposes no small burden upon the Court. To understand the Civil War amendments, the Court must understand the Civil War itself. According to the Court, the amendments gave a formal and permanent effect to the results of that war: "[T]he war being over, those who had succeeded in re-establishing the authority of the Federal government were not content to permit this great act of emancipation to rest on the actual results of the contest or the proclamation of the Executive, both of which might have been questioned in after times, and they determined to place this main and most valuable result in the Constitution." Fortunately, from the Court's perspective, the relevant events are "almost too recent to be called history." In the Court's view, the Civil War must be understood wholly in terms of slavery: "[W]hatever auxiliary causes may have contributed to bring about this war, undoubtedly the over-shadowing and efficient cause was African slavery." Accordingly, the termination of slavery and the establishment of the condition of equality for freed slaves must constitute the basis of every "fair and just construction . . . of these amendments."[12]

Two points follow from this. First, the Court insists that the amendments do not affect the structure of relations between the states and the federal government: "[W]e do not see in those amendments any purpose to destroy the main features of the general system."[13] Second, the amendments are not to be understood against the background of common-law rights to liberty and contract. Instead, the Court finds the amendments to be narrowly remedial, addressing unique problems arising from emancipation. Just when theorists were arguing in an ever-stronger fashion that

American constitutional law was simply an offshoot of British constitutional law, differing in form but not in substance, the Court emphasized the uniqueness of U.S. history and the law that it had produced.[14]

The instability in the Court's model of constitutionalism during this period is clear not only from a comparison of *Slaughter-House* with contemporaneous decisions but also from a comparison of the majority opinion with the dissents. *Slaughter-House* was a close case: the vote was five to four. Justices Stephen J. Field and Joseph P. Bradley both wrote strong dissents that in time became more important than the majority opinion. Both Field and Bradley found the Fourteenth Amendment declaratory of the rights of free citizens in a republican government, and both argued that these broad rights had to be understood within the historical context of the common law. Each suggested a convergence of U.S. and British constitutional law. Both rejected the central claim of the majority's argument—that the amendment established a new right but not a new institutional structure—and argued instead that the amendment reshaped institutional structure while leaving common-law rights in place.

For the dissenters, the war was not about slavery; it was about the place of the states in the constitutional system. Bradley puts this most clearly: "The mischief to be remedied [by the amendments] was not merely slavery and its incidents and consequences; but that spirit of insubordination and disloyalty to the National government which had troubled the country for so many years in some of the States." Field develops this argument by explaining the relation of the privileges and immunity clause of article IV to the similar clause of the Fourteenth Amendment. The rights protected by each clause, he contends, are the same. The difference is in the institution that protects them. The assumption in article IV was that individual rights would be protected by state governments. It demanded only that the states extend equal protection to noncitizens within their jurisdictions. Through the Fourteenth Amendment, the federal government guarantees to citizens that their state governments will recognize their rights: "Now, what [article IV] does for the protection of citizens of one State against the creation of monopolies in favor of citizens of other States, the fourteenth amendment does for the protection of every citizen of the United States against the creation of any monopoly whatever."[15]

Although the dissenters believed the Fourteenth Amendment was innovative with respect to governmental structure, they did not believe it innovative with respect to individual rights. The amendment simply declares those rights that "belong to the citizens of all free governments." Field explains: "The amendment does not attempt to confer any new privileges or immunities upon citizens. .... [I]t assumes that there are such privileges and immunities which belong of right to citizens as such. .... [T]he amendment refers to the natural and inalienable rights which belong to all citizens."[16] This talk of natural rights should not, however, be seen as a return to the founders' abstract science of politics.

Following the pattern of Cooley's contemporaneous writing, the dissenters suggest a conflation of natural and common-law rights. In the same paragraph that Justice Bradley speaks of the "rights of citizens of any free government," he links these rights to the historical development of the common law: "In this free country, the people of which inherited certain traditionary rights and privileges from their ancestors, citizenship means something." To understand the rights protected by the Fourteenth Amendment requires a proper "estimate of constitutional history and the rights of men, not to say the rights of the American people." Justice Field also turns to the common law: "The common law of England is the basis of the jurisprudence of the United States."[17]

The conflation of natural and common-law rights in the dissents is more than the confusion of an epistemological with a substantive claim. The dissenters do suggest that the way to ascertain the character of natural rights is to look to the history of the development of the common law, but the conflation of rights goes much deeper. For Bradley and Field, free government cannot be conceived apart from the historical process that produced it. The "natural rights of every Englishman," which are those of citizens of the United States as well, are embodied and expressed in the historical struggle of a people to give itself an idea of freedom. For example, of the natural right of every citizen to pursue any legal trade— the right at issue in *Slaughter-House*—Field writes, "The struggle of the English people against monopolies forms one of the most interesting and instructive chapters in their history." Similarly, Bradley writes of natural rights that they are "[t]he privileges and immunities of Englishmen [which] were established and secured by long usage and by various acts of Parliament."[18]

In the dissenters' arguments, the new model of constitutionalism entered the reasoning of the Court. What had been two distinct conceptual patterns in prewar constitutional theory—an abstract political science and originalism—were being brought together in a single vision. In this new model, the rights of the free citizens of a republican state have been worked out through a historical process. That, however, did not make them merely positive rights. Justice Bradley could write that despite the theoretically "unlimited authority" of Parliament to repeal any law, a parliamentary effort to repeal the "unwritten" constitution would be grounds for a just revolution. Indeed, he offers precisely that justification for the American Revolution.[19]

What began in the dissents of *Slaughter-House* came increasingly to dominate the Court's understanding of the Constitution. Indeed, the foreignness of the *Lochner* Court to modern sensibilities does not rest on its vision of natural rights but rather on this more complex vision of the relation between reason, history, and adjudication.[20]

The Development of the *Lochner* Court

By the beginning of this century, the Court's characteristic form of constitutionalism represented a commitment to the idea of an evolving unwritten constitution. The legitimacy of the Court's role now turned on its claim to possess that science of political order that is required for constitutional growth—that is, not the abstract republican science of the founders but the same deeply historicized path of reason that theorists of the period were exploring.[21] The disputes within the Court were not over the place of science in constitutionalism or over the place of a historical, as opposed to an abstract, science.[22] They were over the content of the new science and the locus of a scientific, evolutionary constitutionalism.

Just four years after *Slaughter-House,* a change in direction became evident in Chief Justice Morrison R. Waite's opinion for the Court in *Munn v. Illinois,* which examines the constitutionality of a state law fixing the rate schedule for grain elevators in Chicago. No longer does the Court argue that the Fourteenth Amendment is a remedial measure limited to the historical problem of slavery. The Court now accepts the idea that the amendment constitutionalizes common-law protections of property: "[D]own to the time of the adoption of the fourteenth amendment, it was not supposed that statutes regulating the use, or even the price of the use, of private property necessarily deprived an owner of his property without due process of law. Under some circumstances they may, but not under all. The amendment does not change the law in this particular: it simply prevents the States from doing that which will operate as such a deprivation."[23] The vague reference to the beliefs of the framers is not a serious methodological move. The last sentence carries all the weight: the amendment constitutionalizes the common-law understanding of the relation of public authority to private property.

On this view of the substance of the amendment, the Court's role becomes essentially indistinguishable from the role performed by scholars such as Cooley and Tiedeman: surveying the historical data, that is, the common-law cases. The Court begins its inquiry by "[l]ooking ... to the

common law, from whence came the right which the Constitution protects. . . . " It comes to the same substantive conclusion as the scholars:
"[T]he very essence of government [is] found . . . in the maxim *sic utere
tuo ut alienum non laedas*."[24] But just as Cooley and Tiedeman recognized
that the abstract principle alone could not decide cases, the Court, too,
looks to the actual manifestation of the principle in historical phenomena.
It concludes that the controverted regulatory action "presents . . . a case
for the application of a long-known and well-established principle in social science, and this statute simply extends the law so as to meet this
new development of commercial progress."[25]

The conjunction of common law, constitutional law, and social science is explicit, as is their dynamic or progressive character. The Court
believes it must keep common-law understandings of rights current with
social and economic progress. It must provide for the growth of law by
adapting old law to new circumstances. The common law is not a passive
body of ancient customs but both the object and product of the judge as
social scientist.

Just this point is emphasized in that particular doctrine of *Munn*
that the *Lochner* Court later abandoned. In *Munn*, the Court seems to
envision the legislature, not the judiciary, as the locus of progress in scientific governance: "Indeed, the great office of statutes is to remedy defects
in the common law as they are developed, and to adapt it to the changes
of time and circumstances." Adaptation is the central mechanism for
growth, and the institutional organ of adaptation is the legislature. Of its
own role, the Court says: "For protection against abuses by legislatures
the people must resort to the polls, not to the courts."[26]

This remark about judicial deference to the political operations of
government is hardly consistent with the actual inquiry pursued by the
Court in *Munn* to support its substantive conclusion with respect to the
rate regulation. Had institutional deference been the real basis of
the decision, that inquiry into the common law of regulation would not
have been necessary. The remark is similar to the nod toward originalism
at the beginning of the argument. Both are vestigial forms of argument
that the *Lochner* Court abandoned when it placed itself at the center of
the new science of government.

Munn was an early expression of substantive due process under the
Fourteenth Amendment. The same model of constitutionalism emerged
in the area of procedural due process—with the same institutional ambiguity. In *Hurtado v. California,* the Court upholds a decision by the
state of California to proceed by information, rather than indictment, in
the prosecution of certain felonies. Again, the Court is most concerned

to link the scientific examination of the common law with the idea of progress. It rejects a model that looks purely to the past—either the deep past of the common law or the more recent past of the framers—for a determination of the content of due process: "[T]o hold that [historical precedent] is essential to due process of law, would be to deny every quality of the law but its age, and to render it incapable of progress or improvement. It would be to stamp upon our jurisprudence the unchangeableness attributed to the laws of the Medes and Persians." Such an approach is not possible "in this quick and active age."[27] The Court's own inquiry into the common law of procedure is intended to discover "the true philosophy of our historical legal institutions." The inquiry reveals a growing common law: "[T]he spirit of personal liberty and individual right [are] preserved and developed by a progressive growth and wise adaptation to new circumstances and situations of the forms and processes found fit to give, from time to time, new expression and greater effect to modern ideas of self-government."[28]

Growth and adaptation were again key elements of constitutional jurisprudence. Self-government, for the Court as for contemporary theorists, occurred in its most mature form only at the end, not at the beginning, of the long process of legal evolution. The Court states that "flexibility and capacity for growth and adaptation is the peculiar boast and excellence of the common law" and that "we should expect that the new and various experiences of our own situation and system will mould and shape [the common-law inheritance] into new and not less useful forms."[29]

Hurtado carried forward not only the substantive model of constitutionalism from *Munn* but also the institutional confusion of the earlier case. Thus, it refers to "the right of the people to make their own laws, and alter them at their pleasure," as "the greatest security" of constitutionally required due process. But again this suggestion of judicial deference is more apparent than real. Just one page later, the Court writes of its own role as follows:

[T]he limitations imposed by our constitutional law upon the action of the governments . . . are essential to the preservation of public and private rights, notwithstanding the representative character of our political institutions. The enforcement of these limitations by judicial process is the device of self-governing communities to protect the rights of individuals and minorities, as well against the power of numbers, as against the violence of public agents transcending the limits of lawful authority.[30]

Munn and *Hurtado* were major steps forward in the Court's acceptance of the new model of constitutionalism. This theoretical development, rather than their substantive outcome—approving innovative state legislation—linked them directly to the *Lochner* Court.[31]

The specific controversy in *Lochner* concerned a state criminal statute limiting the number of hours an employee could contract to work in a bakery. The Court believed it had to choose between conflicting private and public rights: "[I]t becomes of great importance to determine which shall prevail—the right of the individual to labor for such time as he may choose, or the right of the State to prevent the individual from laboring or from entering into any contract to labor." This proposition takes for granted the constitutional status of the individual's claim of a right to contract. In fact, Justice Rufus W. Peckham's opinion for the Court relies on a single source to support the proposition that "[t]he general right to make a contract in relation to his business is part of the liberty of the individual protected by the fourteenth amendment of the Federal Constitution."[32] That source is his own opinion in *Allgeyer v. Louisiana.*

Allgeyer involved a Louisiana statute prohibiting any resident from obtaining insurance from an out-of-state company. There, for the first time, the Court held a state statute unconstitutional as a violation of a due process right to liberty of contract. The birth of the constitutional right to contract occurs in the following passage:

The liberty mentioned in that amendment means not only the right of the citizen to be free from the mere physical restraint of his person . . . but the term is *deemed* to embrace the right of the citizen to be free in the enjoyment of all his faculties; to be free to use them in all lawful ways; to live and work where he will; to earn his livelihood by any lawful calling; to pursue any livelihood or avocation, and for that purpose to enter into all contracts which may be proper, necessary and essential to his carrying out to a successful conclusion the purposes above mentioned.[33]

The Court here extends the Fourteenth Amendment to cover exactly the sort of economic interests rejected twenty-five years earlier in *Slaughter-House*. Remarkably, in light of the reasoning of *Slaughter-House,* the *Allgeyer* Court does not once discuss the original history of the Fourteenth Amendment; it does not even suggest that historical intent might be relevant. The Court couples the meaning of the constitutional text to the verb *to deem*. To deem is to perform a completely self-referential act: the Fourteenth Amendment means what the Court deems it to mean. The Court, accordingly, stands on an equal, if not higher, footing with the founders. Within the evolutionary model, the present is always an advance on the past.

The only support the Court provides for this step, which may be the most important step in the second century of the Court's work, is two citations: one to a concurring opinion of Justice Bradley in *Butcher's Union Co. v. Crescent City Co.* and the other to some dicta in *Powell v. Pennsylvania.*[34] These sources are obviously slim, and at best, they modestly advance the chain of self-reference. Moreover, all that these sources provide is "general definitions . . . [of] the meaning of the word 'liberty' as used in the amendment." General definitions cannot decide actual cases: "When and how far [the police] power may be legitimately exercised with regard to these subjects must be left for determination to each case as it arises."[35] With this, the Court simultaneously abandons its earlier suggestion of judicial deference to political institutions and recognizes its own need to give concrete shape to the abstract principles of political order. What such a judicial inquiry would look like is illustrated by *Lochner* itself.

The Science of the *Lochner* Court

The institutional authority the Court claimed in *Allgeyer* and demonstrated in *Lochner* rested upon an understanding of itself as a scientific decision maker. Even though identification of constitutionalism and science was not new in U.S. history, the science of the *Lochner* Court should not be confused with the republican political science that dominated the period of the founding. The Court at no point suggests that its science is the same as that of the founders. Indeed, the reverse is true. In *Holden v. Hardy,* the Court declares law to be "a progressive science" and recognizes that "law [is] forced to adapt itself to new conditions of society."[36] The political science of the *Lochner* Court is believed to be legitimate, not because it corresponds to the science of the founders but because it is thought to be good science.

The scientific self-understanding of the *Lochner* Court had an important consequence: its decisions could be right or wrong in their own terms. If the legitimacy of a decision turns on a special kind of knowledge, then it can be evaluated by those with a competing claim to knowledge. This feature accounts for the prestige of treatise writers such as Cooley and Tiedeman, as well as for the characteristic form of their treatises: situation-specific explanations of the constitutional limits on public authority. The Court's acceptance of the new model of an evolving unwritten constitution blurred the distinction between judge and theoretician. A failure in theory now went to the legitimacy of the judicial function. This idea of competing scientific claims was critical to the demise of the *Lochner* Court, whose jurisprudence required deference to the best scientific voice.

The scientific character of the *Lochner* decision can be understood from three slightly different perspectives: that of common law, that of means-end rationality, and that of Darwinian social science. These perspectives are overlapping and mutually reinforcing. Each emphasizes the links among growth, history, and reason.

The Constitution and the Science of the Common Law

Already in *Allgeyer*, the Court recognized a background system of legal arrangements within which the due process clause gained its meaning. The controverted statute interfered, according to the Court, with "lawful ways" of using one's faculties and with the right to pursue "any lawful calling."[37] The standard of the lawful, against which the positive legislation of the state should be measured, was the common law. The authority of the state to exercise public coercion was constitutionally limited to enforcing the set of legal rights embodied in the common law. This convergence of public authority and existing private rights was emphasized in *Reagan v. Farmers' Loan and Trust Co.*: "It has always been a part of the judicial function to determine whether the act of one party (whether that party be a single individual, an organized body, or the public as a whole) operates to divest the other party of any rights of person or property."[38]

The idea that the state is limited to maintaining the common-law system of order was carried forward in *Lochner:* "If the contract be one which the State, in the legitimate exercise of its police power, has the right to prohibit, it is not prevented from prohibiting it by the fourteenth amendment."[39] The Court argues that the legitimate domain of state authority precedes and defines the boundaries of constitutional constraint. To determine what is a legitimate exercise of state authority, the Court must, therefore, look to what has historically been recognized to fall within that authority: "There are . . . certain powers, existing in the sovereignty of each State in the Union, somewhat vaguely termed police powers, the exact description and limitation of which have not been attempted by the courts."[40] Neither was it attempted by the framers of the Fourteenth Amendment nor by any other institutional source of authority.

Even though the courts have attempted no exact description, the Court has to delineate the scope of public authority to give effect to the Fourteenth Amendment. In *Lochner* the Court appeals to the common-law understanding of permissible state ends to give concrete form to the public order assumed by the due process clause. The Court concludes that the police powers "relate to the safety, health, morals and general welfare of the public."[41] These are the traditional, and therefore legitimate, ends of government within which the constitutional protections of the Fourteenth Amendment must be understood.

State authority to interfere with private arrangements is, according to the Court, embodied in and legitimated by the common law. The Court's idea of the common law was not "commonly" understood, however. The standard of the common law was, after all, being used to strike down popularly supported legislation. At the turn of the century, the common law was recognized as the distinct subject matter of legal science—as that body of doctrine that emerged when prior judicial decisions were systematically studied with a view to their principled coherence.[42] Expertise in the science required specialized training. That training was the point, for example, of legal education at Harvard Law School under Dean Christopher Langdell.[43]

The specialized character of the knowledge of common law is evident in the *Lochner* decision. The first part of the argument reads today like a puzzle of minute distinctions, as the Court distinguishes its own precedents from the controverted bakery regulation. It distinguishes the employees of bakeries from the employees of mines, smelters, and coal operations, work in a bakery from "work of a public character," and restrictions on hours of employment from restrictions on working on Sundays.[44]

To the common-law lawyer or judge these precedents represented the integrity of the general rule that the state may not interfere with freedom to contract. Exceptions, as long as they are understood as exceptional, do not threaten a general rule but prove it. The Court's inquiry into precedent, then, was an attempt to determine whether any existing exception "covers the case now before us."[45] Yet the logic of these distinctions is evident only to those in possession of the common-law science. Where the Court saw a rule with a limited set of exceptions, we are likely to see only arbitrary action. This difference in perception is a measure of the distance traversed since *Lochner*. To those who do not possess the science of the common law, the exceptions destroy, rather than support, the general rule.[46]

The Scientific Adaptation of Means to Ends

The Langdellian science of the common law incorporated a principle of evolution.[47] The *Lochner* Court, too, put into explicit focus the need to adapt the common-law rules to contemporary conditions. For this reason, the opinion could not end with a canvass of the existing exceptions to the general rule of liberty of contract. The Court has to ask whether further exceptions are required to adapt the police power to the changing social and economic order. At this point, the emphasis in the opinion shifts from the historical science of the common law to an inquiry into means-ends rationality.

Repeatedly, the Court states that the rule of decision is the "reasonableness" or "rationality" of the exercise of state authority. The basic test is whether "this [is] a fair, reasonable and appropriate exercise of the police power of the State, or . . . an unreasonable, unnecessary and arbitrary interference with the right of the individual to his personal liberty."[48] A reasonable exercise of the police power is one that has a "direct relation, as a means to an end, and the end itself must be appropriate and legitimate."[49] Accordingly, the Court asks whether the statute can reasonably be said to advance any of the legitimate state interests specified by the common-law understanding of the police power.

The Court considers two such ends, against which it measures the rationality of the statute: it might be a labor law or a health measure. In each instance, the form of the argument is the same. No proposition in support of the reasonableness of this means of meeting a legitimate end can be accepted if accepting it would allow the exception to swallow the rule. The opinion is at its strongest in the set of arguments offered to demonstrate the "unreasonableness" of the statute, because the arguments fill in the model of a general rule with exceptions and because in these arguments the "common law" makes contact with the "common understanding." The Court's role of adapting the traditional principles of public order to contemporary conditions required that it mediate not only between past and present but also between scientific knowledge and ordinary belief. The ordinary understandings of the contemporary community were to be shaped by the Court's imposition of a scientifically validated common-law order.

In its consideration of legitimate labor laws, the Court writes that the state can reasonably exercise special care in superintending the contracts of certain categories of employees. Such people are analogized to wards of the state. This statute, however, cannot be upheld as a valid labor law because "there is no contention that bakers as a class are not equal in intelligence and capacity to men in other trades."[50] Bakers, in other words, cannot form an exception to the general rule because they are too much like everyone else. This exception would swallow the rule.

Although the Court is not explicit, clearly it believes that the deficiency to which the state may respond must involve more than dissatisfaction with market outcomes. Striking a poor bargain would not in itself convert an autonomous agent into a ward of the state; some nonmarket deficiency must justify a paternalistic attitude toward the class. This deficiency may affect the outcome of contractual relations, but that outcome does not ground state intervention. The Court uses just this form of argument several years later in order to extend special protection to women: "That woman's physical structure and the performance of maternal functions place her at a disadvantage in the struggle for subsistence is obvious. . . . [S]he is not an equal competitor with her brother. . . . [S]ome legislation to protect her seems necessary to secure a real equality of right."[51]

The *Lochner* Court operated with a norm of *sui juris* agents, which to the Court means free adult males of ordinary insight and ability pursuing the ordinary occupations of life. Class deficiencies are measured against this standard, and the exceptions were fairly clear: women, children, mentally retarded people, and, for reasons that escape the contemporary mind, those who work underground.[52] Delineating these categories was not "a question of substituting the judgment of the court for that of the legislature."[53] It was a question of examining the common understanding to see whether it recognized the exceptionality of the class. That understanding, according to the Court, failed to evince any special reason to protect bakery employees.

This same methodology characterized the second branch of the means-end argument: Did the statute reasonably advance the public health? Again, the measure of unreasonableness was found in the common understanding: "To the common understanding the trade of a baker has never been regarded as an unhealthy one." To recognize it as special would destroy the exceptional quality of regulatory interference with contract: "It is unfortunately true that labor, even in any department, may possibly carry with it the seeds of unhealthiness. But are we all, on that account, at the mercy of legislative majorities?"[54] If the health of the employees was not sufficiently at jeopardy to justify state interference, neither was the health of the general public. The measure would fail "unless there be some fair ground, reasonable in and of itself, to say that there is material danger to the public health . . . if the hours of labor are not curtailed." Given the steps already taken to control the cleanliness of the bakery workshop, a limit on hours was entirely unreasonable: "Adding to all these requirements, a prohibition to enter into any contract of labor in a bakery for more than a certain number of hours a week, is . . . so wholly beside the matter of a proper, reasonable and fair provision, as to run counter to that liberty of person and of free contract provided for in the Federal Constitution."[55]

From the perspective of the *Lochner* Court, the problem with the New York State legislation was its irrationality—that is, it was an exercise of authority that failed to advance any legitimate state interest. But the statute was not an irrational means of accomplishing one particular end—limiting the market power of employers to demand long hours from their employees. To say that the statute is irrational is to reject this end.

Science and the Ends of Government

So far, I have argued that this end was rejected because the Court constitutionalized common-law limits on police power. If this were the whole story, then the science of constitutionalism would still rest on certain historical facts that were themselves not further reducible to scientific explanation. Redistribution of wealth would be an illegitimate end only because it was illegitimate at common law. *Lochner,* however, carried the argument of science one step further. The unspoken premise of the opinion—unspoken by all but Justice Holmes—was that constitutional interpretation occurs within the context of a particular socioeconomic theory. In a famous line, Holmes specified the larger social science theory within which the majority was operating: "The fourteenth amendment does not enact Mr. Herbert Spencer's Social Statics."[56]

In the last chapter, I demonstrated that there is no necessary connection between the concept of an evolving unwritten constitution and the common law. But those theorists—including judges—who needed to see in Anglo-American society the end point of social evolution found a ready vehicle for their evolutionary thought in the common law. For them, reason and rights came together in the modern form of the common law. Although the material sources of the common law—the cases—may be distinct, the science of the common law was not an autonomous discipline but an aspect of a more general social science.[57] The attraction of the common law to constitutional theorists who were pursuing the evolutionary model lay largely in its capacity to embody contemporary developments in social Darwinism. In sum, the Court's perception of the unconstitutionality of statutory efforts at redistribution rested on a larger theory concerning a mature political system. Such a system would minimize state interference with private orderings of property and contract.

Justice Peckham, the author of *Lochner,* had earlier expressed the relation between the common-law concept of liberty of contract and scientific governance. He disapproved of legislative interference in economic affairs as inconsistent with "the more correct ideas which an increase of civilization and a fuller knowledge of the fundamental laws of political economy, and a truer conception of the proper functions of government, have given us at the present day." He appealed to the ideas of political growth and maturity, condemning a "recurrence of legislation which, it has been supposed, had been outgrown not only as illegal, but as wholly useless for any good effect and only powerful for evil."[58] Growth in law and in the science of government were not parallel but identical processes.

This set of assumptions about the scientific validity of laissez-faire governance explains the *Lochner* Court's extreme hostility to redistributive legislation. Such statutory efforts were unconstitutional not because they burdened the economically powerful but because they violated the rationality of the state.[59] The achievement of the modern era was, on this view, the final separation of the public character of the state from the private ends of those in power. This public character was assured as long as the state acted on the model of the night watchman, securing the individual from interference by others. This required a measure of the kinds of interference with individual liberty that must be tolerated as the cost of any social order. Those limits had gradually become clear in the evolution of government; they were embodied in the common law. In using governmental authority to advance the private interests of a particular faction, then, the state retrogressed to earlier forms of political organization. For this reason, public authority that was driven by private interests—even majority interests—was labeled irrational.

In accepting this social science background, the *Lochner* Court also accepted the projection of the concept of political liberty onto an economic model of market capitalism. Contract did not exhaust the Court's idea of autonomy; nevertheless, it dominated the Court's thinking.[60] The Supreme Court was not alone in believing that a political idea of self-government and an economic model of contract could be scientifically linked. The Pennsylvania Supreme Court, for example, described a state law prohibiting payment in the form of commodities as "an insulting attempt to put the laborer under a legislative tutelage, which is not only degrading to his manhood, but subversive of his rights as a citizen of the United States."[61] This linkage of legal and economic ideas of liberty was a frequent theme of contemporary work in social and political science.[62] It turned out to be easier to break this link between economic and legal ideas than the link between the Constitution and social science.

Social Science among the Dissenters

The extent of the commitment of the *Lochner* Court to a new social science of constitutionalism is evident not just in Peckham's opinion for the Court but also in the dissents of Justices Harlan and Holmes. Harlan shares the majority's view of the range of constitutional public purposes. He agrees that a statute that seeks to redistribute wealth from the rich to the poor amounts to an arbitrary interference with constitutionally protected private rights and that the New York statute can be upheld only if it is a rational means of advancing public health. Moreover, he agrees that the issue before the Court deeply implicates social science and should be decided on the basis of scientific truth:

What is the true ground for the State to take between legitimate protection, by legislation, of the public health and liberty of contract is not a question easily solved, nor one in respect of which there is or can be absolute certainty. . . . One writer on [the] relation of the State to labor has well said: "The manner, occasion, and degree in which the State may interfere with the industrial freedom of its citizens is one of the most debatable and difficult questions of social science."[63]

Where Harlan disagrees with the majority is in his understanding of what kind of expert knowledge is relevant to the determination of the issue. He recognizes the claim of the new, statistical social sciences over the claim of the judicial science of the common law. Accordingly, he supports the rationality of the statute by appealing to the work of a Professor Ludwig Hirt, author of "Diseases of the Workers," and to the reports of the New York Bureau of Statistics of Labor. Harlan's reliance on statistical expertise contrasts markedly with the majority's easy dismissal of such evidence when it fails to support the common assumptions of daily life: "In looking through statistics regarding all trades and occupations, it may be true that the trade of baker does not appear to be as healthy as some other trades, and is also vastly more healthy than still others. To the common understanding the trade of a baker has never been regarded as an unhealthy one." Harlan has found the key to the demise of the *Lochner* Court: if social science determines the legitimacy of political authority, then the Court must yield to the better claim to expert knowledge.[64]

More interesting than Harlan's opinion, though surely no more important to subsequent legal developments, is the famous dissent of Justice Holmes. Holmes is, in fact, vague on the rule of decision he would apply under the Fourteenth Amendment: "[T]he word liberty in the 14th amendment is perverted when it is held to prevent the natural outcome of a dominant opinion, unless it can be said that a rational and fair man necessarily would admit that the statute proposed would infringe fundamental principles as they have been understood by the traditions of our people and our law."[65] This statement and much of what the majority has to say are surprisingly similar. For example, both make the same appeal to "rationality" and "fairness." Both look to a long tradition, rather than a founding moment, to understand constitutional order—a tradition that is, presumably, best explicated by an expert. Holmes's reputation was based largely on just such expertise. Both majority and dissent understand the constitutional constraints to allow a "natural" evolution of political order.

Holmes seems to be operating within a competing social-evolutionary model that also provides a framework for understanding the development of rational governance. When Holmes writes that "[e]very opinion tends to become a law," he has in mind a model of the evolution of social order that is just as scientific as the majority's model. The problem Holmes sees with the *Lochner* majority opinion is that judicial intervention will block, or at least deter, the evolution of the community. For Holmes, growth occurs through the competition of ideas, not the economic competition of individuals. He would break the link between economic and political ideas of competition, but not that between constitutionalism and competition.[66]

The dispute between Holmes and the *Lochner* majority was a dispute over the science of social evolution. It was not a dispute over the claim of science to provide the ground of constitutional construction. Both sides assumed that the legitimacy of the Court's constitutional interpretations derived from the adequacy of its political science. The *Lochner* majority followed classic social Darwinism; for them, social evolution took place in the economic competition between individuals. Holmes, however, participated in the contemporaneous critique of the movement. One object of the critique was to reject the model of society as a collection of individuals in competition with each other. To Holmes, society had to be thought of instead as a collective whole.[67] This collectivity, not the individual, was the subject of the scientific theory of evolution generally and of constitutional law more particularly.

My concern here is not to develop early twentieth-century theories of social evolution in detail. Rather, it is to point out the shift in the Court's conception of constitutionalism. The expression of popular will and its record in unique acts of constitutional creation were no longer central to constitutional discourse. The Court now viewed history, not as a field for the preservation of origins, but as the progressive working out of reasonable governance. To support this idea of history as growth, the Court appealed to the science that was available in the contemporary culture—one dominated by ideas of social Darwinism.[68]

The *Lochner* Court was imbued with science. Science appeared at every level of analysis: the sources for its decisions were found in a common law that required scientific exploration; legislation was tested against a model of means-ends rationality; and the normative context of the whole inquiry was provided by a theory of the evolutionary character of political order. For all these reasons, the strength of the *Lochner* Court's position was only as strong as its claim to science. That claim was challenged in a serious way in the first decades of the twentieth century.

The Critique of the *Lochner* Court

Science is a powerful political force at first. An institution that can convincingly claim a privileged access to reason will be unchecked in its assertion of authority. That authority gains strength in part by characterizing the opposition as unreasonable. In a world that values reason, no normative value attaches to the unreasonable; it is simply irrational behavior. Not surprisingly, the *Lochner* Court cast disputes as conflicts between the reasonable and the unreasonable. Its own role was to demonstrate the path of reason in complex factual situations.

The demise of the *Lochner* Court teaches that the claim to scientific governance does not easily translate into stable political authority. Assertions of reason are not self-validating in the political domain. The relation of the larger community to the judicial voice of reason must be supported by a particular set of beliefs. First, the community must believe that judges are scientific decision makers. The Court must not be seen as the voice of any particular interests, whether class based or narrowly personal. Second, the community must believe that the common law represents a rational ordering of society. The science of the common law, which lies at the heart of the Court's special claim to reason, must be seen as the correct body of knowledge for the reasonable ordering of the self-governing state.

In the first three decades of the twentieth century, both beliefs broke down—not through questioning the legitimacy of scientific governance but through applying the new empirical social sciences to the processes of constitutional law. Throughout this period there remained a remarkably stable understanding of constitutionalism as rational governance. Rationality permitted the adaptation of means to ends and thus growth within the constitutional order. What changed was the locus of rationality, and thus the vehicle for growth, in politics. Only in retrospect does the collapse of the *Lochner* Court in the judicial crisis of the New Deal represent the triumph of democratic majoritarianism. At the time, it represented the institutional consequences of the triumph of empirical social science.

The attack on the rationality of judicial decision making in the first part of this century was associated with the rise of legal realism. Although the boundaries of legal realism were diffuse, one idea uniting critical legal thinkers of the period was the rejection—often vigorous and scornful—of the claim that judicial decisions represented the application of a deductive methodology. Different critics focused on different aspects of the claim, some denying the neutrality of abstract legal principles and others denying the possibility of a neutral noninterpretive apprehension of the facts to which the principles were applied.[69] All would probably agree with Morris Cohen's assessment:

The invocation to Reason rather than to the relevant facts of the social scene has become traditional in constitutional law. . . . But when four judges . . . declare that a given law has a reasonable connection with the public health, and five say that no reasonable man can suppose that there is such a connection, one begins to doubt. Not only the reason but also the sense of humor and the courtesy of our judges thus appear to be of a peculiar transcendental variety.[70]

Much of the critique of judicial decision making was rooted in the application of nontranscendental forms of reason to the judges themselves. Two new sciences helped in mounting this critique: economics and psychology.

Charles Beard: Economics and the Constitution

In 1913, Charles Beard published *An Economic Interpretation of the Constitution of the United States*, in which he considers the "hypothesis that economic elements are the chief factors in the development of political institutions."[71] The empirical data against which the hypothesis is tested are those of the origins of the Constitution. Beard's work, however, is not narrowly historical; it rests at the intersection of history and law.

For Beard, methods of historical interpretation are closely linked to methods of legal reasoning. The poor state of American historiography has resulted in an artificial model of legal process: "Sadly as the economic factors have been ignored in historical studies, the neglect has been all the more pronounced in the field of private and public law. . . . In the absence of a critical analysis of legal evolution, all sorts of vague abstractions dominate most of the thinking that is done in the field of law." A failure to understand the role of economic factors in legal evolution leads to poor legal history and, more important, to poor law. The vague abstraction that dominates U.S. legal thinking is the "devotion to deductions from 'principles' exemplified in particular cases." It is, in other words, the central premise of a science of the common law.[72]

Beard's immediate aim is to demonstrate that the framers' "direct, impelling motive . . . was the economic advantages which the beneficiaries expected would accrue to themselves."[73] If the Constitution was a product of a factionalized, self-interested politics, then, to the degree that the courts try to maintain the constitutional order originally established, they are perpetuating an order founded on class interests—a prospect that raises serious questions about constitutional governance as a legitimate form of democratic self-government. This problem would hardly be insurmountable. It could, for example, be argued that despite these origins, the "living constitution" represents only those aspects of the original structure that have evolved to match a contemporary sense of justice.[74]

Beard, however, is not simply challenging popular assumptions about the grounds of the original constitutional order. He is making a more radical claim about legal reasoning. Law and history both rest on purposive interpretations of the social order. To understand these purposes requires understanding the interests of those involved as actors and interpreters. Beard's basic point is that ideas cannot be separated from interests: "[I]nterpretive schools seem always to originate in social antagonisms."[75] Bad history and bad law therefore have a common root: a failure to understand the connection between ideas and interests. Conversely, Beard hopes that historical methods that meet contemporary scientific standards will lead to good law.

Beard spells out the larger implications of his critique in a short essay, "Historiography and the Constitution," published some twenty-five years later. Prominent in this essay is a linking of what might otherwise be seen as three distinct constitutional moments: "making, development [and] interpretation of the Constitution." All three are deeply historical phenomena: "Any treatment of the constitutional process as separate from the conditioning and determining environment is arbitrary and does not correspond to the realities of the total situation." That determining environment includes ideas and interests "evolving and involving in time." "Every treatment that deals with the Constitution or any aspect of it as mere idea or abstraction unrelated to associated interests is unreal, fails to correspond to history as actuality."[76]

Whereas the earlier work applied the economic approach to the origins of the Constitution, Beard now applies the same approach to the process of judicial interpretation: "Any realistic treatment of judicial interpretations of the Constitution will cover the ideas and interests of the judges who make the interpretations."[77] To understand a judge's ideas therefore requires an understanding of the economic interests that are advanced by those ideas, as well as the judge's relation to those interests. Judges are not simply scientific decision makers applying the cold logic of the common law.

Beard offers his critique of the claims of judicial science as an advancement in the scholarly study of the processes of constitutional government. But it will also lead, he argues, to a new judicial self-consciousness, which will, in turn, lead to a more rational order of governance:

[B]y the persistent association of ideas and interests in the historiography of the Constitution, do we not put men and women on guard against treating their own ideas as having the dogmatic force of divine revelation? Do we not aid mankind in emancipating itself from the idolatry of symbolism that is the essence of government by sheer force? . . . [B]y refusing to recognize anyone as possessing a monopoly of divine revelation in matters constitutional, do we not soften the bitterness of conflict and open wider the door for understanding, mediation, and adjustment by the use of intelligence?[78]

Reason still promises resolution of political conflict. The aim of constitutionalism remains the progressive rationalization of political order. To achieve this, the judiciary's false claims to scientific governance must be exposed as another form of interest-driven politics.

Beard offered a doctrine of political psychology, then, not of economic determinism, as applied to constitutional law. The truths of modern economics were intended not just to expose the reality of judicial governance to the community but also to reveal to the judges themselves the interests behind their ideas. Only by understanding the relevance of economic interests can anyone gain that distance from self that will allow the application of intelligence to the problems of governance. This, he says, "is one of the profound discoveries of modern psychology."[79] Beard was not alone in attempting to bring modern psychology to bear on the problems of judicial decision making.

Jerome Frank: Psychology and the Constitution

The most explicit effort to link law and modern psychological science is found in the work of Jerome Frank. Law, he argues, must be seen as "a portion of the science of human nature." The role of modern psychology is not simply to take lawmaking as an object of study; it is not merely to offer a theory of law. Rather, psychology must be taken up into the law itself. Like Beard, Frank sees the study of legal process and the practice of law as deeply interconnected. The judge must engage in self-analysis for law to overcome the limits of the judicial personality: "[T]he judge should be not a mere thinking-machine but well trained, not only in rules of law, but also in the best available methods of psychology. And among the most important objects which would be subject to his scrutiny as psychologist would be his own personality so that he might become keenly aware of his own prejudices, biases, antipathies, and the like."[80]

From the perspective of a modern science of psychology, Frank argues, contemporary law is immature. Where Lochnerian science saw a law that had evolved into a mature political form, Frank sees a law that "stimulates childish emotional attitudes." The hope for formal certainty and abstract deductions in legal decision making represents "the survival of childish resistance to introspection with reference to thinking about law."[81] As the understanding of science shifts, so do the terms and measures of political maturity.

Frank's object, then, is to show that the idea of judicial decision making as a formal, deductive process that leads to objective, determinate results is a myth rooted in "the childish need for an authoritative father." In its place, he offers a model of decision making based upon contemporary psychology: "[S]ince the judge is a human being and since no human being in his normal thinking processes arrives at decisions . . . by the route of any such syllogistic reasoning, it is fair to assume that the judge, merely by putting on the judicial ermine, will not acquire so artificial a method of reasoning. Judicial judgments, like other judgments, doubtless, in most cases, are worked out backward from conclusions tentatively formulated."[82] The key to understanding law is to understand the grounds of these tentative conclusions. These are "based on the judge's hunches [and] the way in which the judge gets his hunches is the key to the judicial process." The judge, of course, gets his hunches the same way everyone else does. They arise from individual traits, dispositions, biases, and habits, as well as from opinions based upon political, economic, and moral prejudices. They arise, in short, from the whole complex personality of the judge: "To know the judge's hunch-producers which make the law we must know thoroughly that complicated congeries we loosely call the judge's personality."[83]

Not only must students of the law know these characteristics of judges to understand why the law is as it is or to predict what it will be, but more important, judges must pursue self-knowledge. The modern judge should offer "detailed autobiographies" or "opinions annotated . . . with elaborate explorations of the background factors in his personal experience which swayed him in reaching his conclusions." Only such a self-examination promises release, to the degree that release is possible, from the "evils" that arise from the unavoidable intrusion of the judge's personality into the process of decision making.[84]

Beard and Frank were united in their claim that apparent social phenomena, including law, must be explained by a scientific exploration of nonapparent phenomena. For both, the critical feature of modern social science is its exposure of the controlling effects of forces that do not operate in the conscious decision-making process of the ordinary actor. For Beard, the large-scale phenomena of history could be explained not by looking to what the individual actors said or believed but by looking at the underlying pattern of economic interests. For Frank, the small-scale phenomena—such as the judicial decision—could be explained by the dynamics of the unconscious. Their arguments together undermined the claim of the Court to be the voice of reason in the state. They exposed the Court as one among a number of competing institutions, with no privileged claim to truth: judges act according to those interests and biases that attach to all human action. Understanding the law required, therefore, understanding the class interests and individual psyches of those who make the law.

Like most legal realists, their work was stronger in its negative aspects—the critique of the Court's decision making and of the judiciary's understanding of the evolution of the law—than in its development of a positive model of constitutional law. Both assumed that a clearing away of the old beliefs would open the way to a more rational, scientific court. There were, however, serious institutional implications in the appeal to the new social sciences. The critique of the character of judicial reasoning was linked, through these sciences, to the critique of the substantive content of the judicial science of the common law as a basis for social ordering. Rational governance might not lie in an improved judicial science but in a nonjudicial science.

Roscoe Pound: Sociology and the Constitution

Perhaps the most trenchant and effective contemporaneous criticism of the *Lochner* Court came from Roscoe Pound. In a series of articles, Pound analyzed the jurisprudential character of the Court's constitutionalism and proposed a new model of scientific constitutionalism: sociological jurisprudence.[85] Pound acknowledged that the *Lochner* Court was operating under a particular conception of scientific jurisprudence. Unlike the legal realists, he rejected the idea that the jurisprudence of the Court could be explained by looking to the "personal, social and economic views" of the judges or to "the party bent of judges." Of such reductionist approaches, Pound said: "[W]hen a doctrine is announced with equal vigor and held with equal tenacity by courts of Pennsylvania and of Arkansas, of New York and of California, of Illinois and of West Virginia, of Massachusetts and of Missouri, we may not dispose of it so readily. Surely the sources of such a doctrine must lie deeper."[86] The sources of this doctrine were, according to Pound, in the hold that a particular understanding of science had upon the judicial imagination. Pound described this as "mechanical jurisprudence," by which he meant "a rigid scheme of deductions from *a priori* conceptions."[87]

Pound explains the connection between constitutional law and mechanical jurisprudence by referring to a larger theory of the evolutionary stages of all domains of scientific knowledge: "The effect of all system is apt to be petrifaction of the subject systematized. Perfection of scientific system and exposition tends to cut off individual initiative in the future, to stifle independent consideration of new problems and of new phases of old problems, and to impose the ideas of one generation upon another. This is so in all departments of learning. . . . Legal science is not exempt from this tendency."[88] A paradigm of normal growth in science explains the *Lochner* Court's constitutionalism.

The substantive content of the Court's jurisprudence, however, cannot be explained apart from the historical context within which this mechanical jurisprudence developed. In his essay "Liberty of Contract," Pound describes this context. He points to the mix of a natural-law theory of individual rights, a socioeconomic theory of individualism, and the individualistic character of the common law, all of which dominated thought during the period in which constitutional law developed. "This bit of history" explains the content of the principles of the Court's mechanical jurisprudence.[89]

The mechanical jurisprudence embodied in the doctrine of liberty of contract has two prominent characteristics, according to Pound: "the rigorous logical deduction from predetermined conceptions in disregard of and often in the teeth of the actual facts" and the collapse of constitutional law and the common law. These two points are linked because a court that cannot investigate the facts of new economic conditions in an industrial society is bound to decide by reference to the common-law understandings of the domain of contract. The court does not perceive the dissonance between the common law and contemporary facts because it sees the common law as the expression of abstract, natural law: "Closely related to the [training of lawyers in natural law], and indeed, a product of the same training, is a deep-seated conviction of the American lawyer that the doctrines of the common law are part of the universal jural order. . . . [T]his feeling operates in constitutional law to lead judges to try statutes by the measure of common law doctrines rather than by the Constitution."[90]

Even though Pound is devastatingly critical of the Court's mechan-

ical jurisprudence, he is sympathetic to the scientific aspiration it represents. The power of his critique arises from his claim that mechanical
jurisprudence is bad science, not that the Court shouldn't be scientific.
Indeed, Pound begins his essay on mechanical jurisprudence by approvingly quoting Pollock's assertion that law in a modern society must be
scientific: "There is no way ... by which modern law can escape from
the scientific and artificial character imposed on it by the demand of
modern societies for full, equal, and exact justice." Pound goes on to
describe "the marks of a scientific law [as] conformity to reason, uniformity, and certainty. Scientific law is a reasoned body of principles for the
administration of justice, and its antithesis is a system of enforcing mag-
isterial caprice."[91] The problem with mechanical jurisprudence is that "in
truth it is not science at all."[92]

Pound's positive reform effort was intended to make constitutional
jurisprudence congruent with contemporary ideas of science. "We have,
then, the same task in jurisprudence that has been achieved in philosophy,
in the natural sciences and in politics. We have to rid ourselves of this
sort of legality and to attain a pragmatic, a sociological legal science."[93]
Sociological jurisprudence applied to law the insights of the new empirical
social sciences, which operated with a pragmatic, instrumental understanding of the role of theory. For example, Pound began "Liberty of
Contract" by citing the works of contemporary sociologists and econo-
mists who saw the judicial doctrine of liberty of contract as "utterly hol-
low," "surcharged with fallacy," or a "mere juggling with words."[94]

In discussing the scientism of the *Lochner* Court, I pointed out that
a scientific constitutionalism opens the way to a charge of error. Indeed,
Pound seized the opportunity to accuse the Court of poor science. If he
was correct, the Court had failed in its own terms. If the Court has failed
to keep up with scientific developments, it could not claim to be the voice
of reason. Instead of contributing to a rational order of governance, it was
blocking the evolution of the rational form of political order.

Pound tied this point to a deeper criticism of the possible role of
the Court. The Court is institutionally incapable of participating in the
new science of politics: "[I]n the ordinary case involving constitutionality,
the court has no machinery for getting at the facts. It must decide on the
basis of matters of general knowledge and on accepted principles of uniform application."[95] Pound repeatedly emphasizes that "there is coming
to be a science of legislation" that will be based upon "long and patient
study by experts, careful consideration by conferences or congresses or
associations, press discussions ... and hearings before legislative committees."[96] The courts "cannot have the advantage of legislative reference

bureaus, of hearings before committees, of the testimony of specialists who have conducted detailed investigations."[97] He summarizes this view by stating his agreement with the contemporary sociologist Lester F. Ward: "We are told that law-making of the future will consist in putting the sanction of society on what has been worked out in the sociological laboratory."[98]

In this description of the character and sources of the new science of law, Pound was providing, in 1908, a model of the argument that would, thirty years later, displace the *Lochner* Court. He accurately described not only the overwhelming of mechanical jurisprudence by the expert sources of a new empirical social science of law but also the institutional consequences of this shift in the locus of reason in the state. A court that accepted the new model of science would have "to assume that the legislature did its duty and . . . keep its hands off on that ground."[99]

Together legal realism and sociological jurisprudence used contemporary developments in the social sciences to undermine the two supporting premises of the *Lochner* Court: that judges are rational decision makers and that the common law offers a model of scientific ordering of society. Both of these schools have had an enduring effect on the character of legal thought. The legal realists' skepticism about judicial rationality, rooted in its turn in unconscious sources of social and political phenomena, has its modern institutional counterpart in the critical legal studies movement. Pound's sociological jurisprudence finds its modern counterpart in the law and economics movement. As at the beginning of the century, there is no easy alliance between these schools.[100] Nevertheless, they share a common, skeptical attitude toward the judicial claim of an independent integrity for the law.[101] In this sense, the law itself may not have recovered from the demise of the *Lochner* Court.

The Demise of the *Lochner* Court

The demise of the *Lochner* Court is often recounted as a story of confrontation between the Court and the political branches in their attempt to regulate the economy.[102] The Court struck down over two hundred laws between 1905, when *Lochner* was decided, and the mid-1930s, when it was effectively overruled. The conflict this generated came to a crisis with the Court's rejection of the program of the New Deal, which, in turn, led to Roosevelt's effort to pack the Court.

More theoretically interesting, however, is the story of the change in constitutional doctrine that allowed the Court to defuse the political crisis over its own role in the constitutional system. Because the Court believed its actions to be constitutionally required, it could not simply give up; it could not announce political defeat. It had to make sense of the changing political and economic circumstances to which it found itself responding. It had to explain to itself—and to those who listened to it— the theory by which the constitutional effort could continue within these changed circumstances.

The story of the jurisprudential dissolution of the *Lochner* Court is an account of a shift in the understanding of the locus of science in government. The institutions subject to judicial review took the Court's invocation of reason seriously, overwhelming the Court with the techniques and products of the new social sciences. In the end, the Court had less of a claim to science and rationality than legislatures and administrative agencies did.

At the turn of the century, the Court expressly claimed the authority to rationalize economic regulation. One model of judicial rationality was exemplified in *Lochner:* the rationality represented by the categories of the common law. But even in those exceptional areas in which the *Lochner* Court permitted government intervention in the economy, the measure of rationality still had to come from within the judicial process itself. In *Smyth v. Ames,* for example, the Court wrote: "While rates for the transportation of persons and property within the limits of a State are primarily for its determination, the question whether they are so unreasonably low as to deprive the carrier of its property without such compensation as the Constitution secures . . . cannot be so conclusively determined by the legislature . . . that the matter may not become the subject of judicial inquiry." This judicial inquiry entailed review of a "voluminous record" extending to all the economic factors bearing upon the regulated enterprise.[103] Each private litigant had the right to test the reasonableness of state action against the measure of judicial rationality.

By 1938 the Court had adopted an entirely different attitude toward regulatory rationality. It continued to give lip service to the possibility of proving "in judicial proceedings . . . all facts which would show or tend to show that a statute depriving the suitor of life, liberty or property [did not have] a rational basis." In fact, however, the Court was now willing to hypothesize supporting facts: "[W]here the legislative judgment is drawn in question, [judicial inquiry] must be restricted to the issue whether any state of facts either known or which could reasonably be assumed affords support for it."[104] This change in managing the rationality of public order can be traced in the Court's attitude toward state legislation examined under the due process clause and federal regulation examined under the commerce clause. In both cases, the shift from an active Court pursuing the goal of rationality to a passive Court applying a deferential standard of reasonableness reflected the rise of administrative expertise and the legislative use of the new empirical social science.

Like *Lochner*, *Nebbia v. New York* involved a New York State statute that interfered with one of the basic relations in a free-market economy. Instead of a contract for labor, it concerned a sale—an ordinary customer's purchase of milk from a retailer. New York State regulated the price at which milk could be sold; Nebbia had sold milk below the state-mandated minimum price.

Formally, the Court appeals to a test that sounds much like that used in *Lochner:* "[T]he guaranty of due process . . . demands only that the law shall not be unreasonable, arbitrary or capricious, and that the means selected shall have a real and substantial relation to the object sought to be attained."[105] The measure of rationality still appears to be the relation of means to ends. In fact, however, the Court's understanding of its own relation to a constitutionalism of scientific governance has changed dramatically.

The most obvious contrast between *Nebbia* and *Lochner* is the Court's treatment of facts. In *Lochner*, the majority expressly ignored statistical evidence and technical expertise with respect to the conditions of employment in bakeries. In *Nebbia*, the Court's opinion begins with a detailed account of the data generated and relied upon by the state legislature. The Court emphasizes the numerous hearings, the hundreds of witnesses, and the thousands of pages of testimony and expert reports. Quoting the Court in full gives a sense of the transformation that is occurring:

[The joint legislative committee] held 13 public hearings at which 254 witnesses testified and 2350 typewritten pages of testimony were taken. Numerous exhibits were submitted. Under its direction an extensive research program was prosecuted by experts and official bodies and employees of the state and municipalities, which resulted in the assembling of much pertinent information. Detailed reports were received from over 100 distributors of milk, and these were collated and the information obtained analyzed. As a result of the study of this material, a report covering 473 closely printed pages, embracing the conclusions and recommendations of the committee, was presented to the legislature. . . . This document included detailed findings, with copious references to the supporting evidence; appendices outlining the nature and results of prior investigations of the milk industry of the state, briefs upon the legal questions involved, and forms of bills recommended for passage. The conscientious effort and thoroughness exhibited by the report lend weight to the committee's conclusions.[106]

Here the Court is acknowledging that the legislature has established an institutional structure responsive to a new understanding of the empirical character of the science of government. These new institutions, however, represent a form of governance that, as Pound noted, is beyond the Court's institutional capacity. If scientific governance requires this kind of research and proceedings, the Court cannot be scientific.

The earlier, common-law science had been historical but not empirical. Of those in government, only the judges had the intellectual training and the political insulation required to pursue this science. The special expertise of the Court was a knowledge of the law, which made contact with contemporary circumstances through the ordinary understandings that judges shared with everyone else. The empirical data generated by the scientific investigations instigated by the legislature now exploded the common-law rationalism of the *Lochner* Court. The new sciences exposed both the common law and the common understanding as deeply irrational.

Not only were the sources and character of science changing; so was the substantive understanding of constitutional order supported by science. Lochnerian science envisioned the union of political and economic models of liberty: a democratic political order required a free-market economic order. The state-generated empirical data in *Nebbia* were intended to undermine the presumed connection between political rationality and the free market. The free market in milk, according to the data, was the source of the public health problems and the economic problems with which the state had to deal.[107] The problem requiring government intervention was no longer the need to bring certain groups up to a free-market standard but the irrationality of the market itself. "The legislative investigation of 1932 was persuasive of the fact that . . . unrestricted competition aggravated existing evils, and the normal law of supply and demand was insufficient to correct maladjustments detrimental to the community."[108]

Accordingly, market competition could no longer be seen as the end point of political evolution. It was, at best, a choice government might make: "So far as the requirement of due process is concerned, and in the absence of other constitutional restriction, a state is free to adopt whatever economic policy may reasonably be deemed to promote public welfare, and to enforce that policy by legislation adapted to its purpose."[109] Once the market was divorced from the constitutional order, the workings of the market could be reconceived as presenting merely technical problems, for which technical solutions were appropriate. Within this factual context, revealed by expert knowledge, it would have been irrational for the Court to claim that a technical response—that is, one founded on the new science of economics—was irrational, arbitrary, or capricious.

The shift in the character of constitutional rationality is symbolized by the Court's review of its own precedents on permissible government interference with private contracts of sale. It turns to these precedents in response to the claim that government regulation may not extend to price control.[110] The Court, however, can no longer make sense of the old common-law categories, which distinguished price control from other regulatory interventions. The new, quantitative science of economics flattens all prior, qualitative distinctions among kinds of economic interventions. Thus, the Court concludes that there is nothing special about regulating prices because all regulation affects prices.[111] Where the *Lochner* Court understood that a general rule might have exceptions—noninterference with contract, for example, yielded to the protection of women and minors—the *Nebbia* Court sees only arbitrariness and inconsistency. The rule disappeared in the exceptions.

With the abandonment of the old categories of exceptionality came the demise of the common-law understanding of constitutionally cognizable harm. For the *Lochner* Court, redressable harm had to be located outside the market transaction. A bad bargain was not itself ground for state intervention. From the perspective of the new science of economics, no such qualitative distinction could hold. The harm that government could address included the outcome of ordinary market transactions: "[G]overnment cannot exist if the citizen may at will use his property to the detriment of his fellows, or exercise his freedom of contract to work them harm."[112] The important point is that this harm now included striking a hard bargain or, for that matter, a weak bargain. This point was given vivid expression in *West Coast Hotel v. Parrish*, decided three years later in 1937, when the Court described the social consequences of employers entering into low-paying wage contracts as "a subsidy for unconscionable employers." The employers had done nothing but exercise their previously protected right to contract. The Court's new view of the harm this causes was based upon "recent economic experience," which is so apparent that "[i]t is unnecessary to cite official statistics."[113]

For the *Lochner* Court, state intervention was limited by a doctrine of public interest that defined redressable harms. In *Nebbia*, the public interest standard collapses into mere tautology; "'affected with a public interest' is the equivalent of 'subject to the exercise of the police power.'" As the dissent points out, "[T]his is but to declare that rights guaranteed by the Constitution exist only so long as supposed public interest does not require their extinction."[114]

Economic expertise therefore provided the context within which the Court could move to an entirely new understanding of its own role. If government is to be scientific in a world in which science is a statistical enterprise, then the Court will have less and less to say. It will, as Pound noted earlier, "assume that the legislature did its duty and ... keep its hands off."

This same pattern is apparent in the Court's escape from its confrontation with the federal regulations of the New Deal. In *National Labor Relations Board v. Jones and Laughlin Steel,* the Court examined a board ruling that the company had engaged in an unfair labor practice by discharging employees for pursuing union activities.[115] The case brought before the Court the issue of the competence of federal administrative agencies in what appeared to be a highly unfavorable context: the company, which employed thousands, had dismissed just ten workers. To uphold the board's action, the Court had to accept the claim that the agency could properly find the dismissal had a sufficient effect on interstate commerce to support federal intervention under the commerce clause.

The *Lochner* Court used the categories of "direct" and "indirect" effect to determine whether a regulatory intervention fell within congressional authority under the commerce clause. In the world of Lochnerian science, the meaning of those categories did not depend upon statistical evidence of actual economic effects. Rather, the constitutional logic of the federal role in the national economy was driven by common-law categories: "The word 'direct' [as in "direct effect on interstate commerce"] implies that the activity or condition invoked or blamed shall operate proximately—not mediately, remotely, or collaterally—to produce the effect. It connotes the absence of an efficient intervening agency or condition."[116] This was the language of common-law tort. Private economic activity was protected from outside interference—whether private or public—as long as it stayed within the boundaries established by the common law. The interests of the federal government were not—in their legal character—different from those of a private person: only when another's actions directly effect those interests was countervailing action permitted. The Court understood public power as falling within an existing pattern of legal order. The logic of this order was best known by the judges, who were the scientists of the common law.

The Court gives perfect expression to this view when it intones:

The distinction between a direct and an indirect effect turns, not upon the magnitude of either the cause or the effect, but entirely upon the manner in which the effect has been brought about. If the production by one man of a single ton of coal intended for interstate sale and shipment, and actually so sold and shipped, affects interstate commerce indirectly, the effect does not become direct by multiplying the tonnage, or increasing the number of men employed, or adding to the expense or complexities of the business, or by all combined.

Just as state interference with private contracts was regulated by the arcane logic of the common law, so was federal interference with economic activity. To perceive this logic required the Court to abstract from the actual economic facts: "[T]he extent of the effect bears no logical relation to its character."[117]

In *Jones and Laughlin Steel*, decided in 1937, this common-law approach to federal power ended. A common-law science of political economy was displaced by a statistical, economic science. From then on, the measure of rationality would be quantitative, not formal. "It is the effect upon commerce, not the source of the injury, which is the criterion."[118]

The Court's rejection of formalism was complete: "We are asked to shut our eyes to the plainest facts of our national life and to deal with the question of direct and indirect effects in an intellectual vacuum." This it would not do. The requisite effect on interstate commerce was no longer the subject of formal categorization but was "to be determined as individual cases arise."[119] Just as *Nebbia* began with a thorough review of the facts of the milk industry, *Jones and Laughlin Steel* begins with a detailed review of the organization of the steel industry.

To the degree that these complex facts were relevant to determining the reasonableness of regulation, the Court was providing the grounds for its own deference to the administrative agency. The agency alone had the technical experience, knowledge, and resources to make the necessary determinations. Reasonable governance was now inseparable from the complex facts of contemporary economic organization; and if so, interference by the Court was more likely than not to be unreasonable. Instead of a paradigm of scientific rationality, *Lochner* now appeared as a model of irrationality. No longer the institutional forum for progress in the implementation of the science of government, the *Lochner* Court was now seen as an obstacle to that progress. Progress remained linked to science, and science, it was thought, would impose a rational order upon the facts. But by the time of the New Deal, the science of government was economics, not the common law.

Conclusion: Continuity between the Old and the New Court

The history of the Supreme Court in the latter part of the nineteenth century and the first part of the twentieth century perfectly illustrates the changing character of constitutionalism. During this period, academic theory became influential. Changes in the understanding of constitutional governance were deeply affected by a theoretical discourse that occurred outside the institutions of government. The *Lochner* Court was the institutional culmination of the theoretical development of a particular idea of an evolving unwritten constitution in the post–Civil War period. Its demise reflected the shift in social science, at the beginning of this century, from broadly historical and evolutionary to narrowly empirical and statistical.[120]

From the larger perspective of the development of constitutional theory, the critical step was the move to an evolutionary model of constitutionalism. The substantive content of that model was quite flexible, reflecting larger disputes about the character of the social order. It would, however, be a mistake to see the turn toward evolutionary models in constitutional thought as simply a reflection of these larger, extralegal developments. There was no need to wait for the development of social Darwinism to put a model of growth into constitutional thought. The common-law resources were always available.

The shift from the mid-nineteenth-century model of originalism to a model of growth is best explained by the increasing difficulty of maintaining the originalist model as the distance from the origin increased. The felt difference between the present and the past eventually had to overwhelm the claim of identity. When that happened, a new way of conceiving of the past was required if history was not to be given up entirely. The evolutionary model offered this: it put into the constitutional order of the state a capacity for remaking that did not require a new foundation, a breaking with the past. The idea of growth privileges the present while continuing to respect the past; it affirms the continuity of the present with the past. Thus, across all the domains of constitutional thought, both theoretical and judicial, the central idea of this period was adaptation: the Constitution must continually adapt to the needs of a developing society. The question that came to dominate constitutional debate was not whether adaptation was required but who would do the adapting.

Nothing about the evolutionary model in itself suggests that progress must be measured by an increasing rationalization of the state. This gloss on the value of growth came from the larger normative environment of the period. However, once growth was identified with progress in the scientific ordering of the state, the pattern of dispute within this conceptual model was set. By the end of the nineteenth century, the basic problem that attached to the constitutional appropriation of the evolutionary model was clear: What is the character of the science by which growth is to occur? The institutional location of that science largely followed from its character.

The science of the common law, with its privileged place for the judiciary, had won this battle by the beginning of the century. Nevertheless, science was a weak foundation upon which to set the legitimacy of the Court's role. Reason could serve as a model of constitutional legitimacy, but the locus of reason was not likely to stay with the Court. Just as one hundred years earlier Marshall's claim to a nationalist, republican political science had been countered by a decentralized republican science, the *Lochner* Court's claim to a common-law science was countered by the rise of empirical social sciences. The commitment to reason as the source of constitutional growth implicitly entails a commitment to the best science. By the time of the New Deal, the best science, as Pound predicted, had a new institutional location. This new science exposed the *Lochner* Court as an irrational actor.

The collapse of the *Lochner* Court represented a vast change in the content of constitutional law, but not in the conceptual model of constitutionalism. The New Deal program, with its central theme of the application of scientific expertise to diverse problems of public and private order, continued to represent an evolving scientific governance. The constitutional model upon which that program relied remained that of an unwritten evolving constitution, which first appeared in the post–Civil War years. The Constitution was not, for New Dealers, a serious constraint on the evolution of scientific governance. Thayer, who stood for the weakest possible view of constitutional constraints on legislative innovation, became their prophet of the correct—that is, modern—view. Not until the 1950s would the claims of scientific ordering begin to be felt as themselves challenging the legitimacy of constitutional self-government.

CHAPTER FIVE

The Locus of
Will in Modern
Constitutional
Theory

I have described three conceptual models in the development of constitutionalism: making, maintenance, and growth. Growth represented a synthesis of the first two models and seemed, therefore, to offer an end point to constitutional development. The capacity of this model to address the complex temporal character of the state, moreover, afforded it a hold on constitutional theory that was not available to the first two models. Making looked only to the present, and maintenance looked only to the past. Growth linked present, past, and future in a coherent whole.

The appearance of completion notwithstanding, constitutional development did not come to an end. Instead, the modern period—beginning after the Second World War and entering its slow death in the 1970s—was marked by a profound crisis in constitutional theory. The enterprise of constitutionalism was in danger of collapsing. Constitutional theory polarized between two positions, both antithetical to the idea of constitutional self-government within the bounds of the historical state. The first position focused on simple majority rule, the second on individual autonomy. The former view could not account for constitutional constraints on a present majority. The latter view could not account for constitutional support of any authoritative governmental structure.

Although political theories of majoritarianism and autonomy are ordinarily seen as opposed to each other, they are united in their reliance on individual will as the source of all values.[1] Reliance on the immediate will of the individual, moreover, sets both in opposition to a constitutionalism based on either reason or history. The dispute between the proponents of majoritarianism and those of individual autonomy was over the locus of will in the constitutional state: Does it lie in the majority or in the individual? Modern constitutional thought moved from the first to the second position but lacked a conceptual apparatus to resolve the dispute. Resolution required movement to yet another conceptual model of order: the discursive community, which is at the core of contemporary constitutional theory.

Constitutionalism in a Majoritarian World

Although a reconceptualization of the character and forum of science was central to the demise of the *Lochner* Court, by mid-century constitutional theory had reconceived the New Deal experience, understanding it now as about the political role of the Court.[2] The emergence of the empirical social sciences delegitimated the old constitutional science and the institution that embodied that science. For a brief period, it seemed as if the Court's new role might be to ensure that the decisions of the political institutions of government were based upon the new social sciences.[3] That role was abandoned when the association of social science and self-government was broken by the rise of European fascism.[4] Instead of focusing on the application of the new sciences to government policy, constitutional theorists now focused on the institutional contrast between an illegitimate Court and the democratically legitimated political branches. The Court was perceived as a deviant institution within a democratic society, and the central issue of constitutional theory became "the countermajoritarian difficulty." Constitutional theorists faced the uncomfortable choice between affirming an institutional role for the Court that seemed to undermine the democratic foundation of the political order and affirming government by consent, which seemed to undermine any role for the Court. To resolve this paradox became the main problem of constitutional theory.

Although today this problem seems obvious, its emergence represented a radical shift in the conceptual framework of constitutional theory. Throughout the latter part of the nineteenth century and early part of the twentieth, the central problem of constitutional theory was the majoritarian difficulty: How could a constitutional system designed to put in place the historically evolving form of reasonable governance be reconciled with popular, democratic institutions? If government was not to become a manifestation of the factional self-interests of the disorderly mob, how could a place be maintained for the majoritarian institutions of government? That theorists in the modern period were preoccupied with the opposite problem is not a measure of enduring truth but of a shift in conceptual frameworks. Even this preoccupation is changing: rejection of the focus on the countermajoritarian difficulty marks the emergence of a contemporary constitutional theory.

Learned Hand and the Platonic Guardians

In 1958, Judge Learned Hand delivered the Oliver Wendell Holmes Lectures at Harvard Law School under the title "The Bill of Rights." Hand begins modestly: "My subject is well-worn; it is not likely that I shall have new light to throw on it; but it is always fresh, and particularly at the present time it is important enough to excuse renewed examination."[5] His subject is judicial review. According to Hand, the subject is important "at the present time" because the Warren Court has begun to disturb the grounds upon which the judicial crisis of the New Deal was resolved. Hand's modesty derives from his belief that he speaks as the representative of the last great moment of constitutional self-consciousness.

What Hand learned from the legal realists and the constitutional crisis of the 1930s was that the Court possesses no special knowledge. In the absence of such knowledge, the justification for judicial review must, he believes, lie in the Court's contribution to preventing "the defeat of the venture at hand"—which is the institutional maintenance of government through a majoritarian political process.[6]

Hand begins by arguing that the practice of judicial review cannot be derived from either constitutional text or original history. The text establishes three coequal branches, each operating as an agent of the sovereign people. Each branch is bound only by its own understanding of the character and limits of this agency relationship. Because, at best, original history is indeterminate, Hand concludes: "I cannot . . . help doubting whether the evidence justifies a certain conclusion that the Convention would have so voted, if the issue had been put to it that courts should have power to invalidate acts of Congress." Neither is Hand sympathetic to the claim that the ordinary function of courts—to say what the law is in the course of adjudication—entails judicial review. "[I]f a court, having concluded that a constitution did not authorize the statute, goes on to annul it, its power to do so depends upon an authority that is not involved when only statutes or precedents are involved."[7]

Nevertheless, he believes judicial review is justified, because it is legitimate "to interpolate into the [Constitution] such provisions, though not expressed, as are essential to prevent the defeat of the venture at hand." Without judicial review, the constitutional system would degenerate into congressional omnipotence or endless interbranch conflict. Either alternative would be "so capricious in operation, and so different from that designed, that it could not have endured."[8]

Because judicial review has its justification in structural, long-term considerations, it need not be exercised in any given case. Its exercise depends upon the needs of the system, rather than the right of the litigants. "[S]ince this power is not a logical deduction from the structure of the Constitution but only a practical condition upon its successful operation, it need not be exercised whenever a court sees, or thinks that it sees, an invasion of the Constitution."[9]

The Court's role, according to Hand, is to maintain the constitutional distribution of authority among the various organs of government. The standards defended by the Court should do no more than articulate the boundaries of each department. The Court has no authority to review the substantive decisions made by each branch within its appropriate domain. Two examples of what Hand had in mind might be the nondelegation doctrine, which requires Congress to do its own work, and the decision in the *Youngstown* case, in which the Court held that President Truman unconstitutionally exercised legislative authority in seizing the steel mills.[10] Both doctrines are neutral with respect to substantive policy, insisting only on maintenance of the constitutional division of responsibility.

Hand's rejection of judicial review under the broad substantive provisions of the Constitution rests upon a general claim about the character of values. Values, for Hand, reflect subjective, individual gratifications. There are no objective norms; individuals bring their own scale of values to the choices made. The task of the legislature is somehow to weigh these incommensurable norms. It must choose between competing claims to gratification and injury and apply those choices through its best guess about the course of future events. That process cannot be measured objectively—neither values nor predictions can be set on any kind of scale.

Any time a court reviews substantive policy choices, then, it is acting in a legislative capacity. It is substituting its guess about the future course of events or its own values for the guess or values of the legislature. It must, because there is no other way to make such decisions. Hand has his eye on the *Lochner* Court, which repeatedly found "arbitrary" and "irrational" legislation that balanced competing social interests. He vigorously attacks the Court's claim that it can resolve conflicts over values by relying on something other than the personal preferences of the judges.

The legal realists debunked the earlier Court's economic, due-process jurisprudence. But Hand sees judicial legislation reappearing in the Warren Court's defense of noneconomic values: "I can see no more persuasive reason for supposing that a legislature is *a priori* less qualified to choose between personal than between economic values."[11] No institutional difference can be supported because there is no substantive difference between the grounds of personal and of economic values. Individual will, not objective reason, is the only basis for choice in both cases.

Hand does not believe that the courts can sustain this policy-making function within a democratic polity. What possible rationale can there be for deferring to the idiosyncratic values of a group of nine old men who are wholly unaccountable to the larger public? From this critique arises his most famous line: "For myself it would be most irksome to be ruled by a bevy of Platonic Guardians, even if I knew how to choose them, which I assuredly do not." For Hand, the judge is on solid ground only when he is a "mouthpiece of a public will, conceived as the result of many conflicting strains that have come, at least provisionally, to a consensus." That consensus is represented in the product of the political branches: positive law. There exist no higher law, no purer reason, and no truth by which to judge the reasonableness of the legislative product.[12]

Hand is not insensitive to the problems of aggregating individual wills through the legislative system: "Of course I know how illusory would be the belief that my vote determined anything; but nevertheless when I go to the polls I have a satisfaction in the sense that we are all engaged in a common venture."[13] He does not pretend to offer a principled defense of legislative choice. But his skepticism at the polls is no match for his cynicism toward the courts. Nothing that the legislature does could match the failings that are the legacy of the *Lochner* Court.

For Hand, reason could not chart the course of policy because each choice is nothing more than a balance of incommensurable, personal values. Nevertheless, reason did not totally disappear. Establishing and maintaining the boundaries among the institutions of government was not a function of will. Reason remained linked to formal institutional design. Hand hoped to defend an objective ground for judicial action by stripping the Court of all substantive content and thus of any will of its own. This effort to couple the constitutional role of the courts to a formal, and hence neutral, process of reason—which allows all substantive decisions to be made by a majoritarian political process—was continued and expanded by Herbert Wechsler.

Herbert Wechsler and Neutral Principles

Just one year after Hand's lecture series, Herbert Wechsler responded to Judge Hand in what was to become one of the most famous articles of modern constitutional theory, "Toward Neutral Principles of Constitutional Law." Hand spoke with a cynicism that arose out of the New Deal experience of the Court; Wechsler writes with a new optimism that the countermajoritarian difficulty can be solved within the terms of the law itself. This contrast of new and old theory is clear in Wechsler's opening remarks. Hand disavowed that he had anything new to say, but Wechsler claims that his argument "will not constitute mere reiteration." He plans to address and resolve "that most abiding problem of our public law: the role of the courts in general and the Supreme Court in particular in our constitutional tradition."[14]

Hand and Wechsler, in fact, shared a good deal. Both agreed that a defense of judicial review must be based on the capacity of the Court to pursue a kind of decision making different from that of the legislature. Both tied this function to the exercise of reason, rather than the assertion of preference. The desire for reasoned decision making led both to a formalistic account of the Court's role. The difference between them rested on their widely different assessments of the potential scope of reasoned decision making.

Hand leveled all forms of practical reason, contending that all normative judgments are based upon the subjective evaluation of competing interests. Wechsler saw that any adequate response to Hand would have to offer a model of practical reason that is independent of the mere assertion of personal choice. To defend the Court required a defense of reason as a source of substantive decision making. Over and over again, Wechsler asserted that the unique role of a court is its capacity to deploy reason in the making of political choices. But Wechsler hardly had a sophisticated idea of what reasoned decision making entails. In fact, the power of the article largely depends on a fundamental ambiguity in his analysis of judicial reasoning.

To offer a reason for a decision is to appeal to a general rule. A reasoned decision is never grounded simply in a personal preference for one outcome rather than another. "Neutral principles" is Wechsler's cumbersome way of referring to this idea of rule-governed choice. Neutrality does not characterize the principles themselves but rather the reasons offered to support a principle and the manner in which it is applied. A principle is not neutral when it is supported only because of a subjective preference for an outcome it generates. Although that outcome might be a reason to support the principle, neutral decision making entails a commitment to support the principle even when its application produces outcomes contrary to the preferences of the decision maker.

Wechsler's description of decision making under neutral principles captures the ideal of justice as equality under law. The special function of the courts, according to Wechsler, is to decide issues on the basis of neutral principles, which means offering reasons of some generality that are supported for reasons that are independent of the outcome in a particular case. He approvingly quotes Justice Felix Frankfurter's description of the role of the judge: it is "the achievement of justice between man and man, between man and state, through reason called law."[15] The appropriate domain of judicial decision making is defined by that set of problems that are best resolved by this method of decision making. In the legal-process school, of which Wechsler was a founding member, this category is defined by the concept of "a case or controversy."[16]

To say that values must be given a principled expression is hardly the same as saying that adherence to this formal idea of neutrality is enough to resolve conflicts among values. At times, Wechsler recognizes this point—in particular, when he focuses on the methodology of constitutional law. He speaks of the role of history, text, and precedent in the determination of constitutional values.[17] The substantive principles that result from these interpretive methodologies are not neutral. Nevertheless, Wechsler hopes to apply his doctrine of neutral principles to the methodologies by taking the argument to a higher level. The "relative compulsion" among these different methodologies must itself be "judged, so far as possible, by neutral principles—by standards that transcend the case at hand."[18]

One neutral methodological principle, for example, might specify that whenever the text is clear, historical inquiry cannot defeat the value choice explicit in the text. But the opposite principle, privileging history over text, is also neutral. Although the neutral-principles doctrine can be applied at increasing levels of abstraction, it will not, in the end, resolve the problem of choice among values.

The neutrality thesis as so far presented is not controversial, although it may be an incomplete account of justice.[19] It has, however, two serious deficiencies. First, it fails to justify judicial review. Whether the Court or Congress should have the last word on the meaning of the Constitution is not resolved by pointing to the greater institutional capacity of the courts to decide according to neutral principles. This is a model for the application of law, but the majoritarian critique of judicial review rests upon a claim that the courts are making new law when they purport to interpret the Constitution. Hand's critique of judicial review of substantive legislative choices made just this point.[20]

Second, the neutrality thesis is so formal that it is unhelpful. Wechsler does not explain how problems of constitutional value choice should be resolved; he only says to deploy those resolutions in a neutral manner. The problems with this formal approach to neutral principles are evident in any attempt to apply the thesis.

Consider the example of affirmative action. Those opposed to affirmative action appeal to Wechsler's rule of neutral principles. They claim that the constitutional value put in place in the desegregation cases was that race may not be a ground for state action—a value best expressed in the rule of color-blindness. Thus, the state cannot make race the basis of any assignment of benefits or burdens. The rule requires the dismantling of segregated institutions, and it also forbids affirmative action programs. To look to who benefits—in one case, whites, and in the other, blacks— represents precisely the kind of ad hoc appeal to outcomes that is the antithesis of judicial neutrality. Even on this view, a state could conceivably act on some occasions in conscious consideration of race. But whatever exceptions exist must themselves be consistent with the principle. Remedial action, for example, might permit race-conscious decision making for a limited time.

Yet the neutral-principles thesis supports the opposite outcome equally well. One can argue that the value at stake in the desegregation decisions is not captured by the principle of color-blindness but by another principle: for example, the state may not use racial classifications to stigmatize, or the state may not use classifications that perpetuate the burdens originally created by slavery.[21] All of these propositions state principles; all can be applied neutrally. If accepted, however, the alternative principles are not likely to lead to trouble with affirmative action.

The equal protection clause does not specify which of these principles correctly expresses the constitutional rule. To determine that requires an appeal to an interpretation, and such an appeal will introduce a complex discussion of political and constitutional theory in which no position has a uniquely privileged claim to principle.[22]

The empty formalism at the core of Wechsler's argument is often masked by an implicit subtheme that suggests that invoking the principle of neutrality is itself enough to resolve problems of interpretation. This deep-seated confusion is most evident in the famous challenge to defend the Court's desegregation decisions, which Wechsler issues at the very end of the article. Wechsler recasts *Brown v. Board of Education,* seeing its basis not in constitutional principles of equality but in constitutional principles of association.[23] For him, *Brown* fails the neutrality test because it prefers the associational interests of blacks who favor integration over the associational interests of whites who prefer segregation. If association is the value at stake, then *Brown* is not neutral. But why not say *Brown* expresses a constitutional principle that race cannot be a ground for state policy when the effect would be to perpetuate a legacy of state-imposed injury and prejudice? At the climax of his essay, Wechsler trips over the word *neutral*.

Freedom of association looks like a neutral principle; it is neutral regarding the preferences of blacks and whites. The alternative principle is not neutral with respect to these competing preferences. It rejects the preferences of the white segregationist, privileging a black's choice to integrate over a white's choice to segregate, in just the way that Wechsler criticizes. But this kind of nonneutrality is true of all constitutional value choices. The protection of speech under the First Amendment, for example, is a value choice adverse to those who prefer censorship. Wechsler has confused his claim about the neutral application of principles with a claim about principles that are substantively neutral. If he is looking for a neutral principle that will decide between the right to associate and the right not to associate, he won't find any. That, however, is not the inquiry to which he committed himself.

Reason alone—in the sense of neutrality, which Wechsler in fact defends—will not resolve the problem of constitutional value choice. Yet the more powerful, implicit claim in his article is that reason can do just this: if the courts are faithful to reason, law and justice will follow. This claim is not defended.[24] The argument must be joined just there, however, if reason is to resolve the countermajoritarian difficulty by establishing values independently of the preferences of a particular judge. At best, Wechsler managed to shift the locus of the countermajoritarian difficulty from the institutional level—why the Court?—to the level of judicial decision making. He asked, What is the appropriate source of the principles the Court is to apply neutrally? The shift in locus is evident in the work of Alexander Bickel, who responded to both Hand and Wechsler in *The Least Dangerous Branch*.

Alexander Bickel: The Politics of Judicial Representation

The dispute between Hand and Wechsler can be summarized as follows. Hand argued that all values are subjective and that democratic government can, therefore, be based upon nothing other than the aggregation of personal preferences. Stripped of an objective source of value, the Court is undermined by the countermajoritarian difficulty. Wechsler promises a way out, arguing that reason can resolve conflicts in a neutral manner. His answer was incomplete, however, because the neutrality of law presupposes a prior value choice. To save Wechsler and respond to Hand required a way of grounding judicial value choices in popular sentiment. Bickel's ambition in *The Least Dangerous Branch* was to provide that ground. Instead of seeking to take the Court out of politics, he hoped to solve the countermajoritarian difficulty by frankly recognizing the majoritarian basis of the Court's work.

Bickel's argument and the constitutionalism of the founders are strikingly similar. Like the founders, Bickel believes that the legitimacy of the U.S. constitutional order rests on popular consent: "[O]n the supreme occasion, when the system is forced to find ultimate self-consistency, the principle of self-rule must prevail."[25] Nevertheless, he understands that the achievement of popular consent is not a guarantee of reasonableness or good government. Just as the founders distinguished between government based on consent and good government—and sought a coincidence of the two—so Bickel distinguishes between "the morality of government by consent and . . . moral self-government." Government in Bickel's view must be "principled as well as responsible." Principled government rests on reason; responsible government is responsive to the will of the people.[26]

The moral and political values of a social order must come from outside the principle of consent, which is given institutional expression in majoritarianism. These values depend upon substance, not on process. The need, therefore, is to identify a political institution that can bring substantive values into the democratic political order without undermining the principle of democratic legitimacy. Madison spoke of this in *The Federalist No. 10* when he wrote of the need for a "republican remedy for the diseases most incident to republican government."

Principles without consent cannot legitimately govern; but consent without principles cannot govern well. For the founders, the institutional structure of establishing a constitution—drafting by a convention of experts, followed by popular ratification—accomplished this synthesis of reason and will. Through ratification, government by, and according to, political science was given popular consent.[27] Bickel hopes to solve the modern version of the countermajoritarian difficulty by identifying and explicating an institutional arrangement analogous to ratification. Instead of focusing on a single moment in which reason and will are synthesized, he projects the synthesis into the indefinite future. For him, there is no single moment at which reason and will are fully integrated. Rather, there are many moments at which popular consent is given to particular, substantive principles. The problem of constitutionalism for Bickel is to create a process by which the society can continually move closer to moral self-government.[28]

Bickel's explanation of judicial review is an account of the Court's institutional role in sustaining and managing this process. He begins his account by distinguishing between two kinds of public values. First are the immediate, intended effects of a governmental choice—the domain of competing factional interests, of the short-term gains and losses at issue in ordinary politics. Immediate interests are best measured by elected political decision makers. The legislature, in particular, is a forum in which such interests are freely expressed and freely compete. This is interest-group pluralism pure and simple.

Opposed to this competition among short-term interests are what Bickel describes as "values we hold to have more general and permanent interest." These values are likely to be lost or misperceived in the competition among interest groups that characterizes ordinary politics. Representative institutions are not good at seeing the consequences of their decisions to these long-term interests. In Bickel's mind, the courts are the institution best suited to "be the pronouncer and guardian of such values."[29]

Bickel takes an institutional difference between elected representatives and judges and links it to a substantive difference between two kinds of values. Legislatures are responsive to shifting, short-term political sentiments—to the self-interest of constituents as understood by those constituents. Judges are insulated from the political pressures that confront legislators. They have the leisure, training, inclination, and opportunity to follow "the ways of the scholar in pursuing the ends of government." The judge's function, however, is not to articulate principles of natural law or to pursue an abstract logic. Rather, the judge must represent the "enduring values of a society."[30]

The institutional difference between legislators and judges, then, has its practical justification in the difference in what they represent. Different aspects of a community's values require different representative institutions; both kinds of norms—short-term interests and long-term principles—are valuable only because they are valued by the community. Bickel has shorn representation from its traditional roots in an electoral process. Judges are representatives no less than legislators are.

Even assuming that Bickel has correctly identified a representative function that the courts could perform well, the argument has not yet offered a justification of judicial review. If the courts make value choices when they engage in judicial review, then what privileges these policies over those made by the more overtly political institutions of government? To describe them as representative of long-term rather than short-term values or as principled instead of expedient is hardly sufficient.

Bickel offers no good answer to the question of why a community cannot prefer short-term expediency to long-term values. He cannot do so as long as he believes that the relative merits of conflicting values is an issue for the people themselves to determine. Unless the courts are representing values supported by popular consent, judicial review cannot be reconciled with a democratic system—no matter how principled its conclusions may be. It is not principle that legitimates the Court's constitutional role but consent.

Principles can displace interests—allowing the Court to displace the legislators—only when those principles receive, or will shortly receive, the consent of the governed. The Supreme Court, Bickel says, "labors under the obligation to succeed." Its political responsibility is to gain general, public consent for the principles that it articulates. When it fails, it has no right to impose those principles, regardless of the abstract merits of the position.[31]

The difference between the Court and the more traditional political organs is that for the Court, the moment at which popular consent is expressed often comes after, not before, institutional action. The Court can thus be the "teacher" in a national seminar about the enduring values of the society.[32] The values that are articulated after such a communal seminar should be more general and enduring than those expressed by political organs before that seminar. Discourse, after all, is a means of clarifying values, resolving contradictions, pondering their implications, and perhaps ordering values in terms of some more fundamental commitments.

Nothing, then, privileges principle and legitimates the Court except the consent of the citizenry. That the Court has, since *Marbury v. Madison,* sustained this function of judicial review is a consequence of the unique character of American politics. Bickel remarks early in the book that "the stability of the American republic is due in large part . . . to the remarkable Lockeian consensus of a society that has never known a feudal regime; to a 'moral unity' that was seriously broken only once, over the extension of slavery. This unity makes possible a society that accepts its principles from on high, without fighting about them. But the Lockeian consensus is also a limitation on the sort of principles that will be accepted."[33] The function of the Court is to hold on to these traditional, shared values and to reformulate them in ways adequate to contemporary experience.

The Court, therefore, takes its principles from its understanding of American history—not from reason alone but from the substance of the U.S. political experience. Through its understanding of history, the Court comes to understand the substantive moral principles that characterize this particular society. Because such principles exist, the Court can expect a fair degree of success when it seeks consent to the application of those principles to contemporary problems. If it fails to obtain consent, the fact that those principles were supported in the past confers no legitimacy on them in the present.

The resolution of the countermajoritarian difficulty hinges on the possibility of obtaining popular consent to principled governance. Of course, according to Bickel, the Court is not a passive bystander. The Court should lead the people to an understanding of the values they already hold and should continue to hold. The Court does not rule through the dead hand of the past but helps to construct the future through education about the moral values of the past.

Bickel, accordingly, resolves the problems exposed by Hand and Wechsler by identifying a democratically legitimated source for the value choices that are to fill in the content of the neutral principles. He resolves the countermajoritarian difficulty at too high a cost for Wechsler's legal-process school, however, when he converts the Court into a political institution that cannot claim a privileged place for law.[34] Whether Bickel offers an adequate response to Hand's skeptical view of the objectivity of the judge's value choices depends upon the accuracy of his political perceptions. If the Court is not acting on principles legitimated by popular consent, Hand's problem with the Platonic guardians remains. Bickel's political perceptions, in retrospect, seem wildly off.

Bickel's resolution of the countermajoritarian difficulty hinges on the capacity of the Court to generate popular support for its substantive positions. The Court is to lead popular opinion to higher levels of principled governance. In general, however, the Court has not been good at managing or leading the political debate. Controversial decisions frequently remain controversial, even after a generation. This is surely true of many modern controversies, including those over abortion, affirmative action, religion in the public schools, busing, capital punishment, and the exclusion of illegally obtained evidence. Bickel's justices can claim legitimacy only when they can claim popular support—or at least a trend in their direction. But in each of these areas of controversy, they are met by counterclaims from the more directly popular institutions of government. Instead of movement toward common, enduring principles, there is institutional conflict over the content of those principles. The Court is on weak ground if all it can cite for support is popular consent to the substantive values that it claims to represent.

Nor is Bickel's thesis more compelling as an appraisal of the longer history of constitutional adjudication. He describes a legislature that focuses on short-term interests, overlooking the consequences of its actions to long-term values. He fails, however, to capture the political debate on the major issues in constitutional history. The defining issues of that history—for example, federalism, slavery, laissez-faire doctrine, racial equality, a right to privacy—have not been missed or misapprehended by the political branches. The debate within the political institutions has not focused on short-term interests but on the conflict over long-term values. The Missouri Compromise, for example, hardly arose from a failure to grasp the long-term consequences of slavery to the national commitment to equality. Antiabortion legislation does not result from a failure to grasp the enduring value of personal privacy. The Court may weigh in on these debates, but it does not alter the level of the debate. No sober second look has ever been able to see a way past these debates. If the Court does not change the quality of political debate and contribute to a consensus at a higher level of principle, the countermajoritarian difficulty remains.

Bickel's analysis failed not only to match the historical character of the constitutional debate but also to capture the fundamental self-perception of the modern Court. Where Bickel would have the Court gain legitimacy through its claim to represent a majority, the modern Court seemed more frequently to identify with those groups and individuals who consistently failed to vindicate their interests through the majoritarian political process. This judicial identification with the dissident minority was more accurately captured in the most successful modern competitor to Bickel's theory: the process-based theories of judicial review, expressed in shorthand in footnote 4 of *United States v. Carolene Products* and given the most complete theoretical expression in the work of John Ely.[35]

John Ely and Process-Based Theories

The countermajoritarian difficulty has been at the center of each work of modern constitutional theory discussed so far. Each dealt with the problems for constitutionalism that arise from the belief that because all values are founded on individual preferences, the aggregation of those preferences through electoral politics is the only legitimate method of determining which values will inform the law. If one accepts this view of values, then the only solution to the difficulty is either to claim that judicial reasoning is value free or to find majoritarian support for judicial review. These alternatives are equally evident in Ely's process-based theory of judicial review.

Ely's basic strategy follows Bickel's: to argue that judicial review remedies a flaw in the process of democratic decision making within the institutional structure of U.S. politics. For Bickel, the flaw was moral short-sightedness. For Ely, it is the self-interest of elected officials and the groups to which those officials are particularly responsive. In this, too, he follows Bickel: he sees political problems as rooted in the social psychology of democratic, representative politics. He overcomes the countermajoritarian problem by giving the Court the role of perfecting the democratic processes of the elected branches of government.

Ely finds the most lucid judicial expression of his theory in the famous *Carolene Products* footnote. The Court, after reserving a special role for itself "when legislation appears on its face to be within a specific prohibition of the Constitution," sets forth two other situations in which a "presumption of constitutionality" might not operate:

> It is unnecessary to consider now whether legislation which restricts those political processes which can ordinarily be expected to bring about repeal of undesirable legislation, is to be subjected to more exacting judicial scrutiny under the general prohibitions of the Fourteenth Amendment than are most other types of legislation. . . .
>
> Nor need we enquire . . . whether prejudice against discrete and insular minorities may be a special condition, which tends seriously to curtail the operation of those political processes ordinarily to be relied upon to protect minorities. . . . [36]

In both instances, the justification for a special judicial role is found in a failure of the ordinary political processes.

The footnote rests on the idea that the outcomes of a democratic political process should be respected only when that process meets certain conditions. Unfortunately, the institutions within which that process occurs cannot be trusted to keep the process pure. Ely's insight is as simple as "power corrupts." The interests of those in power—as well as their supporters—are in inevitable conflict with the larger community. The self-interest of those with power invariably leads to attempts to manipulate the political process to assure continuation of the status quo. That same self-interest affects substantive decisions about the distribution of public benefits and burdens.

For the democratic process to work—for it to produce outcomes deserving of respect—the social psychology of power must be prevented from infecting the process of democratic representation. The political process of representation must be policed by an institution that is not itself a participant in the democratic process but is nevertheless responsible for the success of that process. The institution with that responsibility is the Court, the legitimacy of which is derived from the process it perfects.

The neutrality of the Court, on this view, depends upon a distinction between process and substance. The ordinary political institutions are free to make any substantive decisions they choose—as long as those decisions do not interfere with the integrity of the process of choice. Values remain a product of individual will. The constitutional system, in its ordinary operation, is a system for aggregating individual preferences. Only when the system does not work properly is the Court justified in acting. "In a representative democracy value determinations are to be made by our elected representatives. . . . Malfunction occurs when the *process* is undeserving of trust."[37] Even then, the Court's role is limited to remedying the process; it may not substitute its value judgments for those of elected institutions. The countermajoritarian difficulty is again solved within the terms of majoritarian politics.

Process-based theories require an abstract model of ordinary politics against which to measure the constitutionality of the actual operations of government. That model is generally one of pluralist, interest-group politics under which government decisions are the product of bargaining among diverse factions. Each faction aims to maximize its self-interest by entering into ever-changing strategic alliances with other groups. A bad bargain is revealed as such in the course of the political life of the community. It is then corrected through new factional alignments. Problems arise only when this ordinary process of self-correction is blocked—either by the erection of procedural obstacles to participation or by a refusal to bargain with disfavored groups.

Although Ely often accepts this model, he also appeals to a somewhat more complex model of the political process when he links the two different flaws in the process—blockage and prejudice—to a single model of democratic politics. Ely seems to accept the Madisonian idea that pluralistic diversity is a strategy for preventing faction and not just for aggregating factions.[38] Competition among interest groups should lead to a better understanding of their common interests and of a public good that transcends any particular faction. Exclusion of a faction from the process has larger consequences than the denial to its members of an opportunity to engage in pork-barrel politics. Exclusion leads to a misapprehension of the public good and thus to an injury to society generally.

Even this more complex understanding of democratic self-government cannot save Ely's theory from the same problems that disturbed earlier attempts to resolve the countermajoritarian difficulty. Just as Bickel's theory was undermined by a failure to justify the standard by which he identified the flaw in electoral politics, so is Ely's. Indeed, Ely's problem is even greater because, unlike Bickel, he requires a content-neutral standard by which to measure process flaws. The neutrality promised by process-based theories has been no more successful than the neutrality promised earlier in the theory of principled adjudication; the abstract idea of neutral process is no more capable of resolving conflict than was the abstract idea of a neutral principle.[39] How does a court identify a procedural defect that illegitimately blocks the self-correcting nature of the political process, given that any actual system requires the creation of institutional structures that will inevitably make some possibilities more difficult to obtain than others? Lines must be drawn, for example, to apportion a voting district or to determine a court's jurisdiction. How does a court decide that an issue is appropriate for resolution through the political process, as opposed to adjudication? Every governmental choice will burden some groups and benefit others. Yet not every group that loses within the ordinary political process—even if it consistently loses—is entitled to a judicial remedy. What distinguishes some losers from others, if not a substantive judgment about the appropriateness of the categories? Answers to such questions require a way to measure the ordinary process, which may be unexamined but is hardly neutral.

Even though *Carolene Products* seems to promise a legitimate foundation for judicial review at the fringes of a democratic political process, process-based theories are hard to restrict to the fringes. Instead of securing ordinary politics from the critical judicial eye, process-based theories expose the questionable democratic legitimacy of much that purports to be ordinary. The structural flaws identified as blockage and prejudice are inseparable from the working of actual political institutions. Government rests upon a legacy of laws passed and actions taken by legislative and executive bodies that were themselves the products of uncontroversially illegitimate processes. To take *Carolene Products* seriously would require the rejection, for example, of the entire legislative legacy of a malapportioned legislature.[40] The defects in process extend all the way back to the ratification of the Constitution itself. To free government of these deficiencies would require starting over with a clean slate. Short of that, it is impossible to deny that illegitimate institutions have shaped current political life and the range of possibilities within it.

Ely's process-based theory seems to do either too little or too much. Either it can find no neutral measure of the existing political order or it threatens to undermine the whole political order. The widespread appeal of process-based theories, despite their obvious problems, speaks to the hold of the countermajoritarian difficulty on modern constitutional thought.[41] Process-based theories seemed to offer a means of legitimating the renewed activism of the Court within the terms of the countermajoritarian difficulty. Ely, after all, proposed his recovery of the *Carolene Products* approach as an explanation of the "deep structure" of the constitutional decisions of the Warren Court.[42] For example, increased protection of speech, press, and candidates and especially the concern with voting and apportionment issues are all justified on the grounds that judicial intervention is necessary to remove procedural obstacles to the operations of a pluralist democracy. At the same time, the tremendous growth in modern equal protection doctrine falls neatly within the concern with the effects of prejudice on the workings of democratic political institutions.[43]

Yet much of the modern Court's work remained outside the theory—in particular, the development of a right of privacy and the focus on an adjudicatory model of individual participation in government decision making.[44] Whether its work falls into two categories—one justified on process grounds and one subject to the countermajoritarian objection—depends upon whether a single theory can tie the categories together. Such a theory is available and may in the end explain some of what Laurence Tribe has called the "puzzling persistence" of process-based theories. That single theory looks not to majoritarian, pluralist politics but to individual autonomy.

Individual Autonomy and the Modern Court

Brown v. Board of Education, decided in 1954, signaled the start of modern constitutional law. In this case, the Court squarely faced a challenge to the separate but equal doctrine in the public schools. The lower courts had found that the black schools and white schools at issue had "been equalized or are being equalized, with respect to buildings, curricula, qualifications and salaries of teachers, and other 'tangible' factors."[45] Measured by the standard of separate but equal facilities upheld in *Plessy v. Ferguson,* the Board of Education was engaged in a reasonable distribution of resources.[46]

Bruce Ackerman has recently argued that *Brown's* claim to modernity lies in its synthesis of two previous moments of fundamental constitutional change: the commitment to equality embodied in the Civil War amendments and the affirmation of activist government achieved in the New Deal. "Rather than looking upon the opinion as an inept effort to breathe new life into the living constitution, lawyers may find in it a compelling synthetic argument explaining why *Plessy* had become inconsistent with foundational principles of the new constitutional order established in the aftermath of the struggle between the New Deal Presidency and the Old Court."[47] Ackerman argues that the low-key rhetoric of the *Brown* opinion rests upon the Court's appreciation of the characteristic legal task of interpretation that it confronts: to synthesize the periodic constitutional efforts of the nation. Synthesis is required because, on Ackerman's view, there has been a genuine—albeit informal—constitutional amendment since *Plessy*. Ackerman argues that *Plessy* was not overturned by the slow growth of an evolving constitution but by a moment of constitutional crisis and amendment.

Ackerman fails to recognize that the discourse of *Brown* is continuous with that of the Court in the first part of the century. The Court's explicit response to the problem of school segregation maintains the discourse of social science and the rule of reason typical of the earlier period. The Court also continues to understand scientific governance within a model of growth. It writes: "In approaching this problem, we cannot turn the clock back to 1868 when the Amendment was adopted, or even to 1896 when *Plessy v. Ferguson* was written."[48] This statement does not acknowledge the singular quality of the New Deal, as Ackerman would have it; it acknowledges the evolving unwritten constitution. Unlike Ackerman, who can see no relevant change until the New Deal, the Court notes that 1896 comes later in the process of growth than 1868. Neither point offers a compelling stopping point. Nor does the New Deal.

The Court confirms its rejection of a backward-looking constitutionalism by turning to contemporary social science to give substance to the idea of equality. The Court appeals to "modern authority" for the "psychological knowledge" to support the proposition that racially segregated public schools "are inherently unequal." These modern authorities demonstrate that segregation with "the sanction of law . . . has a tendency to [retard] the educational and mental development of negro children and to deprive them of some of the benefits they would receive in a racial[ly] integrated school system."[49]

Plessy's central proposition—separate can be equal—was undermined not by a new act of a mobilized citizenry but by a contemporary scientific analysis of the social and psychological consequences of existing race relations. To follow *Plessy* in light of the contemporary understanding of the psychology of racial separation would have been like following *Lochner* when the facts of market failure had been revealed. Just as the post-*Lochner* Court came to see that certain economic problems were produced by the market as such and, therefore, were not capable of correction within market terms, the *Brown* Court saw the problem of racial inequality as produced by the system of segregation and thus not capable of correction within that system. Ackerman correctly sees in both an acknowledgment of the constitutionality of the activist state, but he ignores the role that social science had in legitimating that conclusion.

Not only is a theory of informal amendment not required to explain *Brown,* but it obstructs an understanding of the manner in which the substantive transformation of constitutional doctrine occurred. Ackerman contends that *Brown* was a response to a change that occurred twenty years earlier through a popular political movement. In fact, the meaning of the idea of equality upon which the Court began to act in *Brown,* only became clear over the next twenty years. The Court was not explicating something that had already happened. It was itself carrying the development of constitutionalism in a new direction.

Ackerman is not alone in looking in the wrong direction to understand the modern constitutional idea of equality. Theoretical discussion of the modern Court's focus on equality has tended to take the form of a process-based theory supplemented with a substantive norm of group harm. Ely's effort to purify process-based theory of all such norms was a reaction to an earlier recognition that some measure was required if process errors were to be identified. Ely's fear that the countermajoritarian difficulty would undermine each such norm drove him toward a theory of pure process. Conversely, the countermajoritarian difficulty drove earlier writers to link their substantive norms to a process theory. Owen Fiss, for example, wrote:

The injustice of the political process must be corrected. . . . [But] a pure process claim cannot determine substantive outcomes. . . . The political status of the group justifies the institutional allocations—our willingness to allow those "nine men" to substitute their judgment . . . for that of "the people." The socioeconomic position of the group supplies an additional reason . . . and also determines the content of the intervention— improvement of the status of that group.[50]

Paul Brest, while objecting to Fiss's group-disadvantaging principle, nevertheless offered a version of the antidiscrimination principle that relied for its justification on the same twofold appeal to process and effects: "The antidiscrimination principle guards against certain defects in the *process* by which race-dependent decisions are made and also against certain harmful *results* of race dependent decisions."[51] For Brest, process could no more operate independently of results—again measured by their effect on a particular group—than they could for Fiss. These theories differed only at the margins of their application, not in the structure of thought they brought to understanding the Court's constitutional effort. Each sprang from a remedial vision of the Court's role, rooted in the historical failure of particular groups, especially blacks, to succeed in ordinary politics.

The strongest challenge to this view of modern constitutional doctrine has come from Cass Sunstein, who argues that pluralist politics is not the end of constitutionalism. Pluralism, he says, is a degenerate form of politics against which constitutional law is generally directed. A government policy that rests on nothing more than the political strength of factions competing for government largess is constitutionally prohibited. Yet even Sunstein's attack on interest-group pluralism was largely a response to the consequences of this form of politics to less powerful groups. On his view, what is forbidden is "the distribution of resources or opportunities to one group rather than another solely on the ground that those favored have exercised the raw political power to obtain what they want."[52] Sunstein hoped that the democratic political process could be turned toward larger public purposes that encompass all groups. Instead of providing the measure of constitutional politics, the pluralist model now provided the limit. Whether playing a positive or a negative role, this model of group-based politics still gave substance to the theory. However, just this idea of pluralist politics was abandoned by the modern Court as it turned increasingly to an idea of the autonomous, self-forming individual.

The Constitutionalism of Individual Autonomy

Brown was rapidly followed by a series of per curiam opinions holding segregation in a wide range of nonacademic, public facilities unconstitutional.[53] Rather than develop the social science discourse on equality begun in *Brown*, the opinions say nothing or simply cite *Brown*. Not knowing how to explain itself, the Court slipped into silence. *Brown's* appeal to science appears in retrospect to be a transitional device, linking the Court to an earlier constitutionalism but of uncertain weight in the new era.

The Court's desegregation cases cumulatively made clear that the evil targeted in *Brown* was not harm to education but discrimination itself. Segregation was not evil simply because of its harmful consequences to some other value, whether educational achievement or economic well-being. *Brown* and its progeny rested upon a substantive concept of equality under which segregation was an evil in itself. The social science language of *Brown*, however, was of little help in explaining the harm that the Court perceived in segregation. The harm worked in the domain of morals, not statistics. The Court needed a new language with which to explain this moral harm. It found that language in the simultaneous development of a right to privacy. Behind the Court's elaboration of a right to privacy stood an idea of the autonomous individual who creates his or her own identity independently of any assertion of public authority. The evil of segregation for the modern Court can best be understood as a violation of this principle of individual autonomy: racial segregation entails a refusal to acknowledge its victims' right to decide their racial or ethnic identity.

Just as the constitutional theorists of the pre–Civil War period struggled with the question of what it meant to be an American, so the modern Court struggled with the question of constitutional identity: Who is the person that the Constitution protects? In the first part of the nineteenth century, that question was answered by looking to history. The modern Court looked in the opposite direction, finding the constitutionally protected self to be that which individuals make for themselves. Neither a member of a group nor a product of history, the self-made individual stood alone before the government.

The contrast with antebellum thought is striking. The early discourse and the modern discourse both focus on the relation between the state and the individual body. In the early discourse, to understand what it means to be an American requires understanding the fundamental claim that the state makes upon the body and, conversely, the affirmation that the idea of the state achieves through the individual body. The body is taken up into a myth of participation in a transtemporal, national organism.[54] The body is not a private possession but a means to create public life. Individual, family, and state are aspects of a single whole.

The body was again at the center of modern constitutional thought, but in the opposite way. The modern constitutional right to privacy began with the thesis that "a person belongs to himself and not others nor to society as a whole." This view achieved its highest symbolic expression in the Court's affirmation of a woman's right to control her own body, to decide for herself whether to have a child.[55] Given the obvious connection between the historical life of the state and generational reproduction, this is a remarkable symbol of modern thought. The Court recognizes no state interest in embodiment and historicity at all. The total domain of legitimate state interests is reduced to the well-being of private individuals: the woman and the child.[56] The state may protect the individual; it may no longer make a claim upon the individual's body.

Roe's focus on the body is substantively important, but it is also a symbol of the larger relation between self and state in modern constitutional thought. The state no longer has a constitutionally protected interest in the determination of personal identity.[57] Instead, participation in the state becomes one among many other choices that an individual might make in determining for himself or herself the meaning and character of personal identity. This idea of self-determination was first expressed in *Griswold v. Connecticut*, in which the Court states that the purpose of much of the Bill of Rights is to create a "zone of privacy" within which the state may not operate.[58] Although the Court failed to indicate the limits or content of this zone, it did suggest that the function of the zone is to shield the construction of personal identity from the influence of the state. Marriage is protected from state intrusion because it "is an association that promotes a way of life, not causes; a harmony in living, not political faiths."[59] On the Court's view, the choice of a way of life occurs within a zone of privacy, outside the purview of the state.

The idea of autonomous self-creation has no obvious limits, however: any act at all can be vested with vast personal significance by a particular person.[60] To rest a constitutionally protected zone of privacy upon this idea of autonomy threatens virtually every assertion of authority. The indeterminacy of the zone is emphasized in *Roe* itself. There, at the critical point in the opinion constitutionalizing the woman's interest in an abortion, the Court can say nothing more than "This right of privacy . . . is broad enough to encompass a woman's decision whether or not to terminate her pregnancy."[61] Because there are no landmarks by which to get one's bearings within the zone, the Court has to rely upon mere assertion.

This move in *Roe* is reminiscent of *Allgeyer*, seventy-five years earlier, when the Court deemed the due-process right to liberty to be sufficiently comprehensive to include contract.[62] Both cases recognize a privacy right, but each relies upon a different argumentative context. First, the earlier Court grounded the constitutional right in its understanding of the common law. The modern Court also appealed to the common law, but its argument was a parody of common-law constitutionalism. Instead of supporting a right to abort, the Court's discussion of common-law and statutory precedents showed, at best, a diversity of views on abortion, which had not evolved into a single position. In fact, the law, until the years just before *Roe*, seemed to be moving toward greater restraint on access to abortion.[63] The common law could not, therefore, shape the content of the modern right to privacy as it had shaped the earlier right to contract.

Second, the right to contract linked political and economic ideas of authority. The constitutional system tied a democratic political order to the economic order of a free market. The *Lochner* Court preserved a right to contract because it recognized the public dimension of private economic decisions. The successful business executive was, for that Court, appropriately a person of public authority. The right to privacy for the modern Court, in contrast, marked the separation of private life and public authority. To be self-made today means something entirely different from what it meant to the *Lochner* Court. Self-creation no longer makes contact with public life and authority.

Third and finally, the right to contract represented the practical expression of a science of social and political order. It expressed the increasing rationalization of constitutional law within a model of growth. The effort to use public authority self-consciously to shape the market would, on this view, not only lead to private injuries but also constitute a regression in the character of public order. The modern Court's privacy doctrine again represented the opposite set of beliefs. The belief in a common science of constitutionalism was gone. Decisions had to be based on individual preference precisely because a scientific ordering of social life was not possible. Furthermore, the Court made no suggestion that these individual decisions would, in the aggregate, constitute a rational public order.

The modern Court protected a domain of privacy against the intrusion of government, then, not because the private and the public are congruent but because they are so wholly separate. Justice Harry Blackmun, who wrote *Roe*, explains the right to privacy cases as follows: "We protect those rights not because they contribute, in some direct and material way to the general welfare, but because they form so central a part of an individual's life." General welfare and private life no longer run in the same direction. What is at stake, Blackmun argues, is protection of the conditions for "an individual's self-definition," the "ability independently to define one's identity that is central to any concept of liberty."[64]

Autonomous self-creation is not so lonely an activity as the language of privacy suggests. Autonomy, Justice Blackmun admits, "cannot truly be exercised in a vacuum; we all depend on the 'emotional enrichment from close ties with others.'"[65] Self and other must be protected within the zone of privacy because self-definition is as much a social as a personal process. Recognizing the public side of private autonomy, however, raises two problems for a constitutional doctrine of privacy. First, indefinite expansion of the protected zone is again possible. All relationships can shape the self or be invested by the individual with significant personal value. Modern judicial doctrine was, accordingly, marked by a trend of constant expansion: spouses, sexual partners, children, extended families, religious groups, educational institutions, and neighborhoods were all pulled into the zone of autonomous self-creation.[66]

Second, to recognize the place of the other introduces the problem of authority into the zone of privacy itself. The other always appears as both resource and threat. For example, the modern Court's actual treatment of the family often described a conflict between authority and autonomy within the family itself. This conflict is most evident in the series of cases that considered and rejected state efforts to require a minor to obtain parental consent before exercising her right to choose an abortion.[67] Because the right to an abortion was at the center of the modern Court's understanding of the constitutionally protected self, these cases graphically tested the willingness of the Court to extend the model of individual autonomy into nongovernmental domains of social authority. Not surprisingly, the modern Court protected the freedom of the individual— here a minor—against the authority of the family. The state, it held, must make a neutral decision maker available to assess the minor's claim to decide for herself, irrespective of the family's claim to authority. Even if the decision maker decides against the minor's claim to be able to decide for herself, the decision whether to go forward with the abortion must be made in the best interests of the minor—not the family.[68] The family has been assimilated to the state as a coercive authority: it confronts a constitutionally protected, self-defining individual.

The modern Court similarly held that the state must assume the role of neutral adjudicator between competing interests, rather than supporter of familial authority, with respect to decisions to institutionalize individuals.[69] The same pattern has recently begun to emerge in the Court's effort to give constitutional shape to a right to die. The family is set against the individual, and the state must protect the individual's interest in self-formation against familial coercion—even when self-formation means self-termination.[70]

When an issue was cast in terms of the coercive authority of the family over its individual members, the modern Court protected the individual. When the issue was the coercive authority of the state over the family, the Court protected the family. For example, the Court protected the right of Amish families to ignore a state's mandatory education laws. But in reaching this conclusion, the Court specifically noted that no party had placed in issue the individual child's interests in obtaining a secular education. The Court likewise protected the family's interest in defining for itself the scope of the familial unit, against the effort of a state to coerce a certain pattern of familial association.[71]

Consideration of the family illustrates the multiple levels at which the distinction between autonomy and authority can work. Autonomy is a powerful idea that challenges not just state authority but all forms of authority. Even though private associations enjoyed considerable protection in their dealings with the state, they enjoyed considerably less protection when the issue of individual autonomy arose within the association itself.[72]

To the autonomous individual the assertion of authority, in the absence of actual consent, always appears arbitrary. To a majoritarian, any claim of private autonomy appears arbitrary unless grounded on the express consent of the majority. Each perspective is comprehensive, asserting the capacity to order all relationships and social functions. The point is not that compromises cannot be reached or that comprehensive theories are not available but that modern constitutionalism did not rest on such agreements or theories. Modern constitutional theory began with the belief that the majority has the right to set the rules of order. The modern Court, in contrast, seized on the idea of autonomy. It no longer worried about protecting the majority from the autonomous judge but about protecting the individual from authority, including majoritarian authority. When the acknowledgment of authority recurs, a point already reached by the Court in some areas of legal regulation, the period of the modern Court ends. That end always appears arbitrary, for there is no logical stopping point to the dynamic of autonomy.

To protect individual autonomy, the Court separated itself from the authoritative structure of the state. Separation created a need for a new constitutional theory to legitimate the Court's anti-statist activity. Such explanations as were offered invoked the already-available models of legitimacy. The model of abstract political science appeared in the writings of those theorists who appealed to contemporary moral and political philosophy to ground the legitimacy of the modern Court.[73] The model of originalism was most evident in the writings of Justice Hugo Black. A new version of the model of an evolving common law appeared in *Roe v. Wade;* this model has been pursued at the theoretical level in the work of Harry Wellington.[74] Even the model of empirical social science was carried forward in the frequent appeals to cost-benefit analysis.[75]

None of these old models has been convincing. The deficiencies of each have too long been known in the discipline of constitutional law, and the choice of a single pattern of justification seems arbitrary. The need for a new model of constitutional legitimacy has been building since *Brown* was decided by appeal to a model that was rapidly rendered irrelevant.

Equality and Autonomy

The equal protection explosion that started with *Brown* was another aspect of the judicial pursuit of autonomy. The right-to-privacy cases stressed the exclusion of public authority from the process of self-creation; the equality cases stressed the manner in which government may operate without violating the respect due the autonomous individual. The privacy cases put forward the negative constraints on the domain of authority; the equality cases put forward a positive vision of constitutional authority in the modern state.[76] Equality as a norm for governmental behavior has come to mean that the government must treat the individual as a self-generating source of values.

The race discrimination cases are pivotal in understanding the jurisprudence of the modern Court, not because of their concern for the well-being of a historically disadvantaged group but because of their paradigmatic quality with respect to the problem of the exercise of authority through generalizations. Racial discrimination treats the individual as nothing more than a member of a group. Because race is biologically determined, and therefore inescapable and unchangeable, racial discrimination is a paradigm for the failure of government to respect individual self-determination. If personal identity is determined by race, there is no place for self-creation.

This modern idea of equality can have a quantitative aspect: equal respect for each person's interests requires that each person have an equal vote.[77] Equality more often has a qualitative dimension, requiring judicial scrutiny of the manner of government decision making. Securing government respect for individual autonomy entails, first, a limit on the use of generalizations by the government and, second, a denial of the relevance of history to understanding individual identity. These two points are related because generalizations are ordinarily based on historically grounded assumptions. The appeal to racial categories, for example, is not grounded in biology but in historical prejudice.

Modern equal protection doctrine was marked by the systematic expansion of categories—that is, generalizations—that were viewed as an inappropriate basis for state action. At various times, the Court considered race, ethnicity, alienage, illegitimacy, sex, age, political affiliation, mental illness, wealth, and religion as categories raising serious equal protection concerns.[78] The need for government to deal directly with the individual increases in direct proportion to the prohibitions on the use of such general categories. The Court's view was that government must respect "the basic concept of our system that legal burdens should bear some relationship to individual responsibility or wrongdoing."[79]

The importance of the list of categories lies not just in its length but also in its sweep. It cuts across those factors most closely tied to an individual's own self-understanding; race, sex, age, citizenship, and political and religious affiliations, as well as family membership, encompass most people's deepest sense of self. Prohibiting state action on these grounds was not meant to suggest that these categories are irrelevant to personal identity; the point was that choices among these categories—how to order them in terms of their centrality to the individual's own life—are matters for the individual alone.

These judicial decisions cannot be explained as efforts to secure access to the political process for discrete and insular minorities. Too often the groups protected were powerfully organized political actors.[80] Rather, the decisions rested on a constitutional concept of the individual that the government must respect. Thus, even when generalizations were based on accurate statistical generalizations, the failure to look to individual circumstances offended the constitutional norm of equality.[81]

The quintessential expression of this understanding of equality as respect for individual autonomy is Justice Lewis Powell's opinion in *Bakke*. Powell rejects any group-centered theory of equal protection rights—including that of *Carolene Products*—insisting instead that "the rights created by the ... Fourteenth Amendment are ... guaranteed to the individual. The rights established are personal rights."[82] Membership in a group is not relevant to the constitutional right to equal treatment, although in some circumstances it may be relevant to the state's justification for a controverted action. Accordingly, Powell rejects an affirmative action plan that fails to treat "each applicant as an individual in the admissions process" even while he recognizes that ethnic background may be a factor to which the state can give weight. Powell adheres to this position, not because it is practically feasible to distinguish a quota from a goal, but because he understands the Constitution to require equal respect for each individual. This means respect for those qualifications that an individual has achieved through personal efforts at self-creation: "unique work or service experience, leadership potential, maturity, demonstrated compassion, a history of overcoming disadvantage, ability to communicate with the poor." Powell, in short, designs an admissions program responsive to the constitutionally protected self of the modern period.[83]

Corresponding to the rejection of generalization was a rejection of history as a source of individual definition. The constitutionally protected self was not a member of any community, present or past. Association with a community was to be a matter of choice, not identity. History appeared as nothing but a burden on individual freedom.

This denial of the relevance of history to constitutional identity explains, for example, the modern Court's concern with the right to travel. The Court actually protected not a right to travel but a right to stop traveling and take up residence. The right to travel came to mean that every state and local community must remain porous to new entrants.

Each individual has the right to be treated as an equal in any community within which he or she chooses to reside: personal choice, not historical connection, is determinative.

For example, in *Shapiro v. Thompson*, the Court struck down a one-year residence requirement for welfare payments.[84] The Court was wholly unsympathetic to claims that this is a reasonable way to protect local resources from claims by those who have yet to participate in the life of the community. Taking care of one's own was now a constitutionally prohibited form of discrimination—unless *one's own* is defined wholly in terms of immediate residence. If all that matters is the present choice to reside, the new entrant is in exactly the same situation as long-term residents. Welfare was viewed by the Court as a response to individual need and not as an expression of sympathy within an ongoing community.

That *Shapiro* was not just about welfare rights but about the place of history in the constitutionally recognized self was made clear in *Zobel v. Williams*. Here, the Court struck down the attempt by the state of Alaska to distribute some of the windfall benefits from oil production through a negative income tax calibrated on the basis of years of residence. Again, this might have seemed a reasonable way of celebrating the historical struggle of a community to establish itself in a difficult environment. The Court rejected this: the legitimate concern of the state is not to preserve the past, to recognize what current members have accomplished, or to project a vibrant tradition into the future. Justice William Brennan made explicit the irrelevance of history in the life of the state: "[T]he business of the state is not with the past, but with the present: to remedy continuing injustices, to fill current needs, to build on the present in order to better the future."[85]

A state that must be completely porous to new entrants, that can treat no member of the national community as a stranger within the smaller community, has been deprived of a sense of itself as a historical actor. Its history is the history of the nation, no more. If all citizens share a single national history, then history has no relevance to any constitutionally relevant distinction. Within the national community, each person is whoever he or she chooses to be. History, in the end, is inconsistent with equality.

The modern Court's hostility to history was apparent not only with respect to defining the community but also with respect to organizing political power within the community. Most obviously, the Court rejected durational residency requirements for voting.[86] No community could claim a need to educate the new entrant in its values. No resident, no matter how new, could be treated as a stranger. More significant, the

Court rejected the idea that political power could be assessed in terms of historically defined interests. Its reapportionment jurisprudence consistently rejected the idea that differences in individual political power can be justified by appealing to history: "[N]either history alone, nor economic or other sorts of group interests, are permissible factors in attempting to justify disparities from population-based representation."[87] If all citizens are members of a single community, there is no reason to deviate from strict numerical equality among voting districts.

Once again the Court was driven by an extreme vision of individual autonomy. It insisted that the rights at stake are "individual and personal in nature," even though it was always clear that the power of a vote is as much dependent upon the historical realities of the community within which it is exercised as upon the size of that community.[88] The Court's repeated insistence that "people, not land or trees or pastures, vote" represented a rejection of historically defined communal interests as the fundamental elements of political structure.[89] Democracy itself was recast as an exercise in individual autonomy. The individual—not the Madisonian faction, the modern interest group—was the constitutionally cognizable unit, regardless of how poorly that unit might correspond to political reality.

Autonomy and Procedure

To say that the state must respect the individual would mean little if the Court were not willing to specify the procedures that such respect requires. In *Goldberg v. Kelly*, the Court set down this path, reconsidering procedural due process from the perspective of individual autonomy. The respect the state owes individuals—even those dependent on state largess—formed the substantive background of the case: "From its founding the Nation's basic commitment has been to foster the dignity and well-being of all persons within its borders." In the Court's view, the purpose of welfare is to enable all members of the community to create their own lives, to "bring within the reach of the poor the same opportunities to participate meaningfully in the life of the community" as are available to others.[90] This end is undermined by procedures that fail to afford respect to the individual. Accordingly, welfare terminations require procedures designed to assure that each individual's case is considered on its unique merits.

For the *Goldberg* Court, there could be no excuses that the procedures generally work, even though an occasional individual might be improperly denied benefits. Due process "require[s] that a recipient have timely and adequate notice detailing the reasons for a proposed termination, and an effective opportunity to defend by confronting any adverse witnesses and by presenting his own arguments and evidence orally."[91] The state could not disregard the circumstances of the individual claimant, even if, in the vast majority of cases, the procedures were not necessary to reach a correct outcome. It could not do so even if it could show that its method of operation was an efficient—that is, cost-effective—and therefore reasonable way to manage public resources.

The Court rejected Justice Black's argument that "[w]hile this Court will perhaps have insured that no needy person will be taken off the rolls without a full 'due process' proceeding, it will also have insured that many will never get on the rolls."[92] This claim was rejected not because it was false with respect to the distributional effects of the decision but because it was not relevant to the issue of due process. The process due runs to the individual—it is his or her right to be heard—not to the group of the needy.

The Court subsequently extended the same sort of procedural protections at issue in *Goldberg* to a large number of situations in which liberty and property interests were at stake, including adverse state actions against drivers, government employees, parolees, students, and debtors.[93] It determined that the procedures used before the state eliminates a protected interest must afford full respect to the individual's unique circumstances. The procedures must take those circumstances into account, which means that the individual must have a full opportunity to present his or her case. This rule converts the decision maker from an efficient administrator of state resources to a neutral adjudicator of the competing interests of state and individual. Respect for the individual meant placing public authority and individual autonomy on an equal level and allowing each equal resources to make their case.

The connection between the modern Court's concern with the individual in equal protection doctrine and its concern with procedural due process was made clear in the development of irrebuttable presumption doctrine. Under this doctrine, the state is not allowed to operate on the basis of generalizations that are not "universally true in fact."[94] Someone who is uniquely situated must be given an opportunity to show that the generalization is not applicable in his or her case. In *Vlandis v. Kline,* which involved tuition preferences for state residents, the Court wrote: "[S]ince Connecticut purports to be concerned with residency . . . it is forbidden by the Due Process Clause to deny an individual the resident rates on the basis of a permanent and irrebuttable presumption of nonresidence, when the presumption is not necessarily or universally true in fact . . . [and] the State [must] allow such an individual the opportunity to present evidence showing that he is a bona fide resident entitled to the in-state rates."[95] The Court used similar reasoning to strike down a mandatory pregnancy-leave policy for schoolteachers, saying that the state's generalization—pregnant women are not physically able to teach—must be open to challenge in individual cases. As in *Goldberg*, the state was not allowed to make mistakes.[96]

These cases demonstrate the procedural side of the substantive theme of modern constitutionalism. The state must respect each individual as a self-determining agent; it may not treat anyone as merely a member of a group. This theme is even clearer in the modern Court's criminal procedure jurisprudence.

In *Gideon v. Wainwright* and *Miranda v. Arizona*, for example, the Court manifested a belief in an unbridgeable gap between the individual criminal defendant and organized society.[97] Again, due process required evenhanded treatment of these polar interests. In *Gideon*, the Court notes that "[l]awyers to prosecute are everywhere deemed essential to protect the public's interest in an orderly society."[98] The interest in an orderly society, however, is no longer seen as a value sufficiently comprehensive to include the interests of the individual criminal defendant. That the interests of the state are protected by lawyers creates an asymmetry in the clash between the individual and authority that must be corrected. Accordingly, the Court overrules *Betts v. Brady*, which rejected a right to appointed counsel. *Betts* relied heavily on a presumed unity of interests between the defendant and the larger society, given visible expression in the judge's control of the case: "Such [nonjury] trials . . . are much more informal than jury trials and it is obvious that the judge can much better control the course of the trial and is in a . . . position to see impartial justice done."[99] In *Gideon*, the authority of the state is no longer aligned with a comprehensive scheme of justice. Instead, it is aligned against the individual, who must be protected.

This concept of individual autonomy is even more apparent in *Miranda*, where the Court appeals to a norm of "human dignity," which is offended by thinking of the defendant as a member of the community subject to its instruments of coercive authority: "It is obvious that interrogation [in custody] . . . is created for no purpose other than to subjugate the individual to the will of his examiner. This atmosphere carries its own badge of intimidation. To be sure, this is not physical intimidation, but it is equally destructive of human dignity." What is at stake in *Miranda* is "the respect a government—state or federal—must accord to the dignity and integrity of its citizens."[100]

The dichotomy of a state interest in criminal law enforcement, on the one side, and individual dignity, on the other, is rejected by the dissenters. Both Justices John Harlan and Byron White understand the interest in law enforcement as socially comprehensive and thus supportive of—rather than opposed to—the individual's interests. Justice Harlan writes: "Society has always paid a stiff price for law and order, and peaceful interrogation is not one of the dark moments of the law." Individual defendants can be asked to pay a price for the general social interest, in which they, too, have a stake. Justice White writes that "the most basic function of any government is to provide for the security of the individual. . . . Without the reasonably effective performance of the task of preventing private violence and retaliation, it is idle to talk about human dignity and civilized values."[101] Individual dignity is not opposed to, but is dependent upon, the coercive authority of the state. Justice White correctly identifies the underlying motive of the majority as a dislike for all confessions. That dislike springs from a belief that individuals who confess have done the work of the government, placing themselves on the wrong side of the divide between authority and autonomy.

Just as the irrebuttable presumption doctrine joined the modern Court's procedural and substantive jurisprudence on the civil side, so the death-penalty cases joined procedure and substance on the criminal side. In these cases the Court struggled with the question of how, in the administration of the death penalty, the state could be made to respect the unique, self-determining individual. Substantively, this required the Court to chart a position for the states between the arbitrary and the mandatory exercise of authority.[102] Unbridled discretion, no less than the complete absence of discretion, denies respect to the individual. State policy had to be finely tuned to the circumstances of each case. Application of the death penalty had to accord "significance to relevant facets of the character and record of the individual offender or the circumstances of the particular offense."[103]

Respect, from the point of view of the individual, means that the defendant is allowed a full opportunity to demonstrate "who he is" to a neutral adjudicator. Procedurally, this means that a defendant can present any kind of mitigating evidence to a sentencer and that a defendant must be allowed to respond to all of the state-generated information considered by the sentencer.[104] If the development of the death-penalty jurisprudence of the modern Court affords a rich example of how it managed the confrontation between authority and autonomy, the Court's more recent retreat from managing the confrontation symbolizes the passing of the modern age of constitutionalism.[105]

Conclusion: Constitutionalism without History

Forty years ago, at the beginning of the modern period, the countermajoritarian difficulty dominated constitutional theory. By the 1970s, constitutional discourse was no longer about the will of the majority but about the will of the individual. Not the reasonable exercise of democratically grounded authority but the respect authority must accord individual self-determination dominated inquiry. The Constitution was now understood to protect the conditions of individual self-determination against the authority of the state. Nevertheless, the two sides of this apparent contrast between majoritarian politics and individual autonomy had a common thread, one that ran through the process-based approach that was so attractive to modern constitutional theorists.

Carolene Products provides such a strict measure of the legitimacy of political order that it effectively projects popular sovereignty into the future. The conditions necessary for the expression of popular sovereignty have yet to occur. Nevertheless, because process-based theories rely upon a remedial idea of the judicial role, they require a determination of what that future politics should look like. It is to be a pluralist politics in which every group is the direct result of the aggregation of individual choices to invest meaning and energy in one interest rather than another. The political status of a group must be based upon individual choices; individual choices may not be a function of group definition. The aim of constitutional law under such a system would be to maintain the conditions of individual freedom within a pluralist politics. Those conditions can be specified in two dimensions that correspond roughly to the two prongs of *Carolene Products:* prejudice and process.

First, all groups and potential groups must be leveled. Politics will produce legitimate results only when the self who makes choices is free to form himself or herself independently of any historically given identifications. The meaning given to history is to be determined by the individual, not the state. In *Carolene Products,* the illegitimate burden of history is specifically captured in the expression "discrete and insular minorities." These are not simply minority groups that have been unsuccessful in the political process; some groups may never gather much support in a society. Rather, the lack of success must be attributable to the prejudice directed against the group. Prejudice is a product of history: disagreement becomes prejudice only through a history of antagonism that becomes settled expectation. By defining the individual in terms of group history, prejudice operates as a barrier to individual self-definition. Prejudice prevents an individual from exiting the disfavored group.

One remedial role of the Court, accordingly, is to remove the burden of history as an external restraint on private freedom of choice. From this perspective, history includes family, race, religion, and community. Politics must become a domain in which people make themselves rather than manifest what they already are. A society without history would be a society of free individuals: each person would be free to create the self on the basis of present choices. Only under those conditions can there be a coincidence of individual self-definition and political order, of subjective freedom and public authority. The future to which *Carolene Products* looks for the manifestation of popular sovereignty is not a future connected to the past as the evolving life of the community. Unleashed from history, public authority—the state—no longer offers a target for revolution. This image of the state is the economist's model of a pure, competitive market without externalities, projected into the future as a dream of political order.

History is a source, but not the only source, of an illegitimate politics of groups. Failure to respect individual self-definition can be just as much a function of the administration of government as a function of historical prejudice. In the former case, however, the neglect of the individual is likely to be a consequence of efficiency, rather than prejudice: it is easier for government to work with generalities than with individuals. This is true even when government policy has been set by a perfected political process. To secure politics as a domain of individual self-expression requires protection from a government instrumentalism in which some individuals are treated only as placeholders for a group interest.

Whenever government acts on the basis of a general category, it allows the group to define the individual, rather than the individual the group. The failure to respect individual choice and self-definition can, therefore, be rooted in the prejudice of history or the convenience of the many. In both cases, the denial of individual self-definition, the separation of political authority from subjective freedom, is the same.

The true neutrality of *Carolene Products*—in fact, the only possible neutrality—rests upon an idea of individual self-definition. A court that accepts this idea of neutrality will be compelled to undertake a reconstruction of politics, as well as a severing of politics from history. A legitimate politics will be one in which each individual is given an opportunity to express his or her own conception of the self, to differentiate that self from others, and to demand that government respond to that autonomously generated self. To the extent that generalizations are permitted, each individual will be assured an opportunity to make a case for exceptionality. Each will have an opportunity to prove that the general rule does not apply in a specific case.

Carolene Products, accordingly, works at two different levels. Its apparent theory is one of interest-group pluralism; its deep theory is one of individual self-definition. The apparent theory requires the Court to remedy defects in the current political process by removing barriers to participation and protecting the interests of discrete and insular minorities. To accomplish this, however, the Court must give up the claim of neutrality and act within a set of values embodied in contemporary understandings of protected groups and appropriate processes. The deep theory, in contrast, promises a kind of neutrality, but at the cost of setting the Court in virtually irreconcilable opposition to existing authority. Government is the product of a determinate history. All governmental choices—both procedural and substantive—result in the privileging of some groups and the injuring of others. The deep theory has no way to justify these distinctions. All act as external constraints on autonomous choice. The apparent theory, therefore, is workable but not neutral; the deep theory is neutral but not workable. This is the paradox of *Carolene Products.* The paradox represents the two sides of a classic debate: Should the expression of will be located in majoritarian decision making or in individual autonomy?

Modern constitutionalism developed between the two sides of this dilemma. The dilemma is irresolvable within the terms of modern theory, because that theory starts from the premise that all values are subjective, determined solely by individual will. As long as constitutional problems centered on regulation of the economic market, majoritarianism seemed the obvious response to problems of social conflict. This answer drew support not just from utilitarian instincts but also from a belief that government intervention in the economy would ultimately benefit all through the correction of market failure.

Majoritarian politics no longer seemed an adequate response when constitutional problems came to focus on issues of equality and privacy. Now the perception shifted: If all values are subjective, with what right does anyone or any institution determine another's values? The only legitimate ground for a claim of authority is consent. But in these areas a theory of consent is most difficult to construct.

Autonomy and majoritarianism are equal responses to the location of value in the individual will. Both are reactions to the dominant place of science and reason in the prior model of constitutionalism. Both understand the constitutionally protected individual from the perspective of individual will. Each approach follows from the same first principle, and each seems equally obvious and uncontroversial to its defenders. Majoritarianism appeals to those who believe that because value is only a matter of individual preference, everybody's preferences should be counted equally in a system of aggregation. Autonomy appeals to those who believe that because values are a matter of individual choice, individuals must exercise responsibility for their choices. Preference for one or the other approach is a matter of emphasis—whether one perceives a need for social decision or a need for individual responsibility.

Selecting either theory threatens the historical continuity of the constitutional enterprise. The individual will that is the heart of both theories—either alone or in aggregate—exists only in the present. Both the majority and the autonomous individual are self-forming: to both the historical givenness of the Constitution appears as an illegitimate constraint. For one theory, it constrains majority choice through burdensome procedures and supermajority requirements. For the other, it constrains individual autonomy through recognition of authoritative political structures.

The task of contemporary constitutional theory is to build a new model of legitimacy that can link the autonomous individual to the majority. Theory confronts the need to construct a model of politics that can satisfy the demands of individual autonomy yet support the historical state as an institution wielding coercive authority. Supplying that need is the concept of community, which dominates constitutional discourse today.

CHAPTER SIX

Community in
Contemporary
Constitutional Theory

$\mathbf{M}$odern constitutional theory seemed to pose a choice between a majoritarianism that could not be bound by concerns with individual autonomy, on the one hand, and an individualism that could not be bound by a majority, on the other. This opposition defines the problem at which contemporary constitutional theory is directed: to find a synthesis that can overcome the divide between the one and the many, the individual and the majority. Contemporary theorists have turned in response to a concept of community, which functions not as a geographical place but as a conceptual model of order. In the community that has captured the imagination of contemporary constitutional theorists, the only relevant activity is discourse. This community talks itself into a historical identity.

Instead of seeing a problematic relation of part (citizen) to whole (state), in which either the part or the whole threatens to subsume the other, the new communitarian understands the relation of the individual to the political order as that of microcosm to macrocosm. Personal identity is created and maintained in the same process by which communal identity is created and maintained. The historically specific discourse, which is at the center of communitarian theory, simultaneously creates the individual and the community. Neither has priority—temporally, conceptually, or normatively. Individual and community are two aspects of a single, ongoing, historically situated discourse.

The emphasis on community reflects, to some degree, larger trends in political and moral theory,[1] but it can also be understood from within the discipline of constitutional theory as a final step in the dialectical development of constitutional discourse. Finality, however, does not mean either an end to the history of constitutionalism or a resolution of all the problems of creating a legitimate system of constitutional self-governance. The step is final because it represents the point at which theory works itself pure. To do so requires the theory of law to split decisively from law as a system of authority. Theory is pure here because the model of community collapses the reflection on constitutional authority into the authority of constitutional reflection: the discursive community that is the model of constitutional authority is a reflection of the theorist's own activity.

There are two main schools of contemporary constitutional theory: the new republicans and the interpretivists. Both understand community as discursively constituted. The community arises out of a historically specific discourse that focuses on the practices and values that its members find themselves sharing with each other. Although both schools use this model of community to reconceptualize the relation of the individual to the state, each asks and responds to different questions. The new republicans ask how the existing institutions of government should operate. They respond with a theory of community that supports a normative critique of institutional practice. The interpretivists ask how law is possible. They respond with a theory of meaning that rests upon the discursive community.

Each school suggests a unique problem for constitutional theory. The problem for the new republicans is the institutional location of the community of discourse. Each of the new republicans I discuss places that community in a different institution of governance. The problem for the interpretivists is to differentiate among many such communities of discourse. Each of the interpretivists I discuss reaches a different resolution, privileging or refusing to privilege one discursive community over others.

Ultimately, all the new communitarians fail for the same reason: the authoritativeness of law, including constitutional law, is inconsistent with the egalitarianism of the community of discourse. My account of each theorist, accordingly, involves a juxtaposition of authority and community. In each instance, I argue that we are left with either an unsupported claim of authority or an anarchy of diverse discursive communities.

The Shifting Place of the New Republican Community

Bruce Ackerman: The Recovery of a National Community
Bruce Ackerman's work represents a self-conscious effort to break with modern constitutional theory. Accordingly, he critiques the two

dominant ideas of modern academic theory: the countermajoritarian difficulty and the political burdens borne by discrete and insular minorities that afford the background for process-based theories.[2] Modern theorists' conceptualization of these problems, according to Ackerman, springs from the attempt to ground political legitimacy, including the Court's, in consent. He argues that the idea of consent that informs modern theory is too thin to account for the complexity of American politics. Constitutional theory must instead distinguish constitutional politics and ordinary politics. The distinction lies in the twofold character of political discourse. With this conclusion, Ackerman turns decisively away from the focus on individual will found in modern theory and toward the conceptual model of a community of discourse.

Ackerman accuses modern constitutional theorists of accepting what he calls the "levelling" premise: the assumption that no normative distinctions can be drawn among the various ways in which the people of a community make political decisions. "[B]y definition, the leveller treats all acts of political participation as if they were accompanied by the same degree of civic seriousness."[3] If no qualitative distinctions can be made, the only relevant distinction is between past and present. In a democracy, normative priority must be given to a present majority. The alternative would effectively empower a present minority to control a present majority. Accordingly, the leveler cannot explain the backward-looking character of constitutional law.

Pursued to its logical conclusion, leveling will produce a theory of constitutional law in which the function of the Supreme Court is to protect and perfect the structures of ordinary politics. Reflecting on the development of modern theory, Ackerman suggests that Bickel's effort to maintain a place for principle will inevitably be displaced by process-based theories of constitutionalism.[4] Because normal politics is informed by a competition among private interests, in which each faction strives to use government to minimize its burdens and maximize its benefits, leveling reduces the public order to a coordination of conflicting private interests.[5] Leveling, then, represents a political worldview that drains the Constitution of any special public meaning, undermines the necessary conditions for the democratic legitimacy of a substantive judicial review, and reduces citizens to private individuals using politics for the pursuit of personal ends.

For Ackerman, American constitutionalism makes sense only on the basis of a political dualism, which breaks with the leveling present to recover a republican past. Constitutional politics is republican politics, which must be distinguished from the ordinary politics of day-to-day life.

The difference between these two forms of politics is the difference between a politics founded on a community of discourse and a politics of private individuals. New republicans understand the public order as a domain in which individuals construct their identity through the dialogic creation of a community.

Next to the leveler's reduction of all politics to the normal politics of self-interest, Ackerman juxtaposes a qualitatively different manner of public life that occurs at unique moments in the history of the nation. These moments of constitutional politics are characterized by their "public-regarding forms of political activity, in which people sacrifice their private interests to pursue the common good in transient and informal association."[6] Constitutional politics is distinguished from normal politics by virtue of its end, which is the common good, and its institutional nature, which is transient and informal association. Most important, the character of public life changes dramatically with the move from normal to constitutional politics.

In normal politics, interaction is competitive: "[F]actions try to manipulate the constitutional forms of political life to pursue their own narrow interests."[7] Those interests exist apart from and prior to political action. In contrast, constitutional politics pursues interaction through debate: the citizen finds "deeper meaning on those rare occasions when the American people . . . after sustained debate and struggle . . . hammer out new principles to guide public life."[8] These principles constitute the identity of the public body and the citizens who compose it.

Ackerman frequently appeals to the language of self-identity in describing constitutional politics. At unique moments of crisis, citizens "invest a certain aspect of their personality with heightened significance"; they "redefine, as private *citizens,* [their] collective identity"; "constitutional law . . . has always provided us with the language and process within which our political identities could be confronted, debated, and defined"; "the Constitution is best understood as . . . an evolving language of politics through which Americans have learned to talk to one another in the course of their centuries-long struggle over their national identity."[9] Constitutional politics is not a means to a personal and private end that exists apart from the process itself. Self-creation is an end in itself. Ackerman is reformulating the classic republican idea of the constitutive function of life in the polis, now within the model of a discursive community.

The difference between constitutional politics and normal politics, then, is the difference between the republican vision of community as the domain of self-creation through mutual, dialogic engagement and the liberal vision of the public order as a mechanism for the advancement of private ends. "The first, recalling the grandeur of the Greek polis, insists that the life of political involvement serves as the noblest ideal for humankind. The second, recalling a Christian suspicion of the claims of secular community, insists that the salvation of souls is a private affair."[10] Ackerman's sympathies are clear: "Normal politics must be tolerated in the name of individual liberty; it is, however, democratically *inferior* to the intermittent and irregular politics of public virtue associated with moments of constitutional creation."[11] The private epiphany of grace is replaced by the constitutive process of public dialogue. The inferior politics of the ordinary reflects the inferior virtues of liberalism compared to those of republicanism.

The constitutional role of the Court follows easily from this account of a dualist politics: "To maintain the integrity of higher lawmaking, all dualist constitutions must provide for one or more institutions to discharge a preservationist function."[12] In times of normal politics, the Court preserves the substance of communal self-identity achieved in prior moments of constitutional politics. The Court represents the community's better self—the public identity of its private constituents.[13] The Court speaks for the people as the ordinary institutions of political representation do not, for "the people" as such do not really exist in normal politics. They exist only at those critical moments of history when the entire nation engages in an identity-generating dialogue. "Above all else, a dualist constitution seeks to distinguish between . . . decision by the American people [and] by their government." With this, the countermajoritarian difficulty is "dis-solve[d]."[14]

Whether Ackerman has indeed dissolved the countermajoritarian difficulty depends upon the connections he can demonstrate between the institutional structure of government and the theory of community upon which he relies. If connections cannot be established, then whatever the theoretical merits of a community of discourse, it cannot ground the authority of constitutional law. These connections cannot, in fact, be established, because the theory of community cannot deal adequately with the temporal character of constitutional authority. Time generates three closely related problems for Ackerman's theory, which I will call the problems of continuity, interpretation, and revision.

Ackerman's dualism is projected onto U.S. history. The people who speak in a moment of constitutional politics are rarely the people of the present: most of the people, most of the time, pursue normal politics. Whatever or whoever this popular sovereign—We the People—was at these past moments, it was not anyone living today. Indeed, it probably excluded most of the people alive when We the People were acting. The participants in the constitutional politics of 1787 did not include women, blacks, or the propertyless.[15] Nor did universalism pertain in the constitutional politics of the post–Civil War period.[16] Ackerman's description of constitutional politics as a politics of the national community has, in reality, a very low standard of participation.

Ackerman's response to this critique might be that the quality of political life, not the universalism of participation and assent, distinguishes constitutional from normal politics. But a focus on quality raises troubling issues about the continuity of the community. If quality is what matters, it must matter because substantively correct political principles are more likely to be discovered through constitutional politics. But if this is so, then the continuity of the particular community is threatened; truth, not history, becomes the measure of constitutional identity. This answer converts a theory of the discursive community into an epistemological claim about the kind of inquiry that is likely to lead to the discovery of natural law. Constitutional politics would then have normative significance wherever and whenever it occurs. The French Revolution would be as relevant to American constitutionalism as the American Revolution. The normal politics of contemporary life in the United States could be displaced by the meanings revealed in the revolutionary politics of Southeast Asia or Latin America. The claim for quality cannot be so abstract as to undermine the sense that it is U.S. history that is important.

By projecting constitutional politics into the past, Ackerman creates a further problem of constitutional interpretation. His justices must interpret the content of past constitutional moments in which they did not participate and in which their identities were not directly formed. Their access to the former accomplishments of "the people" is mediated through the tools of historical inquiry. Constitutional provisions—particularly what Ackerman identifies as unwritten "structural amendments"—do not carry their meanings openly. Ackerman proposes a theory of interpretation that focuses on the need for a "principled synthesis" of past moments of constitutional politics: "[T]he interpretative problem that gives modern constitutional law its distinctive shape [is] the task of synthesizing the high law-making achievements of the many generations of Americans who have managed to rework the terms of our constitutional identity since the founding."[17] To the degree that interpretation is controversial, however, the identity and even the singularity of We the People are thrown into question. The effect of all such controversy is to reintroduce the problem of the authority of the decision maker. The stronger the distinction between past and present, between the object of interpretation and the interpreting institution, the more the Court is isolated in its claim to represent the people. How, after all, can citizens be sure that the Court has got them right?

Finally and most important, Ackerman fails to deal adequately with the deficiencies in popular participation in past constitutional moments. These deficiencies pose an obvious problem for his claim that constitutional politics is a process of simultaneous self-generation by the citizen and the community. Even at moments of constitutional politics, there may be a substantial gap between "the people" and the people. Citizens not involved in the process may "consent" to the creation of "the people" by others. Even that consent may be more implicit than explicit. This is hardly a politics of self-creation.

The asymmetry between "the people" and the rest of the citizenry becomes even more problematic when considering the temporal character of Ackerman's account. Ackerman argues that a successful effort to pursue constitutional politics must meet a supermajoritarian condition.[18] Without widespread participation, the requisite legitimacy does not exist for a revision in the content of the higher law that expresses national political identity. But imagine that the total number of people engaged in constitutional politics in 1787 or 1868 was X and that currently some $X + Y$ number of people are engaged in constitutional politics. According to Ackerman, the Court remains bound by the results of the earlier moment, unless $X + Y$ meets a quantitative standard derived from the contemporary community. Why? What does the past have over the present, if it is neither numbers or truth?[19]

Ackerman's answer to the problem of revision seems to rest ultimately on a theory of implied consent: all those not presently engaged in constitutional politics have implicitly consented to the understanding of the Constitution reached at prior moments of constitutional politics. Without the participation of a current majority, there is not a sufficient consensus for a change in constitutional doctrine.[20] At this point, Ackerman's theory comes dangerously close to the leveling premises of modern theory. Ackerman, too, seeks a measure of current popular consent to the principled discourse of the Court, but any reliance on implied consent poses a particular difficulty in light of his commitment to dualism.

Ackerman acknowledges that under conditions of normal politics, citizens are frequently apathetic, ignorant, and selfish in their attitudes toward public issues.[21] If so, why should their attitudes be respected over the constitutional politics of a contemporary minority? Of course, Ackerman does not contend that apathy, ignorance, and selfishness define constitutional self-understanding. To avoid having to make such a contention, he appeals to an implied self-understanding whose content derives from prior moments of constitutional politics. Only in this way can the self-understanding of those *not* engaged in the communitarian dialogue of constitutional politics deserve respect equal to that given those who are so engaged. Ackerman has substituted an implied self-understanding for implied consent, but the object and the effect are the same.

Once he acknowledges that the legitimate authority of the past depends upon the beliefs of the contemporary generation, there is little reason to favor theoretically implied beliefs over actual beliefs expressed in the political process. In other words, any reliance on implied consent will reintroduce the countermajoritarian difficulty. To avoid the consequences of leveling, Ackerman must not simply envision a political dualism in the historical life of the nation but project that dualism into the political psychology of every citizen at every moment. He tries to save his theory by positing a kind of political schizophrenia in which citizens pursue constitutional and normal politics at the same time. Such a view undermines his cyclical interpretation of constitutional history. More important, the communitarian dialogue of self-creation is just not present as a national phenomenon during times of normal politics. To say it is implicit merely acknowledges its nonexistence in any sense sufficiently vital to constitute individual and communal identity.

Each of these problems of continuity, interpretation, and revision is a reformulation of Bickel's countermajoritarian difficulty. That they can be reformulated as questions about Ackerman's theory suggests that his discovery of "the people" as a dialogic community is not a sufficient answer to the problems of modern constitutional theory. To satisfy the demand for a national dialogue rich enough to constitute identity, he must project that dialogue into the past. By doing that, he renders the dialogue incapable of supporting the authoritative claims of constitutional law in the present.

The problems with Ackerman's theory come from his attempt to couple a model of republican dialogue with a claim of institutional authority. Ackerman tries to locate authority in a national dialogic community. His marriage of the quantitative and the qualitative elements of political life may be possible at unique moments of history. Outside those unique moments, the choice must be made between numbers and dialogue. Is constitutional authority founded on the consent of a majority or on a qualitatively distinct discourse? Ackerman hopes to avoid the choice by insisting that numbers and dialogue remain united in a national identity. But the cost of maintaining that view is too high. He must give up real dialogue for an implied dialogue, and real community for an implied community.

Ackerman attempts to dissolve the countermajoritarian difficulty by offering a republican theory of a national self-identity. Other new republicans have far less confidence in the capacity of the people to enter a dialogic community. When forced to choose between the discourse and the people, they choose the discourse.

Frank Michelman: The Supreme Court as a Discursive Community

Frank Michelman's work spans the movement from modern to contemporary theory.[22] His early work provides a rights-centered individualism; his later work develops the idea of a self-generative, discursive community. My concern is with an influential essay entitled "Traces of Self-Government," which offers a republican interpretation of the Supreme Court. More recently, he has moved away from this Court-centered perspective. Nevertheless, that someone would attempt to locate the discursive community in the Supreme Court was inevitable. Only a limited number of institutional settings are available to republican theorists.

Michelman, like Ackerman, sees the theoretical turn to the discursive community as a break with modern theory: "[T]he republican tradition, and its relation to American constitutionalism, points away from the countermajoritarian difficulty as the true focus of democratic concern."[23] In place of Ackerman's vision of a national community of dialogue, however, he proposes an alternative dialogic community that is the locus of republican self-government: the community constituted by the nine members of the Supreme Court.

Rousseau, Michelman argues, was right: the maximum size of a discursive community is that "in which every member can be known by all."[24] Ackerman's claim that We the People can constitute a self-generative community of dialogue must therefore be in error. As "a people," the nation is irretrievably lost to normal politics. If We the People never existed, the Court's authority cannot come from the past acts of the people. Ironically, Ackerman's attempt to find a community in the past leaves the current members of the national community subject to a very uncommunitarian vision of judicial authority.[25] The Court speaks authoritatively, but not with the voice of We the People.

The loss of a national republican community does not mean to Michelman that republicanism has no place in the constitutional system. The task is to find the institutional place at which that constitutive discourse can occur and to ground the authority of that institution in its discourse. Michelman's argument has three steps. First, he identifies republicanism with self-government and self-government with freedom. Second, he asserts that the Constitution does not attempt to establish a national political process on the republican model. Third, he defends a place for republicanism in the constitutional scheme by offering the discursive community as the proper model for constitutional adjudication by the courts, and especially by the Supreme Court.

Michelman explains the fascination of contemporary theorists with republicanism by noting its powerful response to "the Cartesian Anxiety: The sense of entrapment between nihilism on the one hand, and domination on the other." Nihilism and domination are both the product of what Michelman calls "negative freedom." Negative freedom is the view that "moral choice proceeds not from publicly certifiable grounds or reasoning, but from the inexplicable private impulses of individuals, objectively unfounded and rationally unguided."[26]

From the perspective of a theory of negative freedom, a choice is valuable only to the degree that it reflects an individual's ends. In the absence of an external, objective standard, action reflects either the subject's own arbitrary choice—nihilism—or someone else's choice—domination. The difference is only in the identity of the person choosing, not in the nature of the choice. Between nihilism and domination there is, on this view, no third possibility.

Michelman argues that contemporary answers to the dilemma of negative freedom appeal to the idea of a historically situated, dialogic community: themes of "dialogue," "history," "responsibility," and "identity" together "characterize a modern project of ethical reconciliation through dialogue, in search of freedom." Normative disputes are to be resolved "by conversation, a communicative practice of open and intelligible reason-giving" in which the decision maker must take immediate responsibility for the construction of a "normative history," within which the dispute may be situated and so resolved.[27] The unique, historical dialogue that constitutes a community provides the public, objective ground for a theory of "positive freedom." Republicanism is the expression of positive freedom as a political doctrine.

Republicanism remains a doctrine of freedom because the normative rules are given by the citizens to themselves. Yet republicanism is not nihilistic: the norms have an objectivity grounded in the discourse of a community. "This view of the human condition implies that self-cognition and ensuing self-legislation must . . . be socially situated; norms must be formed through public dialogue and expressed as public law."[28]

The political and moral norms of the community are not external demands, dominating individual choice; rather, they are themselves an expression of individual identity. Public law can be identified with self-legislation because in coming to know the law, the individual achieves self-cognition. People are speakers, members of a discursive community, before they are individuals.

In all of this, Michelman is covering the common ground of contemporary theory, even if that ground sometimes resembles a marsh, rather than dry land. He admits that "[r]epublicanism is not a well-defined historical doctrine" and that "it figures less as canon than ethos, less as blueprint than as conceptual grid, less as settled institutional fact than as semantic field for normative debate and constructive imagination."[29] Nevertheless, his originality arises just to the extent that he does offer an institutional blueprint.

Michelman's account, so far, has treated the possibility of a republican politics of self-government. To make the move from possibility to actuality, Michelman asks, "[W]here, if anywhere, can we find self-government inside the Constitution?" This question is "undeniably baffling . . . because the document so obviously charters not a participatory democracy but a sovereign authority of governors—representatives—distinct from the governed." The republicans, on his view, lost the original constitutional debate. The antifederalists objected to the proposed Constitution because they believed that the creation of a national, representative government would deny the communitarian conditions necessary for republican self-government. Those conditions include direct participation in the discourse that constitutes the normative identity of the community. The antifederalists correctly perceived that power would pass to national representatives and that citizens would be excluded from the public deliberation required to maintain positive self-government. The institutions of government would stand over the citizenry not as expressions of self-identity but as coercive authorities.[30]

Michelman reduces Ackerman's effort to reconstruct a national republican tradition to a questionable claim of judicial authority: "In the final analysis, the People vanish, abstracted into a story written by none of us . . . unless we happen to be justices."[31] Positive freedom cannot be achieved by compliance with a set of authoritative rules, even if they emerge from someone else's dialogue—even if one labels that someone We the People. To speak of the Court "representing" the content of past moments of constitutional politics is, according to Michelman, to move from self-government to external authority.

Michelman abruptly cuts through the puzzle created by the juxtaposition of actual constitutional authority and a theory of republican self-government. Even though the Constitution does not establish a republican citizenry, it does, he claims, establish a republican Supreme Court. If theorists are searching for a model of positive freedom—for a republican community of self-government founded on a model of discourse—they need look no further than the Court: "[T]he courts, and especially the Supreme Court, seem to take on as one of their ascribed functions the modeling of active self-government that citizens find practically beyond reach."[32] Michelman preserves the possibility of positive freedom somewhere in the system by converting the Court into a community of discourse. The Court is uniquely privileged to engage in the discourse of republican self-government.

Judging, for Michelman, is not primarily the application of law to the disputing parties. It is an activity of self-government within the community of the Court itself: "Judges [must be committed] to the process of their own self-government."[33] A republican Supreme Court carries on a dialogue in which the justices give the law to themselves individually only in and through the creation of a communal identity. In this Court, voting on an outcome is subordinated to a discourse on the moral unity of the community of the Court itself.[34] Judicial identity is a consequence, not a precondition, of the discourse.

Michelman follows the Bickelian tradition in looking to the unique institutional capacities of the Court as the starting point for his analysis. But what for Bickel was a community of scholars with the leisure for sustained intellectual inquiry—a private, individualistic image—becomes for Michelman a dialogic community engaged in the self-generative process of positive freedom. Michelman, like Ackerman before him, also takes up Bickel's insight that the Court must be understood as a representative institution. Yet Michelman's republican Court is representative in quite a different sense from either Bickel's forward-looking Court or Ackerman's backward-looking Court.

Both Bickel and Ackerman invited doubts about the correctness of judicial decision making by recognizing a gap between the representative (the Court) and the represented (the people). Michelman proposes to escape this problem by conflating the Court and what it represents. For Michelman, the Court represents the possibility of a dialogic community to the rest of the nation and thus the possibility of positive freedom and self-government. It represents this possibility by exemplifying it. The Court represents the possibility of freedom to the necessarily unfree, political selves of the national community. "Unable as a nation to practice our own self-government (in the full, positive sense), we ... can at least identify with the judiciary's as we idealistically construct it."[35]

Michelman envisions a republican Court in a generally nonrepublican system of government. This is a strange new sort of mixed government. Instead of combining the rule of the one and the many or aristocracy and democracy, it combines positive and negative freedom, republican self-government and representative authoritarianism. As an institution, the Court combines positive freedom with authoritative domination. Michelman does not deny the authoritative character of the Court from the perspective of those outside its communal discourse, that is, those subject to its authority. He has not explained how that authority flows from the dialogic character of the judicial process. To ask what privileges the discourse of this particular community is possible and indeed necessary: Why is the outcome of the dialogue of the Court authoritative? More precisely, why should it be authoritative?

Michelman's answer to the problem of legitimacy seems to be simply that positive freedom is better than negative freedom, and positive freedom within the Court is the best that can be done within the existing institutional framework of constitutional government. Neither proposition is self-evidently true. That positive freedom relieves the Cartesian anxiety may suggest that any individual would be wise to choose—if it is a matter of choice—positive, over negative, freedom. But that hardly establishes that positive freedom is better than negative freedom in a political organization, especially if the suggestion is that a minority's positive freedom be accepted at the cost of a majority's negative freedom. If negative freedom is all that is possible within the domain of national politics, then the choice between nihilism and domination may not be a matter of indifference. Michelman suggests that political freedom within the national community raises a problem of second-best solutions, but the reason for his claim to have found the appropriate solution is not clear. In short, even if the distinction between positive and negative freedom is accepted as Michelman elaborates it, nothing follows with respect to any particular institution of government or even with respect to government organization in general.

Similarly, the proposition that he has discovered as much positive freedom as can be found in the constitutional structure does not appear to be true even on Michelman's own premises.[36] To have more positive freedom only requires accepting less authority. The federalists and anti-federalists fought this battle over where to draw the line between authority and positive freedom. The battle is joined vividly once again in the conflict between the "jurisgenerative" and the "jurispathic" that Robert Cover describes. The Constitution has not made a final choice between authority and anarchy. Where to draw the line is always an open question for debate.[37]

Sometimes Michelman seems to argue that recognition of the positive freedom of the Court is a step in a process leading to the positive freedom of the larger body politic. "[I]f freedom consists of socially situated self-direction—that is, self-direction by norms cognizant of fellowship with equally self-directing others—then the relation between one agent's freedom and another's is additive: one realizes one's own only by confirming that of the others. This seems to hold no less for a judge than for any other agent."[38] Yet Michelman has already argued that the proposition cannot be true at the national level, because the institutional character of a national citizenry makes positive freedom in national politics impossible. The issue will never be incremental progress toward national republican self-government but always the choice between national authority and the anarchy implicit in the endless possibilities of distinct new communities emerging to claim positive self-government for themselves.

Michelman attempts to meld authority and community. On the one hand, he affirms that "[j]ustices engaged in adjudication and judicial review are not for this purpose citizens; rather they are organs of the state, the ultimate oracles of its law."[39] On the other hand, he urges a model of adjudication as dialogic self-government within the community of the Court. The concepts conjoined are ultimately incompatible. That the Court can engage in such a dialogue is beside the point; whether it does so has nothing to do with the legitimacy of its exercise of authority over everyone else.

New republicans imagine self-government to be a process in which an individual's personhood is constituted through participation in the dialogue of a historically situated community. Between those within and those outside that dialogic community there may be no common measure by which to evaluate disagreement. The conclusion of the dialogue is not self-validating to those outside the community. Yet Michelman has placed most of the nation irretrievably outside the self-governing community of American political life. The republican constitutional theory he offers can do nothing to legitimate the structures of authority already in place in the constitutional system. Instead, it creates an incurable problem of republican elitism.[40]

Cass Sunstein: Congress as a Community of Discourse

Contemporary constitutional theorists of the new republican and interpretivist schools share a concept of positive freedom founded in the discursive community. For all of them, that community transforms ordinary politics into a process of self-government through self-creation. The new republicans differ from interpretivists in their effort to frame this model of community in terms of political institutions. The weakness of the new republicans is most evident just at this point: they are unable to agree on the institutional setting within which this self-constitutive dialogue occurs. Instead of Ackerman's extraordinary institutions that arise in moments of a national constitutional politics or Michelman's Supreme Court, Cass Sunstein looks to Congress as the locus of the republican community.

Sunstein mixes historical, legal, and moral arguments to support his claim that the constitutional responsibility of Congress is not to exercise authority in response to constituent pressures but rather to deliberate mutually about the common good. His historical argument borrows from recent work on the importance of republican, rather than Lockean, themes to the framers. He sees the framers, particularly Madison, as appropriating much of the argument of the antifederalists with respect to the need for a politics based upon a "face-to-face process of deliberation and debate."[41] The disagreement between federalists and antifederalists, according to Sunstein, lay primarily in their conflicting visions of where and how a republican politics could be pursued.

For the antifederalists, republican politics had to be immediately participatory. For them, citizenship meant the display of civic virtue through participation in the ongoing discursive inquiry into the public good. If citizenship required this kind of participation, then the field for its exercise was necessarily the local community. For the federalists, in contrast, the only hope for a politics not corrupted by private interests was to relocate the community of discourse to the level of the national political institutions, specifically the national legislature: "Representatives would have the time and temperament to engage in a form of collective reasoning. . . . The representatives of the people would be free to engage in the process of discussion and debate from which the common good would emerge."[42] This geographical shift was the unique contribution of the framers to traditional republican theory. It made possible a theory of republican politics compatible with the development of the modern nation-state.

Unlike Michelman, who suggests that republicans largely lost the constitutional debate, Sunstein argues that republicanism was not itself at stake. The ratification debate was essentially among republicans, who disagreed only on the location of dialogic self-government. At issue was a modern innovation in republican theory, not the classical understanding of a republican politics founded on a psychology of civic virtue and a discursive approach to the public good.

Shifting from history to law, Sunstein argues that throughout constitutional law the pluralist model of interest-group politics has been consistently rejected.[43] For a statute to be the product of a fair competition among competing private interest groups is not a sufficient argument for its constitutional legitimacy. The political process alone is never due process. Rather, the common ground of diverse constitutional norms is that legislation must be justified by reference to a public purpose, which is something other than the politically strongest private interest. Legislators are constitutionally required to deliberate and to select public values.

The constitutional prohibition on the legislative pursuit of what Sunstein calls "naked preferences"—the distribution of public resources solely on the basis of political power—is "the best candidate for a unitary conception of the sorts of government action that the Constitution prohibits."[44] This conception of constitutionalism places responsibility for republican governance squarely on the legislature. The role of the judiciary is not to pursue a republican politics of discourse within the community of the Court but to police the process of republican politics within the legislative branch. Where Michelman envisions a republican Court facing a nonrepublican legislature, Sunstein envisions a nonrepublican Court facing a republican legislature.

The heart of Sunstein's argument, however, is neither the historical nor the legal claim, both of which are just controversial descriptive propositions. Even if he is correct regarding both, it hardly follows that the republican aspects of the constitutional system should be encouraged. Even Sunstein admits that these aspects are not exclusive.[45] The choice requires a normative argument that "better" law will emerge from a legislature that understands itself as a discursive community.

Posing the issue in this way demonstrates the difficulties created by Sunstein's mixture of conventional legal argument and republican theory. The attractiveness of the idea of a community of discourse derives from the concept of personal autonomy it offers—positive freedom—and the possibility of grounding the legitimacy of a political order in that concept. Republicanism promises to bridge the gap separating the citizen from the state with a model of dialogic engagement in which the individual and the community, the speaker and the discourse, are simultaneously created. Once that community of discourse has been located in Congress—Sunstein's legal and historical move—the normative appeal of positive freedom, of giving the rule of law to oneself, loses its power outside the elite membership of that institution. This dilemma arises each time the discourse is localized in a particular institution.

Congress may be free, but the law still appears to the ordinary citizen as the imposition of an authoritarian, external rule. Instead of emphasizing republicanism as positive freedom, as the giving of the rule of action to oneself, Sunstein is forced to emphasize the public good. He says that statutes founded on legislative deliberation will be better than those that represent naked preferences—a proposition that invites skepticism. This skepticism, moreover, distinguishes contemporary thought from the republicanism of the founders. For them, the public good revealed through mutual deliberation had the objectivity of a scientific truth. Republicans no longer attempt to make any such claim to abstract truth. Some evidence to support Sunstein's normative claim is therefore needed, as is an explanation of the measure of the public good he uses in making his claim.

Sunstein is not completely immune to the attractions of the traditional republican idea of positive freedom. He emphasizes, for example, that in republican politics, preferences are not exogenous (formed prior to and apart from the political process) but endogenous (formed within the political process).[46] They are shaped, therefore, through the legislative discourse. Preferences are a central aspect of personhood, so self-identity is, at least to some degree, a product of legislative discourse. But whose preferences and whose identities have been shaped? If Sunstein means those of the legislators, then he must explain why the rest of the citizens should prefer to have statutes based on others' preferences as opposed to their own prepolitical, exogenous preferences. If he means those of citizens, then he must explain how a dialogue in which the citizens are not participants can have this self-generative effect. Finally, if he means the preferences of the state, then he must explain the meaning of this personification of the state. Sunstein usually seems to take the first option. He is overwhelmingly concerned with legislative motivation. If he is speaking of the dialogic creation of legislative preferences, then the republican argument for positive freedom never bridges the gap between rulers—the positive freedom is theirs—and citizens. To the governed, legislative outcomes are likely to remain more important than legislative process.

Because Sunstein is unable to link positive freedom and self-government of the national community, the strength of his argument must rest on his claim that a republican legislature will produce better laws: "The republican conception . . . reflects a belief that debate and discussion help to reveal that some values are superior to others. Denying that de-

cisions about values are merely matters of taste, the republican view assumes that 'practical reason' can be used to settle social issues."[47] To
defend the normative value of a republican Congress, Sunstein finds that
he must defend an objective public good. Yet his argument is weakest
here.

The weakness is twofold. First, his own theory indicates that the
nature of the good looks different to those within and those outside the
community of dialogue. This difference is the point of his distinction
between exogenous and endogenous preferences. The legislators are likely,
therefore, to have a different understanding of the public good than the
citizens who do not participate in the legislative community of discourse.
Not everyone sees the legislatively articulated public good as good for all.
Nor is there likely to be a common measure by which to evaluate these
different perceptions. Second, because of the failure to find a common
measure, Sunstein offers a remarkably thin idea of the community of
discourse from which the public good emerges. For Sunstein, that community is accomplished as soon as something is said. What is said may
be virtually anything.[48] All that appears to be prohibited is a vote without
discourse. Yet Sunstein admits that framing a reason, even a public-
sounding reason, for every choice is not difficult, including choices based
on personal preferences.[49] If the measure of community is simply the
giving of reasons, the republican community becomes too weak to support
a notion of positive freedom and altogether too weak to support a substantive vision of the public good.

Sunstein's normative account of the republican community of dialogue risks collapsing into the trivial point that it is better to think before
one acts. Legislation that is carefully considered beforehand is likely to
be more effective and to meet social goals more adequately than legislation
that is not considered beforehand. One does not have to be a republican
to agree with that.[50]

Sunstein has stumbled over precisely the problem of authority that
has troubled each of the constitutional theorists of community. He wants
to simultaneously recognize legislative authority and a community of dialogue. The two ideas, however, operate in different dimensions. The legislature may or may not be a self-generative, dialogic community, but
whether it is has nothing to do with the authority the institution exercises
over the rest of the political community. Sunstein strives for compatibility
between the ideas of dialogue and authority by so weakening the idea of
community that little is left but the authority of the state.

None of these problems is specific to Sunstein; all are equally applicable to Michelman's theory that the Court is the locus of the com-

munity of discourse. He, too, needs to argue that the nation gets better law from such a Court, even from the perspective of the nonrepublican majority: "[Judges'] actions may augment our freedom. As usual, it all depends. One thing it depends on, I believe, is the commitment of judges to the process of their own self-government."[51] He is right; it does all depend. But it does not depend upon the judges' own realization of self-government.

The same problem of juxtaposing the republican community and the nonrepublican life of everyone else plagues Ackerman's theory. The difference is that for Ackerman, the problem appears in a temporal, rather than institutional, form. But as Michelman demonstrates, the temporal problem becomes an institutional problem as soon as one focuses on the issue of who should interpret a past act of We the People.

The problem of authority has not been resolved by the new republicans. Each offers an image of positive freedom through self-government within a dialogic community. But that community fails to make contact with the authority of constitutional law as it operates in the polity. Citizens experience that authority as temporal and institutional. Constitutional law is a historical enterprise; in recognizing its authority, citizens recognize the continuity of the present with the past. In respecting the Constitution as law, they respect the authority of past political acts over present community preferences. To be effective, temporal authority must be mediated through institutions that apply law in the present. The new republicans have tried to meld authority and community at both points: Ackerman uses community to explain the temporal dimension of constitutional authority, and Michelman and Sunstein use community to explain how existing institutions should act. But none explains or justifies authority by appealing to community. The interpretivists recognize the problem of authority more directly but offer no better solution.

The Interpretivists' Use of Community

The discussion of the new republicans reveals a fundamental problem in communitarian-based theories of constitutional law: too many communities can be fit within the dialogic mold. Because of the institutional presuppositions the new republicans bring to their inquiry—the community must be located within the existing institutional structure of constitutional authority—they never directly confront this problem. But just as choosing among these limited possibilities appears arbitrary, so do the institutional limits on the domain of choice. The constraint on what communities are possible comes from a source external to the communal-dialogic foundations of the theory. The interpretivists differ from the new republicans in confronting the possible proliferation of dialogic communities. Although they do not all accept an anarchy of communities, each must find a way of explaining authority in light of the anarchic implications of the dialogic community.

The tension between anarchy and authority is at the center of Robert Cover's essay "Nomos and Narrative." The same tension is at the center of Owen Fiss's work on interpretation and adjudication.[52] Fiss and Cover both understand community to create the very possibility of law, but they reach radically different conclusions. Cover embraces anarchy; Fiss pursues authority. Each is attracted to a particular form of community: Fiss to the professional community, Cover to the religious community. The professional community offers Fiss a source of stability and authority, whereas the religious community offers Cover only the pluralism of sects.

Of all contemporary interpretivists, Ronald Dworkin offers the most philosophically rigorous and complete account of the meaning and significance of a historically specific discourse in the creation and maintenance of law.[53] He aims to ground the legitimacy of law in a particular kind of political community and to ground the privileged place—the authority—of that community within a theory of interpretation. Because his theory of community is so complete, his failure reveals a great deal about the possibility of successfully using the model of dialogic community to support legal authority.

Owen Fiss: Hierarchy and Authority in the Professional Community

"Adjudication is interpretation," Fiss announces in the opening line of his essay "Objectivity and Interpretation." This is a statement about the conceptual foundations of law. The need to explain how law is possible arises, Fiss says, from the nihilists' challenge in contemporary legal theory. The nihilist properly "fastens on the objective aspiration of the law and sees this as a distinguishing feature of legal interpretation." Because the nihilist cannot find that objectivity in constitutional law, the objectivity that characterizes adjudication must be explained and justified in a defense of constitutional law. This defense is the purpose of the turn to interpretation.[54]

Fiss's account of adjudication as interpretation relies on the familiar features of the discursive community. Prominent in his account are what he terms "disciplining rules." To be a judge is to respond to legal texts through the application of disciplining rules, "which constrain the inter-

preter and constitute the standards by which the correctness of the interpretation is to be judged."[55] The rules, not the texts, define the discipline.
What is appropriately considered a legal text is itself a function of the
rules. A text does not stand wholly apart from the rules, although a variety
of disciplines may share a common text. For example, not just lawyers
but historians as well read the constitutional text.

The disciplining rules are both descriptive and normative. They
make possible an agreement on what it means to judge and how the
judicial role is properly performed. Adjudication has a settled—and thus
objective—meaning for those who accept these rules. The group of individuals who share the same understanding of the disciplining rules is
the "interpretive community." Rules and community are interrelated:
"[T]he disciplining rules that govern an interpretive activity must be seen
as defining or demarcating an interpretive community consisting of those
who recognize the rules as authoritative."[56] Individuals outside the interpretive community are, regardless of their legal situation, outside the
jurisdiction of the judge: they may be coerced by the violence of law, but
they do not acknowledge the authority of law. In contrast, for individuals
inside the community, the exercise of legal authority can be measured
against objective standards.

Community, then, is the anchor of interpretation. Because adjudication is interpretation, adjudication rests on community. Adjudication
shares the objectivity of the interpretive community. Fiss refers to this as
"bounded objectivity": "It is bounded by the existence of a community
that recognizes and adheres to the disciplining rules used by the interpreter and that is defined by its recognition of those rules."[57] Without an
interpretive community, the subjectivity of interpretation and the objectivity of text would split apart into an irreconcilable dichotomy. Judges
who operate outside the rules of a community are not judging at all; they
are "abusing" their public office for private ends.

For Fiss, the account of interpretation in adjudication is no different
in its essential meaning-generating function from the account of interpretation as the central explanatory device of all social activity. In other
social activities, however, meaning may be contested through the freedom
"to leave one community and to join or establish another."[58] In law, Fiss
argues, there is only one interpretive community. Were there a plurality
of competing communities in law, the nihilists' challenge could not be
met. The objectivity of law must be defended by identifying a single,
authoritative community within the larger society. Fiss does this by privileging a particular community: the legal profession. "The judge's choice
is constrained by a set of rules . . . that are authorized by the professional

community of which the judge is part (and that define and constitute the community)."[59]

According to Fiss, lawyers know how to read the constitutional text. They know the range of legitimate sources and the appropriate moves that can be made with those sources. They can recognize a professionally competent reading, even when they disagree with it. Fiss repeatedly emphasizes that objectivity does not require agreement, just constraints on the subjective freedom of the judge.[60] Professional training and membership in the legal community are the sources of those constraints.

To respond to the nihilists' challenge, however, requires a demonstration of more than limits on the subjective freedom of the judge. Constraints that are a function of the judge's participation in a religious community, for example, may be objective—they may limit the possibilities of judicial choice—but such constraints are hardly reassuring to the nihilist or to anyone else worried about the political legitimacy, rather than the political psychology, of adjudication. Objectivity in adjudication must legitimate judicial interpretation. Legitimacy cannot arise from constraint alone.

A defense of the authoritativeness of judicial interpretation must, therefore, explain the relationship between the professional community of lawyers and the larger national community. Without such an explanation, the objectivity offered by the former may, from the perspective of the latter, appear just as arbitrary as the judicial subjectivity that Fiss fears. Imagine, for example, a professional community that operates under the disciplining rule of the founders' intent while the larger community interprets democratic self-government to require the consent of a present majority. The professional community would be wildly out of step with the political community.[61]

Fiss recognizes that he has not provided an account of objectivity that bears on legitimacy when he writes: "Interpretation is countermajoritarian, even if properly understood. On the other hand, a proper conception of interpretation will help us understand the pervasiveness of the countermajoritarian dilemma and thus, in my judgment, reduce its significance."[62] In truth, however, Fiss does not explain that pervasiveness.

Fiss's assertion that the countermajoritarian dilemma is pervasive presumably rests on his claim that interpretation occurs within a bounded community. In most fields of interpretation—for example, literary criticism—there are a plurality of such communities. Objectivity holds within each but not across all. Fiss denies this pluralism in legal interpretation: "There can be many schools of literary interpretation, but . . . in legal interpretation there is only one school and attendance is mandatory."[63] The countermajoritarian difficulty arises, however, not because of the theory of interpretation but because of the identification of a particular community as the authoritative source of interpretation in constitutional law. The difficulty is produced by the denial of an "exit" option and the insistence on "loyalty" in the face of disagreement.[64] Authority, not interpretation, is the source of the countermajoritarian difficulty of constitutional law.

Fiss does acknowledge strong interactions between law and morality that encourage the judge to interpret the legal text in a way consistent with popular morality. A judge who understands the disciplining rules of the professional community to require an interpretation of the text that renders the Constitution "immoral" is inviting the broad question of legitimacy: "[W]hy must we respect the Constitution?"[65] Such an interpretation, Fiss argues, represents a bad strategy, though not necessarily a bad interpretation. A political system can tolerate just so much dissonance between its moral and legal communities. The authority of law is, in this sense, always tenuous. Judges are well advised to look to the likely reception of the interpretive products of adjudication in the larger community.

Although the forces of public morality may contribute to the actual outcome of adjudication, they are outside, not within, interpretation itself. These forces constrain interpretation apart from the disciplining rules of the legal community. They are the price that law pays for failing to provide a compelling ground for its own authority. If moral rules were a part of legal interpretation, then the relevant interpretive community would be the one within which morality held sway, not the professional community of lawyers. Fiss emphasizes the insulation of the legal community when he writes that "the judge is to read the legal text, not morality or public opinion, not, if you will, the moral or social texts."[66]

For Fiss, the source of the authority of the interpretive community remains elusive. To be sure, he writes that "[i]t is important to note that the claim of authoritativeness . . . is extrinsic to the process of interpretation."[67] But this statement, though perhaps true, is fundamentally inconsistent with Fiss's whole project, which is to respond to the nihilists' challenge. That challenge links authority directly to objectivity. The nihilists' point is that judicial subjectivity or arbitrariness is incompatible with the proposition that judicial authority represents a legitimate rule of law. Fiss cannot simply detach objectivity from authority, as if the latter did not depend critically upon the former. If the objectivity of interpretation remains arbitrary to those outside the professional community of lawyers, the nihilists' challenge to legal authority remains in place. Moreover, Fiss cannot defend his appeal to interpretation—made to ground his theory of adjudication—by pointing to the potential of interpretation to offer a unified theory of social meaning, and then suggest that the unique aspect of law, its authoritativeness, must be explained on noninterpretive grounds. The claim of interpretation is more complete.

In the end, Fiss suggests that authority is a function of the constitutional text itself, as if the uninterpreted Constitution were available. "The ultimate authority for a judicial decree is the Constitution, for that text embodies public values and establishes the institutions through which those values are to be understood and expressed."[68] But the Constitution did not first establish institutions and embody values and then become an object of interpretation. Institutions and values are themselves products of interpretation.

Although Fiss has little to say about the authority of the legal community over other interpretive communities, he has much to say about authority within the law. Authority is critical to his account of the legal community because he recognizes that whatever objective constraints the disciplining rules provide, they are not sufficiently strong to prevent profound disagreement among judges and lawyers. Disagreement over the application of a disciplining rule or even over the existence of a rule is resolved by the structure of authority within the legal community. "The presence of such procedures and a hierarchy of authority for resolving disputes that could potentially divide or destroy an interpretive community is one of the distinctive features of legal interpretation."[69] The community remains unified, instead of splintering into many communities, because of the authority structure.

Fiss has linked authority and communal identity, but he still must link authority and interpretation. What makes the interpretation offered by an institution of authority within this community correct? Or is correctness a function of authority?

Disagreement is not occasional or exceptional in law. The prevalence of an adversarial process suggests that the constraints produced by the disciplining rules are hardly ever sufficient to resolve a serious legal dispute. Members of the profession know how to frame a suitably objective argument for either side in a case. This expertise is given effect in the practice of brief writing. It is given a continuing, visible presence in the practice of writing dissents. Dissenters may lack votes, but they do not lack the objectivity of the disciplining rules. Fiss suggests that the rules themselves can resolve such disagreements, but his claim is implausible.

The nihilists' claim that there are no constraints on the judge's decision provides Fiss with an easy target. The more difficult target is the legal realists' claim that the constraints are insufficient to ground a choice between two contrary outcomes.[70] True, not everything can be said, but usually enough can be said to support as objective, within the bounded professional community, either of two possible outcomes of a controversy.

Because disagreement within the disciplining rules is built into the structures within which legal interpretation occurs, Fiss must go beyond objectivity to "correctness." Indeed, he often couples the two concepts: the disciplining rules "constrain the interpreter, thus transforming the interpretive process from a subjective to an objective one, and they furnish the standards by which the correctness of the interpretation can be judged." This statement suggests that objectivity and correctness are on a continuum: the correct decision arises from a further application of the same rules that provide objectivity. Fiss says as much when he writes, "The image I have in mind is that of a judge moving toward judgment along a spiral of norms that increasingly constrain."[71]

Conflict in constitutional interpretation is so profound that Fiss's claim seems simply inaccurate. Correct decisions are not likely to be distinguished from wrong decisions by their greater attention to the disciplining rules. Neither the quality of historical research nor the attention to precedent, for example, distinguishes right interpretations from wrong ones. Disagreement is more likely to arise from the application of different disciplining rules. When one judge wants to return to original history, another to follow more recent precedent, both are objective within the norms of the professional community. If there are second-order rules for resolving these conflicts, Fiss has not elaborated them. His argument supports a simpler but far less useful claim: authoritative institutions exist to resolve conflicting legal interpretations, but there are no authoritative rules of interpretation for resolving such conflicts.

If the rules do not lead to a single, correct outcome—and they are not likely to in the absence of a coherent ordering—Fiss must choose between equally problematic alternatives.[72] First, conflict may indicate that more than one professional community interprets the Constitution. If communities are defined by their disciplining rules and if conflict over the rules is sufficiently profound, then it would seem to follow that there are a number of communities.

The problem with a theory of multiple communities is not internal to interpretation. Nothing about the concept of interpretation precludes a plurality of legal communities, just as there are a plurality of communities of literary interpretation. The problem with the theory is political. If more than one legal community exists, which one legitimately exercises authority? A splintering of the legal community will undermine the authority of the professionals.

Fiss, accordingly, rejects pluralism within the legal community. He labels a community that forms around an alternative set of disciplining rules a "clique": "The legal community transcends cliques; some cliques may dissolve over time, others may come to dominate the community."[73] Some cliques win, others lose. Now, however, he is speaking of force as the mark of authority, not the objectivity of interpretation. Interpretation may support some sort of objectivity, but not authoritatively imposed uniformity.

The only option that remains is for Fiss to define the disciplining rules of the community to include acceptance of an institutional hierarchy of authority. But the argument would then be circular. The disciplining rules are meant to ground the objectivity of the institutions of legal authority—especially that of the Supreme Court as exercised in constitutional adjudication. This option, however, suggests that only the authority of the courts can ground the rules. Instead of legal disagreements being resolved by the disciplining rules of the community, disagreements over the disciplining rules would be resolved by an appeal to the courts.[74] On this view, the objectivity of judicial decisions is not explained. The decisions are right because it is the role of the courts to be right. Here, authority stands alone without the support of interpretation.

In the end, neither the authority of the legal community nor the authority of an appellate court majority within the professional community has been grounded in interpretation. At every turn, Fiss's arguments can be challenged by the claims of other communities of interpretation. The proliferation of communities may occur both outside and within the professional community. Each community, from the standpoint of interpretation, stands on the same ground. Authority characterizes adjudication, but interpretation does not characterize authority. No one has better grasped the splitting apart of authority and interpretation than Robert Cover.

Robert Cover: Interpretation and Anarchy

In "Nomos and Narrative," Cover describes a conflict between the jurisgenerative and the jurispathic, between the "paideic" world of the "nomos" and the violent world of the "imperial." His sources are unfamiliar—or at least out of place in the legal context in which he is writing. Large parts of the essay are devoted to biblical exegesis, and the specifically legal texts that do appear tend to be lawyer's briefs rather than judicial opinions. The essay represents an extreme assault on ordinary legal sensibilities and an immediate challenge to Fiss's confident reliance on the language and habits of the legal community. Yet the object of the new vocabulary is once again the community of discourse.

Cover immediately announces his central idea: "We inhabit a *nomos*—a normative universe." Both words of this definition—*normative* and *universe*—are critical. The normative character of the nomos distinguishes it from the physical universe: the nomos is the domain "of right and wrong, of lawful and unlawful, of valid and void." By describing the nomos as a universe, Cover asserts that the normative is objective. The nomos is a universe because it constitutes a world in which people find themselves. "This *nomos* is as much 'our world' as is the physical universe of mass, energy, and momentum. . . . [O]ur apprehension of the structure of the normative world is no less fundamental than our appreciation of the structure of the physical world." People find themselves in a world of meaning in the same way that they find themselves in a world of space and time.[75]

The twofold character of the nomos is captured in Cover's account of its locus and source. The nomos exists in and arises out of discourse. Discourse supplies a normative meaning by creating "history and destiny, beginning and end, explanation and purpose."[76] Discourse cannot be private; it requires a community. The scope of the community of discourse defines the scope of the universe that is the nomos.

Cover's nomos rests securely on the familiar model of the discursive community. The nomos represents the discourse on values that constitutes the history of a particular community. That history provides an "explanation and purpose" for its past and present social life. A community that looks to a unique, normative past will understand itself as carrying an inherited set of meanings into the future. History and destiny are inseparable.

Individuals, according to Cover, do not create values through private, subjective choices; they discover their values in a universe of which they are a part and in which they are never alone. "The intelligibility of normative behavior inheres in the communal character of the narratives that provide the context of that behavior. Any person who lived an entirely idiosyncratic normative life would be quite mad."[77] The communality, and so objectivity, of the normative universe for Cover is disclosed in his constant return to the idea of discourse and variations on discursive action: speech, myth, narrative, communication, and signification.[78]

Cover writes, "The *nomos* that I have described requires no state"; but the legal system of the state nevertheless requires a nomos. Like every social practice, law has a meaning or, on Cover's view, many meanings, which explains why the law is as it is. Meaning can arise only within a nomos. "[L]aw and narrative are inseparably related. Every prescription is insistent in its demand to be located in discourse—to be supplied with history and destiny, beginning and end, explanation and purpose." Indeed, law is nothing more than "a resource in signification," a device for communicating meaning within a shared nomos. A complex society is, for Cover, one in which the legal norms perform a multiplicity of signifying acts as they are given meaning in a number of discursive communities. Fiss's professional community is, according to Cover, just one nomos among many, all of which construct the meaning of law.[79]

This superabundance of law, or, more precisely, of legal meaning, creates the problem of constitutional authority from the perspective of the state. Cover describes that problem as not the creation but the limitation of law. Without limits, the jurisgenerative forces that create meaning would create anarchy. "It is the problem of the multiplicity of meaning— the fact that never only one but always many worlds are created by the too fertile forces of jurisgenesis—that leads at once to the imperial virtues and the imperial model of world maintenance."[80] A common text is not itself a constraint on the construction of meaning; it is an invitation to the jurisgenerative forces of the community.

Cover has in mind the plurality of sects that give meaning to the common text of the Bible. The text is the starting point of interpretation, the beginning, not the end, of meaning.[81] The same creative forces are at work in the law. Constraint on the potential anarchy caused by jurisgenesis must come from outside the text and outside the process by which meaning is given to it. No interpretation is authoritative as an interpretation; no single meaning has more authority than any other. Authority is not built into the structure of the nomos; more precisely, the claim of authority appears legitimate only to those within the community. This same conflict between internal and external perspectives undermined the work of the new republicans; no measure is common to those inside and those outside the interpretive, self-governing community.

For Cover, the imperial virtues of world maintenance are necessarily jurispathic. Their function is to control the anarchy of legal meanings. They cannot do this by creating an authoritative meaning, because all meaning is a function of the nomos:

The precepts we call law are marked off by a social control over their provenance, their mode of articulation, and their effects. But the narratives that create and reveal the patterns of commitment, resistance, and understanding . . . are radically uncontrolled. They are subject to no formal hierarchical ordering, no centralized, authoritative provenance, no necessary pattern of acquiescence. . . . [A]n interdependent system of obligation may be enforced, but the very patterns of meaning that give rise to effective or ineffective social control are to be left to the domain of Babel.[82]

Thus, the meaning of every legal norm, including constitutional norms, is "essentially contested."[83] The Court may have a nomos of its own, but that just makes it one among many communities. It acts "in that respect, in an unprivileged fashion."[84] Its privileged place of authority comes not from a unique capacity to create meaning but from a unique power to deny other meanings. Elsewhere, Cover writes that "legal interpretation occurs on a battlefield . . . which entails the instruments both of war and of poetry. Indeed, constitutional law is . . . more fundamentally connected to the war than it is to the poetry."[85] Discursive communities are diverse; they are not hierarchical. "The meaning judges thus give to the law . . . is not privileged, not necessarily worth any more than that of the resister they put in jail."[86]

Cover offers an ironic reversal of the political theory of *Carolene Products*. The Constitution does not save the discrete and insular community from the defects of the political process; rather, the discrete and insular community saves the Constitution from the burden of meaninglessness. The pursuit in *Carolene Products* of an ahistorical, homogeneous politics of equality represents not the virtue of the legal system but its vice. *Carolene Products* is little more than a benign form of the jurispathic state. The nonbenign form is the violence that supports authority. Both forms come together in the Court: "Because of the violence they command, judges characteristically do not create law, but kill it. Theirs is the jurispathic office."[87] The choice is between the creative anarchy of meaning and the violence of authority.

There is no easy way out of this conflict. There may be no way at all. If meaning arises only within the diverse nomoi, then a national politics—and so a national political community—always rests upon the violence of the jurispathic. The cost of statehood is the destruction of meaning. Cover describes this destruction as the exercise of the imperial virtues of the state, but it is hard to see his use of the term "virtues" as more than ironic. Political life in the modern nation-state cannot preserve individual integrity, because it must destroy a range of meanings that give shape to individual identity. The individual who appears in the nation-state is just as much a product of violent abstraction from the community of meaning as the state itself. Indeed, individual and state are linked, for the violence of the jurispathic will always appear simultaneously as the freeing of the citizen from the burdens of local, communal history.[88] A world of individual, autonomous agents is a world in which a central political authority dominates all other communities. The public order of the free, private individual is the national state, which is the political world of the jurispathic.

Cover's world of jurisgenesis is closer to the feudal world of sect, family, and guild than to the liberal world of free individuals interacting within a nation-state. It is no accident that his key example of a meaningful political life is provided by the Mennonite community. The vision of the autonomous, private individual espoused by modern liberals is at the center of Cover's attack upon the state.

In spite of the shock to modern political sensibilities, Cover's narrative of anarchy is faithful to the theory of discursive community that is so powerfully attractive to contemporary legal theorists. He alone puts the juxtaposition of anarchy and authority, of community and law, at the heart of his work. Unless interpretation can somehow be made to support authority, Cover's accusation that the work of the courts is the death of law signals the limits of the usefulness of the interpretive approach. Ronald Dworkin's work represents just such an effort to ground legal authority in the interpretive community.

Ronald Dworkin: Authority and the True Community

Dworkin's comprehensive jurisprudential work, *Law's Empire*, places community at the foundation of the law. Community, he says, is the conceptual ground of interpretation. If law is an interpretive exercise, as he argues, community is the conceptual ground of law. Community also legitimates law. Without what Dworkin calls a "true community," the commands of law will not provide a normative ground for action. Only in a true community do citizens have a moral obligation to comply with law. Community, then, makes law possible, as well as legitimate. The move from a community of interpretation to a true community is Dworkin's attempt to move from a theory of meaning to a theory of authority. Unfortunately, the community of interpretation undermines the special claims to authority of the true community.

Interpretation and Community. Dworkin's positive account of law begins at a familiar point: law is an interpretive concept because the law is always understood as the meaningful product of a creative act. Meaning does not inhere in an interpreted object independently of the interpreter. There is no world of meaningful objects to which interpreting subjects are subsequently introduced. The process of interpretation always joins subject and object. More precisely, subject and object—including citizen and social practice—are partial abstractions from a prior whole, which is the creation of meaning through interpretation.

The interpretive attitude toward a social practice, Dworkin argues, can only take hold in a community of a certain kind. He lays out the conditions of such a community in a description of the three "stages" of interpretation. First, there must be substantial agreement on the "rules and standards" that inform the pattern of behavior to be interpreted.[89] These are the practices and the beliefs about those practices that shape the ordinary understanding of the community. A community that exhibited no consistent patterns of behavior would not offer an object of interpretation but only a field for political invention. This would be the proverbial state of nature. Either moral and political theory would meet no resistance—they would write on a blank slate—or theory would be overcome by the resistance of anarchy. Interpretation, then, presupposes a "preinterpretive" community, which is that pattern of social practices and beliefs in which a group of people find themselves already located. Among the practices understood and followed in this preinterpretive way are those identified as law.

To say that a pattern of social practices is preinterpretive is not to say that it is uninterpreted: "[S]ome kind of interpretation is necessary even at this stage. Social rules do not carry identifying labels."[90] Only to an interpreting subject does social behavior appear as a practice putting into effect a common rule. Someone who could find no unifying rule would see chaotic or random behavior. Even to identify a social practice as an object for explicit interpretation requires interpretation. Preinterpretive practice, therefore, does not describe a behavioral regularity without conceptualization but a social life in which the interpretive attitude has not been made explicit.

In the second stage of interpretation, the interpretive attitude becomes explicit. It does so in response to conflict, which may be over the meaning of a practice or over what the practice requires. An interpretive attitude takes hold fully when both dimensions—meaning and practice—are open issues. Practice must be responsive to meaning, just as meaning must be responsive to practice. Reciprocity between meaning and practice, interpretation and the object of interpretation, characterizes the "interpretive attitude."

Interpretation exists in this tension between historically given practice and normative intelligibility. An interpretation must "fit" the social practice; it must "count as an interpretation of it rather than the invention of something new." Yet an interpretation is not an explanation of the causes of the practice, as if the practice were a natural phenomenon. It is, instead, a justification of the practice. In isolating the most important elements of the practice and explaining how they contribute to a valuable end, a justification offers a perspective from which to criticize the details of the practice.[91]

The third and final stage of interpretation is the reconstruction of social practice to better serve the justification offered. A justification is offered not only as an explanation but as a ground for reform. The complete interpenetration of practice and meaning is given expression in Dworkin's careful choice of words: "[T]here must be a postinterpretive or reforming stage, at which [the interpreter] adjusts his sense of what the practice 'really' requires so as better to serve the justification he accepts at the interpretive stage."[92]

The interpretive attitude, in short, denies that a practice was really something before the act of interpretation. Rather, the nature of the practice is itself a product of this reciprocal relation between meaning and practice. There is no way to get to the object prior to or apart from the interpretation. The reformist stage of interpretation is not a separate moment of reform that comes after an interpretive inquiry into a social practice. Reform is part of interpretation, the product of which is the social practice of a community.

Dworkin's emphasis on reform as part, and not consequence, of interpretation is a reminder that the analysis of the stages of interpretation is merely an explanatory device. The stages do not represent a temporal sequence but a conceptual structure. The identification and explication of this structure forces a reconsideration of the place and character of community. Community, understood as a shared set of practices and beliefs, was the starting point of the analysis. It provided the preinterpretive basis for the possibility of an interpretive attitude toward created objects, including law. At the end of the analysis, it becomes clear that community is itself an interpretive concept.

Community is not separate from interpretation; it does not provide an independent, objective foundation for interpretation. Community is simultaneously the condition of interpretation of social practices and the end of interpretation. Like Plato's Ideas, which inform discourse before they are set forth as objects of discourse, or Kant's categories, which structure understanding before they are understood, Dworkin's community informs interpretation before it is itself the object of interpretation. If community is both the origin and the end of interpretation, it must play a unique role in Dworkin's theory.

Because community is the product of interpretation, it cannot validate interpretation—as Bickel thought it could. One can no more get to the real community prior to interpretation than one can get to the real painting before any interpretation. Community does not exist as a historical and geographical entity independent of the subject who understands it. Community exists only in the citizen's imagination—the faculty by which object and value, practice and meaning, are combined.

Integrity and Community. Dworkin identifies the preinterpretive understanding of the practice of law as not using force "no matter how useful that would be to ends in view, no matter how beneficial or noble these ends, except as licensed or required by individual rights and responsibilities flowing from past political decisions about when collective force is justified." An interpretation of law must therefore explain how a legal judgment "provides a justification for the use of collective power against individual citizens or groups."[93] Dworkin takes up the task by offering an interpretation that focuses on the virtue of "integrity." Law is an expression of integrity as a political virtue.

In its simplest form, integrity is the virtue of "treat[ing] like cases alike." Integrity is a second-order virtue, attaching to other political or moral virtues. Dworkin mentions, in particular, fairness, justice, and procedural due process.[94] These are substantive values, about which there are substantial disagreements in traditional moral and political theory. Integrity is a response to the possibility of such disagreements. Agents have integrity when they rely upon the same understanding of a substantive value in diverse circumstances. They have integrity with respect to justice, for example, if they act on a single understanding of justice in all of their interactions with others.

A political community has integrity when it applies its best understanding of justice, fairness, and procedural due process in a consistent fashion, despite the presence of moral conflict within the community. A state would lack integrity if it were redistributive one week and libertarian the next or if it resolved conflicts over procedural due process by assigning juries in some cases but not in others and did not justify the different requirements of procedural fairness in each.

Integrity in adjudication requires judges to act as representatives of a community that has the virtue of integrity. To do so requires that they understand the community as a single moral agent. For this reason, Dworkin writes, "[p]olitical integrity assumes a particularly deep personification of the community or state."[95] Judges must give an account of the principles of justice, fairness, and due process that operate in the community as if the principles were the work of a single actor putting a single moral view in place. The account must offer a justification of past practice, which is then juxtaposed to the facts of the current controversy. The result of this process is a statement of what the law is in this situation.

To interpret law as integrity, then, is to assert that the state expresses itself through law as a single moral agent. The personification of the state reveals a fundamental dualism in a citizen's moral vision. On the one hand, citizens can understand themselves as individuals who occasionally contribute to a group decision. From this point of view, the community is an aggregate of individual actors, each morally accountable only for his or her own actions. On the other hand, a public act can be understood as the moral responsibility of the community considered as a moral agent in its own right. On this point of view, individual responsibility arises from membership in the community. Citizens take this point of view when they feel responsible for public actions against which they may have voted or, even more dramatically, for public actions that preceded their own membership in the state.[96]

Different areas of experience are dominated by one moral point of view or the other. To interpret law, with its deep personification of community, as integrity is to argue that the possibility of law requires the communitarian point of view. That the state can be morally identified as prior to, and larger than, the sum of its parts allows it to be seen as continuous through time, despite its changing membership. Integrity makes not only law but political history possible.

Dworkin is describing the identification possible between an individual and the state. The moral independence of the state is essentially connected to the moral dependence of the individual. This moral point of view appeared in my discussion of the model of organic maintenance in chapter 2. Within that model, citizens understand national history as an expression of their individual identity, regardless of any actual connection to that history. They hold themselves responsible, and are held responsible, for the actions of the state, even when they can do, or could have done, little about them. Dworkin claims that this personal identification with the historical state exists wherever there is a system of law; it is not limited to a particular moment in the development of legal discourse.[97] When citizens take this attitude, the personified community is understood as an expression of individual political identity. Thus, integrity is central to the ability to see political life as self-government: "The ideal [of self-government] needs integrity . . . for a citizen cannot treat himself as the author of a collection of laws that are inconsistent in principle, nor can he see that collection as sponsored by any Rousseauian general will."[98]

Both interpretation and integrity rest on the idea of a community of discourse, which dissolves the distinction between the one and the many. Community, Dworkin warns, does not represent a metaphysical entity but a conceptual structure; it does not exist apart from the interpretive judgment that creates history through integrity. Community exists only in the imagination of the interpreter, in the internal dialogue of the interpreter: "[S]ocial interpretation [is] a conversation with oneself."[99] There may be as many communities as there are stories that can be told with integrity. There must be, for there is no way to get to the community-in-itself as an objective source of political legitimacy.

Legitimacy and Community. According to Dworkin, the legitimacy of the use of coercive authority by the state is dependent upon the moral claim made by law: "Do citizens have genuine moral obligations just in virtue of law?" If there is no moral obligation to obey the law, then there is no moral ground for enforcing compliance. Dworkin argues that the moral ground of law must be found in what he calls "obligations of community"—responsibilities that arise from the individual's understanding of himself or herself as maintaining a "role" within a social order. Such obligations are found, for example, among family members, friends, and colleagues. In each case, moral obligation derives from a complex history of association, which cannot be reduced to an expression of either consent or abstract right.[100]

Participation in such a social order is both positive and normative. Much of what members believe they ought to do, according to Dworkin, arises from the factual circumstances in which they find themselves. Moral obligations run to members of one's own family, for example, simply because of what it means to be a member of that family. As a social practice, family is simultaneously an object and a product of interpretation. Familial obligation may be the subject of intense debate, even within a particular family. Nevertheless, each member has an obligation to act consistently on the basis of his or her own best understanding of what it means to be a member of the family. Dworkin emphasizes the coincidence of "is" and "ought" in these communities by describing the moral obligation that they generate as a "natural duty."[101]

Dworkin's jurisprudential strategy is to place the question of the legitimacy of the law within a similar context of obligation that is "natural" without being universal (it is not an abstract theory of natural law) and particularistic without being contractual (it is not a theory of consent). Accordingly, he must first specify the qualities of community that generate a natural duty or obligation of role. Second, he must demonstrate that a political community can possess those qualities. Finally, he must demonstrate that the kind of political community that possesses those qualities interprets law as integrity: "[A] political society that accepts integrity as a political virtue thereby becomes a special form of community, special in a way that promotes its moral authority to assume and deploy a monopoly of coercive force."[102] Dworkin argues each of these propositions, but the total argument is hardly a success.

First, he argues that obligations of role can arise only in communities that meet four conditions. The community must demonstrate a concern that (1) is special to members of that community, (2) runs "directly from each member to each other member," (3) reaches to the general well-being of each member, and (4) is egalitarian. A community that meets these conditions is a "true community."[103]

Second, he argues that a political community that accepts what he calls the "model of principle" meets these four conditions. In this community, political life is "a theater of debate about which principles the community should adopt as a system, which view it should take of justice, fairness, and due process."[104] Here he is describing the discursive community at the heart of contemporary theory.

Finally, he argues that this community of principle understands law as integrity: "A community of principle accepts integrity."[105] The whole argument can then be run backwards: to interpret law as integrity is to create a community of principle, which is a true community within which legal obligations coincide with moral obligations of role.

The weakness of this argument begins with Dworkin's specification of the conditions a community must satisfy to generate obligations of role. He argues that a particular conception of justice, including an equal concern for the well-being of each individual, is such a condition.[106] This claim remains unfounded. Worse, the claims for a true community threaten to trivialize the theory of interpretation and community that he has built.

The theory of legitimacy that one would expect from Dworkin would focus on the collapse of the distinction between the individual and the community. This collapse is central to his account of both interpretation and political integrity. Dworkin suggests just such a theory of legitimacy when he writes that "[p]olitical obligation is . . . not just a matter of obeying the discrete political decisions of the community . . . [but rather of] fidelity to a scheme of principle each citizen has a responsibility to identify, ultimately for himself, as his community's scheme."[107] Because the community does not exist apart from the individual's imaginative construction of it as a meaningful, normative entity, the question of legitimacy does not appear as a question of obligation to a social order that confronts

COMMUNITY IN CONTEMPORARY THEORY

the citizen from outside the self. The theory of legitimacy rests upon the claim that the individual, by acting as a member of the state, gives expression to his or her own identity.

The citizen's self-understanding is deeply embedded in a historical web of roles that make up the community. There can be no separate moment in which the individual's associational role is morally evaluated because there is no way to get beyond the interpretive construction of community. This idea is behind Dworkin's statement that integrity "fuses citizens' moral and political lives."[108] That is, people do not first make themselves as moral subjects and then come to politics possessing a moral identity against which to measure the demands of law. Obligations of legal role are constructed in part out of beliefs about justice and fairness.

If this is a correct reading of the theory of legitimacy implicit—and at times explicit—in Dworkin's account of interpretation and community, then Dworkin's implicit theory undermines his explicit claims for liberal egalitarianism in a true community. Dworkin's account of interpretation and community provides a theory of legitimacy from an internal perspective. It explains why the law appears legitimate to a member of the community. It does not explain why or whether the law is legitimate from an external perspective. Ultimately, however, Dworkin is not satisfied with the internal account. He tries to press the theory further in order to provide an external account of legitimacy. But to do that, he must justify the authority of law in a way that his theory cannot support.

Nothing in the implicit theory of legitimacy suggests a particular moral and political life. Associative communities that support obligations of role are not generally noted for their commitment to individual equality. Obligations of role traditionally have had more to do with understanding one's place in a social hierarchy—"my station and its duties"—than with a commitment to individual equality.[109]

The difference between an internal and an external perspective is clear in Dworkin's example of the traditional family, in which he immediately discovers a conflict between justice and the obligations of role a dutiful daughter may confront.[110] Dworkin sides with justice, saying that only a community that supports an egalitarian interpretation of justice can sustain the identity of individual and community that is the ground of legitimacy. From the internal perspective, this is simply not true: for centuries families have sustained obligations of role without an egalitarian understanding of justice. To support this claim, Dworkin needs a theory of justice that provides an external measure of the community. Yet Dworkin has already argued that justice is simply another interpretive concept, grounded in the same conceptual account of community as law. In the end, there is only conflict among communities; there is no neutral or objective perspective, because there is no escape from interpretation.

Dworkin's move toward an Archimedean point of justice is again implicit in the attitude he takes toward how a community treats a non-member. Communities are discrete; their identity is formed in part by opposition to nonmembers. This distinction between appropriate behavior within and outside the community is always an important part of the self-understanding of a community.[111] Dworkin says that justice provides a moral standard against which to measure the communal attitude toward outsiders.[112] But from where does this idea of justice come? If justice is an interpretive concept, then it, too, arises from the imaginative bringing of meaning to social practice, which is the construction of community. On this view, there is no abstract definition of justice by which to measure the practices of a community either within or without its boundaries. There are only competing communities of meaning: "Our lives are rich because they are complex in the layers and character of the communities we inhabit."[113] Nor is there a neutral perspective from which to evaluate the whole. If this is lacking, and Dworkin's theory of interpretation does seem to imply its lack, then he has not explained why the community called the state should be allowed coercively to enforce its particular concept of justice. At this point, Dworkin needs more than an account of how history is possible, which he offers; he needs an account of why the conditions that make history possible lead to a particular historical outcome. Such an account would explain why the liberal idea of justice is the end of history.

Dworkin's account of the conceptual conditions of interpretation is stronger than his argument for a liberal concept of justice. By insisting on an external measure, Dworkin risks trivializing his own account of the role of community in interpretation. The concept of community that he describes is not contingent upon the emergence of the liberal idea of individual equality. It marks instead a conceptual structure that makes human history possible. History as an imaginative construction is dependent upon just those features of a community that Dworkin identifies in setting forth the conditions of interpretation.

Because the members of a community generate their history through the imaginative construction of meaning, they always find themselves in communities that entail obligations of role. Participation, which is based on neither will nor reason alone, is the ground of legitimacy. It is why members accept the communal use of force both within the community and against other communities. Indeed, Dworkin's account would be stronger had he thought to link the internal coercion sanctioned by law with the external coercion expressed in war. Force, in both cases, is an expression of individual identity. It is not surprising, therefore, to find Dworkin speaking the language of Rousseau: like Rousseau, he suggests that a community can force its members to be free. Legitimacy, on this view, precedes justice, just as the conditions of interpretation precede any particular community.

This answer to the problem of legitimacy is hardly a reason for optimism in constitutional theory. Instead, Dworkin's answer exposes the limits of this interpretive turn. The felt ability to measure community against justice makes each citizen a potential stranger to the community once again. Dworkin appeals to that critical ability, but his explanatory apparatus cannot account for it. Or, even worse, the same apparatus can be applied to justice, in which case the critique becomes the expression of yet another interpretation. Interpretations multiply, with no ground for hierarchically ordering them. Authority and community split apart as multiple possibilities for interpretation emerge. Dworkin suppresses this potential anarchy by appealing to an idea of a true community, yet the authority of that community remains unsupported.

That Dworkin stumbles here demonstrates again what has been evident in the analysis of each of the communitarians: a theory of community cannot provide an adequate ground of authority. Instead of speaking directly of authority, Dworkin speaks of legitimacy, but the point is the same. The argument for legitimacy is designed to ground the authority of the legal rules of a particular community. A ground, however, is precisely what communitarian theories cannot provide.

While Dworkin provides the most compelling and analytically complete account of community, he comes no closer to providing an adequate account of authority. Each new communitarian attempts to understand— most attempt to justify—the authority of law through a theory of discourse. The most such an account can provide, however, is an account of the appearance of authority within a particular discursive community. It cannot provide an argument for the authority of law to anyone outside that community or even to whoever leaves the community by assuming a critical attitude toward its claims. That each person can take this attitude and question the justice of law reveals the need for an Archimedean point or, as I will argue in the conclusion, for an understanding of a community of critical inquiry that is not bound to the state.

The End of
Constitutional
Theory

Constitutional theory begins with the idea that the Constitution should be constructed on the basis of political science and ends with the idea that constitutional authority arises from a community of discourse. These ideas are the beginning and end of a single discourse on the nature of self-government. To understand the dynamic character of that discourse requires understanding the problem that temporality poses for the idea of self-government. Constitutional theory is the discipline that reflects upon the relation between the idea of self-government and the problem of temporality. The stages in the development of constitutional theory represent the variety of conceptual models within which the joining of time and self-government becomes possible.

Three issues require additional consideration. First, my intellectual history of constitutionalism has focused on a level of analysis that I have called conceptual models of order. What is the theoretical status of these models that justifies organizing the argument around them? Second, the single conversation about U.S. constitutionalism that I have described develops by moving from one conceptual model of order to another. Of what significance is this pattern of development? Third, although I may have demonstrated that no contemporary theorist adequately links authority and community, what is the basis of my claim that they cannot be linked? This claim restates my assertion that constitutional theory has reached an end. Explaining the disjunction of community and authority should clarify this point as well.

The Meaning of a Conceptual Model of Order

A conceptual model of order is an organizing pattern of thought that occupies a position somewhere between what Thomas Kuhn calls a paradigm and what Michel Foucault calls an episteme. For Kuhn, a paradigm is an example of scientific practice that provides a model which gives rise to a coherent tradition of scientific research. A Kuhnian paradigm founds a community of scientific inquiry and sets its substantive agenda. For Kuhn, paradigms are not abstract patterns but rich scientific explanations.

For Foucault, an episteme is a conceptual framework that explains what counts as knowledge across the full variety of contemporaneous fields of research. The explanatory ambition of epistemes is much broader for Foucault than the explanatory ambition of paradigms is for Kuhn. An episteme operates at a much higher level of abstraction. Like Kuhn's paradigms, however, epistemes are attempts to characterize the epistemological worldview of a period. Both Kuhn and Foucault are responding to the fundamental insight that the terms within which experience is organized and explained change over time. Both understand that to speak about the history of knowledge, one needs large-scale models by which to measure sameness and difference. Not only does the substantive content of knowledge change over time, but the idea of what counts as knowledge changes.

The idea of a conceptual model of order responds to this same need. The use of conceptual models is an effort to focus on the historical period as the appropriate object of inquiry. The idea of a conceptual model of order, however, operates at a different level of abstraction from either Kuhn's paradigms or Foucault's epistemes. It has neither the substantive, detailed richness of a paradigm nor the sweeping generality of an episteme. More important, the models upon which I rely do not share the contingent character of these alternatives. In spite of the difference in the levels of generality at which Kuhn and Foucault operate, their organizing patterns of thought cannot be separated from the pattern of historical practice within which they are embedded.

In this respect, the idea of a conceptual model of order is closer to the Kantian idea of a category. The models I identify are frameworks of thought that are constantly available. They inform ordinary experience before they provide a structure for theoretical explanation. The models themselves are not dependent upon historical experience; they make it possible. Accordingly, they are not the possession or product of esoteric theory. They do not depend upon developments in the sciences or in the theory of knowledge. To understand the model of making, for example, requires only an understanding of the everyday experience of an object as an artifact. Similarly, the models of maintenance, growth, and community are rooted in the commonplaces of everyday life. Theory enriches these models by elaborating upon their terms and explaining how they operate in certain contexts.

Unlike Foucault's episteme, a conceptual model of order characterizes only some aspect of the intellectual experience of an age. The models of order operate independently in diverse areas of experience. For example, to understand the political order in terms of the model of making does not suggest that making is the model within which all other contemporary social phenomena are construed. Someone might understand the Constitution as an object to be made yet take an attitude of organic maintenance with respect to religion and understand the scientific community within the model of growth. Indeed, different aspects of political experience can be simultaneously understood within different models.

A conceptual model defines the questions asked about the phenomena and sets the limits on what counts as an answer. The terms within which disagreements occur are set by these underlying commonalities. For this reason, in identifying and describing conceptual models of order, I often look to the antagonists of a period to discover what they share. The most basic agreement among antagonistic constitutional theorists is in their understanding of how the Constitution constitutes a community.

For example, I argued in chapter 1 that the constitutionalism of the founders relied on the model of making. They understood the Constitution as an object to be made by political artisans, whose work was informed by an abstract set of ideas. These three terms—artisan, object, and idea—constitute the model of making, but the model does not specify the content of any of these terms. For the framers, that content arose from certain beliefs about political science and political legitimacy. The use of the model of making as an organizing pattern of thought suggests where disputes, as well as agreements, might be found within the discourse of the period. The framers, for example, generally agreed over the identity of the appropriate political artisans: the citizenry in general. At the same time, they vigorously disagreed over the content of the true or correct political science. In chapter 2, I argued that the constitutionalism of the pre–Civil War period revealed a general commitment to an organic model of maintenance. This directed attention to the founding and required the development of a political mythology of popular sovereignty, linking politics and blood. In spite of the consensus that political identity must be sought in the moment of constitutional birth, there was violent disagreement over the meaning of the founding.

The problem of order addressed in this book concerns the temporal experience that the individual achieves in and through the state. Each model of order presents a conceptual framework for understanding how something either maintains or fails to maintain its identity over time. The two simplest models by which to answer this question of identity are those of the artifact and the organism.

Artifacts occupy time as instantiations of ideas. They represent the organization of temporal experience through an intentional act of an artisan who finds a measure for his or her action outside the experience of specific objects and events in time and space. The dependence of the artifact upon artisan and idea means that artifacts do not maintain themselves well over time, for time always presents the problem of decay. No idea can be perfectly expressed in the changing matter of space and time; no artisan can perfectly capture an idea in a work product. To maintain an artifact requires constant recourse to the idea that it represents, a constant remaking on the basis of the original, abstract pattern. This dependence of the artifact upon the artisan does not by any means suggest that the model of making can be used only for objects the making of which occurs within ordinary experience. Nature is understood as an artifact in some of the oldest stories of creation. In these stories, a god functions as the artisan mediating between the idea and the objects of temporal experience. In the beginning was the word, but it took a god to give it shape in space and time. Without ongoing divine intervention, the world will decay and return to its original state of chaos.

The idea of organic unity represents an entirely different understanding of the organization of temporal experience. Unlike the artifact, which requires an artisan to mediate between timeless form and time-bound matter, the organism maintains its own identity through a changing material experience. To be alive is to be self-replicating, not just in the sense of reproducing the self in the other but in the sense of maintaining a constant identity of form within the body. Ideal form for an organism cannot be separated from its temporal embodiment. Separation of form from matter is not an abstract ideal but disintegration and death. The idea of organic maintenance must not be confused with a post-Darwin idea of organic evolution. The model of organic unity is not a model of change. On the contrary, it is a model of the maintenance of form in the face of a temporal threat of chaos.

Just as the model of making is not limited to everyday artifacts, the model of organic maintenance is not limited to natural organisms. Social institutions demonstrate a constancy of formal identity in time, despite changes in their material constituents. They are self-perpetuating, relying on no external subject to mediate between form and matter. Finally, they are self-authenticating, referring only to their own past—what they have been—for a measure of what they will be.

To the ideas of the artifact and the organism alike, time threatens chaos. Neither idea allows a positive place for change; both see change as the opposite of order. In this sense, both represent efforts to stop time. Time need not be understood as essentially chaotic, however. Change can itself be understood as an organizing principle. The model of growth expresses temporality as an intelligible principle. On this model, the threat of chaotic disorder comes from stasis, from being changeless in a changing world. Just as the model of making requires a way to measure ideal form, so the model of growth requires a normative measure of progress. Growth cannot be distinguished from change without some such measure. But what that norm will be is not determined by the model. The openness to diverse measures means that this model, too, can be used to organize diverse areas of experience; social and individual life, as well as nature, can be understood on the model of growth.

Community represents a distinctly different model of order. Although its differences run in a number of directions, they all follow from its self-reflexive character. The other models can be applied to the experience of the self. Individuals can experience the self as a made object—made either by another or by themselves, as when someone decides to learn something or to gain a certain proficiency through the deliberate creation of a habit. Similarly, the self can be understood as a self-sustaining organism or as a growing person. In each instance, the self is approached as just another object to be understood. A gap remains between the knowing subject and the object known.

The model of community arises when the subject realizes that the known object is a product of interpretation, that no meaning exists apart from the discursive act that gives expression to meaning. With the realization that the self is simultaneously the source and product of all these patterns of discourse, self and other collapse into a single whole—the community. Community is the domain of discourse from which all meaning emerges. The self no longer appears as a subject grasping external objects. Rather, the self is in a continuous process of self-creation through meaning-giving discursive activity.

This model of community requires yet another understanding of temporal experience: time now appears as a dimension of meaning. As such, it cannot be an external condition on meaning. It is instead a product of the same discursive community that is the source of all meaning. Time is no longer a threat to be overcome, nor is the present dependent upon the past, as in the model of growth. Rather, the past is dependent on a present act of discourse. Temporality derives from the construction of a meaningful history; it has no meaning apart from that interpretive construction.

Just as the other models can be applied to a wide range of phenomena, so can the model of community. For example, discussions of contemporary physics often appear strikingly similar to work in contemporary constitutional theory. What are ordinarily experienced as objects in space and time are now understood as the products of interpretive acts within a discursive community. Nature, like political history, is the result of, and not a prior condition on, the interpretive acts of a community.

When deployed in constitutional theory, each model produces a distinctly different understanding of the self of self-government and of the relation between the individual citizen and the intergenerational project of constitutional governance. Under the model of making, the citizen is a political artisan giving expression to a science of politics. Under the model of organic maintenance, the citizen is the child of the founding fathers whose current task is to preserve the constitutional inheritance and to pass it on to future generations. The citizen is part of a transtemporal organic whole, which in U.S. constitutionalism is the popular sovereign. Under the model of growth, the real Constitution is the unwritten evolving pattern of reason in history, which precedes any particular act of constitutional construction and links the individual citizen to the larger body of Anglo-American political and legal history. The task of the citizen is no longer maintenance of the past; it is the mature realization of the immature efforts of prior generations. Finally, under the model of community, the citizen is a member of a discursive community that constitutes personal identity and political order. Citizen and Constitution are two perspectives on the same discourse.

Although the abstract models are independent of American political experience, or any other political experience, their content in the history of U.S. constitutionalism has been determined by a substantive conflict that reflects what has been a major theme in political thought since the Enlightenment. That theme is the opposition between reason and will as the foundation of the political order: Is the modern state founded on consent or on a science of government?

At the beginning and end of the development of U.S. constitutionalism, a synthesis of reason and will occurs. In between, that synthesis dissolves, and a dynamic of opposition emerges. Organic maintenance is marked by will: constitutional self-government requires the preservation of the intent of the founders. Growth is marked by reason: constitutionalism is the evolving path of reason in the history of the state. The crisis that follows the end of the model of growth is marked by a reemergence of will as the single source of moral and political values.

Who, then, is the U.S. citizen? The answer depends on when the question is asked. It also depends on who is asked. There has been no single answer, and there surely is no single correct answer.

Dialectic and the Self-Conscious Creation of Meaning

The U.S. constitutional experience is a rich source for research into the conceptual structure of the understanding of political life because it has been self-consciously deliberative in its approach. Constitutional theory shares with the very first inquiry into the possibility of a just political order, Plato's *Republic*, the notion that political life is a function of speech about political life. Plato begins his effort at political construction with words that aptly describe the American attitude toward constitutional construction: "Come now . . . let's make a city in speech from the beginning." For two hundred years, Americans have been discussing this city in speech.

The demarcation of a number of distinct conceptual models within this discourse raises the obvious question of whether they are exhaustive. Demonstrating that there are no alternatives is not possible. One might, for example, consider a model of causal sequence as it operates in scientific accounts. This appears to be yet another model for arranging temporal experience. Whether it can explain meaningful experience within time is more doubtful. Surely no social institution can be understood as the product of an endless and unbroken sequence of cause and effect. For this same reason, reconciling determinism within a causal sequence with an idea of personal responsibility has been a problem in moral theory. Not until the causal sequence is overcome through a meaningful act—for example, an act of making—can history be experienced as a domain of value.

Whatever the problems of causality as a conceptual model of order, nothing follows with respect to a claim of exclusivity for the models I have described. Support for such a claim can come only from an inquiry into the relations among the models. Although that inquiry falls short of a proof of exclusivity, the sequence of development that appears in constitutional history has a comprehensive logic.

The sequence is all the more noticeable given that the models are all available simultaneously in ordinary experience. Simultaneity is possible not just across domains of activity—for example, the church and the state—but even within the single domain of political meaning. For example, the model of the organic state within which individual identity is understood as part of a transtemporal popular sovereign appears to be an aspect of political experience that can be called upon at virtually any time. Although some individuals may be willing to sacrifice themselves for an abstract idea, only the organic model can explain the willingness of masses of individuals to give their bodies to the state. Only on this model is it possible to understand how the individual's death for the political order can be an affirmation of personal identity. That the state can regularly call for personal sacrifice as an instrument of policy suggests the enduring power of this model. Less dramatically, the state in one aspect or another may always present a problem of making or making anew, whether the problem addressed is welfare policy or the construction of an equitable and efficient tax code.

Simultaneity notwithstanding, the inquiry into the development of constitutional theory suggests an ordered progression in the appeal to the various conceptual models of order. One model rather than another characterizes the constitutional theory of a particular period. The other models do not disappear entirely. There is no mechanism for removing old patterns of thought from the constitutional corpus, and people inevitably repeat arguments once they have entered the discussion. But by focusing on the dominant structure of thought in a given period, one can see significant changes. In what sense, it must be asked, do the changes represent progress or even a progression?

The constitutional experience begins with a call to engage in a new making. Only on the model of making can a clean break with the past and the beginning of something new be announced. Revolutionaries, once they have destroyed the old state, must become political artisans. Then they seek to put in place the very ideas upon which their critique of the established regime rested. In the period of the founding, political order was an artifactual construction, based upon a common deliberation. The object of that deliberation was conceived as the truth of political science. The task of the first generation was to become political artisans who could mediate between that abstract truth and the actual state. History lay in the future: it was given a new shape by this act of making.

Making, however, is a model of order that can dominate constitutional theory only in moments understood as beginnings. As long as constitutional thought remains dominated by the model of making, the state remains in a condition of revolution. The products of the past make no special claim. At best, they can be reevaluated on the basis of contemporary political science. They have no special privilege but represent one among a variety of possibilities that threaten chaos unless ordered through the mediating activity of the political artisan.

To make a state successfully requires transcending the model of making. The political artisan must recede, and the state must maintain its own identity through time. This idea is given symbolic expression in stories of the departure of the lawgivers—for example, Solon and Moses—from the ongoing community. In the United States, the movement from making to maintenance required the emergence of a new understanding of the Constitution among the citizenry. No longer were citizens participants in political construction. The inherited constitutional order was no longer a problem to be evaluated by a fresh appeal to political science. Instead, citizens had to understand themselves as the inheritors of an order that made a claim upon them. The political order was not a product of their deliberation and choice; rather, they had to understand themselves as its product.

The separation of the citizen-artisan from the object of his art, the Constitution—a separation that is central to the model of making—must be overcome for the state to have a continuous historical existence. Myth serves this function of collapsing the distinction between self and state, between present and past. The issue is not whether myth should displace political science in the citizen's understanding of the political order. Recognizing the role of myth is a necessary aspect of an account of the kinds of temporality within which the state appears to the citizen. Myth describes the quality of belief under the model of organic maintenance. Maintenance of the state through time requires that the idea of the state be embodied in the citizens, and embodiment requires a myth of transtemporal participation. In U.S. constitutional theory, establishing the myth was the function of the linked ideas of originalism and popular sovereignty. The popular sovereign appeared as the single subject of national life, knowing no temporal or geographical distinctions. As part of the popular sovereign, each citizen participated in the origins of the nation as an act of self-creation.

Logic does not require that revolutions end or that they end successfully by consolidating a new political order. But if they do end successfully, then the model of making must give way to the model of maintenance. Logically, the model of organic maintenance need not give way to the model of growth. Yet the myth of a timeless presence is likely to be undermined eventually by the strain between the idea of transtemporal sameness and the experience of differences brought about by change across the full range of social experience. As contemporary interests, events, and institutions appear increasingly different from those of the past, a new model is needed to link the present generation to the history of the state. A total collapse of the historical dimension of the constitutional project is always possible. A return to revolutionary politics, with its demand for a political remaking, may occur. But in the absence of a new revolution, a model of change that can synthesize past and present is required. This is offered in the idea of growth.

In the model of growth, the sharp distinction between making and maintenance is overcome. Instead, maintenance within the model of growth depends upon making. That which cannot adapt to new circumstances cannot maintain itself under the conditions of change that attach to any historical phenomenon, including the state. To describe anything as growing is to describe a relation of dependence between the present and the past. The present cannot make itself; it can only emerge from the past. The model of growth does not, however, afford grounds for a respectful maintenance of the past. Just the reverse. The past is a less developed stage than the present. To try to return to the past is to engage in political regression.

The model of growth can hold only as long as there is a belief in a normative value against which to measure growth. Without that value, growth becomes mere change. In constitutional thought at the beginning of this century, that norm was the idea of scientific governance. Once that system of values collapsed, it was no longer possible to measure growth, to distinguish growth from arbitrary change. Modern constitutional thought arose from the collapse. The history of the constitutional order no longer made a meaningful claim on the individual. History became the dead hand of the past, nothing more. Constitutional thought polarized, divided between an idea of majoritarianism and an idea of individual autonomy. Proponents of both ideas understood the sole source of meaning to be the present will of the individual. Both sides saw the historical dimension of constitutionalism as a source of arbitrary authority.

The dialectical development of the understanding of political order can halt at any point. Conceptual innovation need not occur in the face of unresolved problems. Nevertheless, the U.S. constitutional experience of collapse at this particular point in the development of theory is significant.

The model of growth shares with the model of maintenance the idea that individuals must understand themselves as a part of a much larger whole. The individual is an element of the state. What changes in the movement from maintenance to growth is the understanding of the existence of the state in time, not the understanding of the relation of part to whole within which individual identity is established. The collapse of constitutionalism in mid-century represents a rejection of this part-whole relation. Individuals now understood the self as the source of their own values. Instead of the individual's being a part of the state, the state became a part of the individual's autonomously formed life.

Constitutional theory began with a respect for the autonomous, self-forming individual. This idea was harnessed to the political project of making a constitution through an appeal to joint participation in a deliberative act of creation. Once the state gained a historical presence, individual autonomy was subordinated to the whole; but because the constitutional enterprise began with the idea of the self as an independent political artisan, the idea of the self as part of the state remained problematic. The idea of a self that stands apart from and critically evaluates political institutions did not disappear entirely. Constitutional discourse carried forward a memory of this idea of self-government as a deliberate making.

The collapse of a historical constitutionalism, therefore, represented the reemergence of the autonomous, self-forming individual. This could have led to a repetition of the cycle, a return to the model of making a constitution on the basis of contemporary political science. Instead, constitutional theory advanced to a new model of synthesis: community. The idea of community represents an effort to overcome the dichotomy of part and whole, of autonomy and authority, that led to the collapse. On this model, the community has no existence outside the historically bounded speech of a group of speakers. They, in turn, have no identity apart from the content of that speech. The relation of part to whole is now displaced by the relation of speaker to speech. These relations are different perspectives on a single discursive activity that is the source of all meaning.

The theoretical inquiry into political order that begins with the invitation to make a city in speech has now become the model of political order itself. Theory and authority coincide in this discursive community. Theory has gone full circle. The reflection on authority has come to rest in the authority of reflection. But what kind of authority is this? What is its relation to the authority exercised by the state in everyday life?

The End of Constitutional Theory

If a conceptual model of order represents a formal structure of thought, then the claim that constitutional theory ends with the development of a particular model seems implausible. How can form determine a substantive outcome? In truth, the distinction between form and content does not adequately express the relation between a model of order and a substantive understanding of political life. Each model limits the range of possible responses to the question of whether self-government is possible. The model of community, however, creates limits that cannot be reconciled with the exercise of coercive authority.

The model of making is not dependent upon the idea of an abstract science—although it is dependent upon the idea of an abstract truth. It is certainly not dependent upon any particular variety of political science. Indeed, the model of making encourages debate over the content of the science that should inform political construction. Although the model does not determine the content of ideal form, it does preclude any understanding of political life that denies the relevance of such abstract ideas, whether that is a politics of individual will or of historical development. Similarly, the model of maintenance does not itself limit the potential meanings of the organic state. A state conceived in liberty can be understood in terms of organic maintenance, just as well as a state conceived in religious conviction. The model does, however, preclude a political life of revolution and remaking the political order in light of a new theory. The model of growth does not carry within it a normative measure of growth. Growth might be in the comprehensive rationality of the state; it might also be in the development of a set of ethnic virtues. But, again, the model of growth precludes forms of political understanding that deny any place to objective, normative standards.

In each of these instances, the model of order structures the temporal character of the political order, defines the questions to which theory will have to respond, and sets limits on the range of possible answers. These models of order are not specific to the democratic state. Every state must explain the relation between political order and time, as well as the claim that political authority makes upon the individual. The openness of these models to diverse contents makes them available to a wide range of political orders. These structures of thought no more determine the character of a democratic state than they determine the character of an authoritarian state. Much of the argument of this book concerns the content given to each model of order in the U.S. constitutional experience—a content I have located largely in the interaction of reason and will in the attempt to explain self-government.

In respect to openness to diverse and opposing forms of political life, the model of a discursive community differs from the others. The power of the model of a discursive community rests upon an idea of positive freedom—a substantive idea with profound political implications. Even though the discourse of this community is open to virtually any subject matter or idea, the model of the discursive community is incompatible with every assertion of authority that arises from outside that discourse. Positive freedom means the creation of self and other through a mutual discourse. Community members—speakers—who take the idea of self-creation seriously cannot know in advance the conclusion to which the dialogue will lead. They cannot know in advance even the parameters of the dialogic engagement. The state has no monopoly on the conditions of such engagements. Rather, the ideal of freedom represented by the discursive community is potentially present in every experience with an other. The freedom and spontaneity of dialogue represents the constant possibility of an alternative community to that of the state and hence the limits of the legitimacy of state authority.

For the community of discourse to be the locus of positive freedom, it cannot be limited in advance. Some implicit limits may inhere in the language and history of community members, but these have no special authority. Not everything can be said, but neither does anything special have to be said. The internal limits never preclude a surprising turn in the conversation. Without external political constraints on the discourse, members of the community cannot know whether the product of the dialogue will be affirmation or denial, a unifying or a splintering, of the inherited political order. To be free in this dialogue, citizens must deny the state any privileged place. Authority is one voice, but with no greater privilege than any other. Each of the other models left open the possibility of various characterizations of state authority, but the model of community is incompatible with any idea of state authority.

Of all the new constitutional communitarians, only Robert Cover seems to have accepted the full implications of the communitarian model of a legitimate political order. The others may see the need for the theory of self-government to work itself pure through a theory of the discursive community, but they have not accepted the idea that their model cannot support the historical state as an agent exercising coercive authority. As constitutional theorists, they remain bound to the Constitution, despite the subversive character of their own theories. Each seeks somehow to constrain the discourse or to privilege one particular discourse. These limits on discourse are necessary to support the authority of the state. The limits may come from a theory of justice or from a theory of institutional role. In each case, the choice of limits must be justified by something other than the idea of a discursive community.

Law is a structure of authority, and constitutional law is a structure of ultimate authority. Law may tolerate much discussion, but it wields the ultimate authority to decide. Legal decisions are binding on the members of the community. Yet those binding decisions do not enter into a real community of discourse with any privileged place. Truth, not authority, is the measure of discourse. Truth, however, is the end, not the beginning, of discourse. The possibility of making the self anew, of rejecting all claims of authority, hangs over every true discursive engagement.

Yet law represents authority—in a democratic as well as in an authoritarian state. Those responsible for enforcing the law understand themselves as standing apart from the rest of the community by virtue of their authority. Their authority derives in part from their unique responsibilities for maintaining the identity of the state through time. For them, the discourse has stopped, at least to the degree that there are limits on what can and cannot be said and, perhaps even more important, on who can and cannot speak. Not everything is up for grabs; not every possibility is open to those responsible for the law. If these limits attach to the guardians of law, the theorists of law must split from the practitioners. Theory must go on to seek the resolution of antinomies within which law must live. Law exercises authority, even in the absence of a theoretically complete account of the legitimacy of that authority. At the bar of legitimacy, democracy is no more successful than any other form of political authority.

To found a theory of the legitimacy of constitutional law in the community of dialogue may seem wholly reasonable in terms of the development of theory. It may, however, seem wholly unreasonable in terms of the law: it looks like an effort to found law in the destruction of the conditions of law. Authority and discourse are both powerfully attractive ideas, but their equal attractiveness does not make them reconcilable. And if they are not, then perhaps we all confront a genuine tragedy. Theory will inevitably move beyond practice, but no one lives wholly in theory. Even Socrates had to suffer the deeds of authority. Those who seek to find a harmony of discourse and authority should recognize the Socratic risks that accompany genuine discourse.

Notes

CHAPTER ONE: To Make a Constitution

1 FERC v. Mississippi, 456 U.S. 742, 788 (1982) (O'Connor, J., concurring in part and dissenting in part).

2 I am not as concerned with the actual political effectiveness of *The Federalist* as with its powerful expression of a dominant constitutional worldview. Thomas Jefferson, for example, characterized *The Federalist* as "the best commentary on the principles of government which ever was written." Letter to James Madison (Nov. 18, 1788), in 5 The Writings of Thomas Jefferson 52, 53 (1895).

3 Representative of modern republican readings of *The Federalist* are G. Wills, Explaining America: The Federalist 224 (1981); C. Sunstein, *Interest Groups in American Public Law*, 38 Stan. L. Rev. 29, 31 (1985). Pluralist readings are represented in the work of M. Diamond, *Ethics and Politics: The American Way*, in The Moral Foundations of the American Republic 75, 92 (R. Horwitz 3d ed. 1986); R. Dahl, A Preface to Democratic Theory (1956); P. Bourke, *The Pluralist Reading of James Madison's Tenth Federalist*, 9 Persp. Am. Hist. 269 (1975).

4 On this contemporary conflict, see generally A. MacIntyre, After Virtue (2d ed. 1984); R. Wolff, The Poverty of Liberalism (1968); Liberalism and Its Critics (M. Sandel ed. 1984); A. Gutmann, *Communitarian Critics of Liberalism*, 14 Phil. & Pub. Aff. 308 (1985).

5 *See* The Federalist No. 40, at 253 (J. Madison) (C. Rossiter ed. 1961) [hereinafter all citations to *The Federalist* are to this edition] (submission of proposal of Philadelphia Convention "to *the people themselves*" will cure formal problem of convention overreaching its mandate).

6 *See* The Federalist No. 9, at 71–72 (A. Hamilton); *see also* D. Adair, Intellectual Origins of Jeffersonian Democracy 141–48 (1943) (discussion of Hamilton's convention speech).

7 The Federalist No. 1, at 33 (A. Hamilton). Publius himself often refers to the "experimental" character of the political order. *See, e.g., id.* No. 14, at 104 (J. Madison); *id.* No. 37, at 231 (J. Madison); *id.* No. 38, at 233 (J. Madison); *id.* No. 49, at 315 (J. Madison). Publius argues that the actual possibility of an experimental politics in the United States is itself, from a more abstract perspective, a function of the "accidental" conditions attending the postrevolutionary period. *See* D. Epstein, The Political Theory of the Federalist 19–21 (1984). The ironic relation of science to accident—science is an effort to control the accidental quality of life, but the opportunity to use science results from the accidents of history— carries forward a theme of Machiavellian political theory. *See* J. Pocock, The Machiavellian Moment 172 (1975).

8 The Federalist No. 1, at 33 (A. Hamilton).

9 On the same theme, see *Washington's First Inaugural,* in Inaugural Addresses of the Presidents 21, 24 (R. Bowers ed. 1929) ("[T]he propitious smiles of heaven can never be expected on a nation that disregards the eternal rules of order and right, which heaven itself has ordained: and . . . the preservation of the sacred fire of liberty, and the destiny of the republican model of government, are justly considered as deeply, perhaps as finally staked, on the experiment entrusted to the hands of the American people").

10 In June 1783, George Washington addressed the relation between political science and popular choice in a circular letter to the state governors: "The foundation of our Empire was not laid in the gloomy age of Ignorance and Superstition . . . but at an Epocha when the rights of mankind were better understood and more clearly defined, than at any former period; the researches of the human mind after social happiness, have been carried to a great extent, the treasures of knowledge, acquired by the labours of Philosophers . . . are laid open for our use, and . . . may be happily applied in the Establishment of our forms of Government. . . . [I]f . . . Citizens [of the United States] should not be completely free and happy, the fault will be intirely [sic] their own." *Reprinted in* D. Adair, Fame and the Founding Fathers 93 (T. Colbourn ed. 1974).

11 The Federalist No. 49, at 313 (J. Madison).

12 Publius acknowledges the obscurity of some areas of political science and the resultant difficulty of reaching the scientifically correct solution of particular political problems. *See, e.g., id.* No. 37 (J. Madison).

13 *Id.* No. 1, at 33 (A. Hamilton); *id.* No. 9, at 72 (A. Hamilton) ("The science of politics . . . like most other sciences, has received great improvement"). *See also* 1 A. Tocqueville, Democracy in America 7 (P. Bradley ed. 1945) (Reeve ed. 1862) ("The first of the duties that are at this time imposed upon those who direct our affairs is to educate democracy . . . to substitute a knowledge of statecraft for its inexperience, and an awareness of its true interest for its blind instincts. . . . A new science of politics is needed for a new world").

14 The Federalist No. 36, at 224 (A. Hamilton). *See also id.* No. 57, at 350 (J. Madison) (on need for rulers who possess both "wisdom to discern, and . . . virtue to pursue, the common good").

15 *Id.* No. 51, at 322 (J. Madison). *See also id.* No. 55, at 346 (J. Madison) ("As there is a degree of depravity in mankind which requires a certain degree of circumspection and distrust, so there are other qualities in human nature which justify a certain portion of esteem and confidence. Republican government presupposes

the existence of these qualities in a higher degree than any other form"). The idea that government reflects the character of the populace was an essential proposition of Montesquieu and his theory of the *esprit général. See* C. Montesquieu, The Spirit of the Laws 20 (T. Nugent trans. 1966) ("There is no great share of probity necessary to support a monarchical or despotic government. . . . But in a popular state, one spring more is necessary, namely, virtue"). On Montesquieu's influence on the framers, see G. Wills, *supra* note 3, at 180.

16 *See* H. Arendt, On Revolution 91 (1965) ("[The founders'] thought did not carry them any further than to the point of understanding government in the image of individual reason and construing the rule of government over the governed according to the age-old model of the rule of reason over the passions").

17 The Federalist No. 10, at 78 (J. Madison); *id.* No. 1, at 33 (A. Hamilton).

18 *Id.* No. 49, at 317 (J. Madison). Reciprocity between the psychological and political orders was a strong theme of the antifederalists, particularly in their arguments for a decentralized structure of politics within which virtue could flourish. *See* M. Dry, *Anti-Federalism in* The Federalist, in Saving the Revolution 40, 45–46 (C. Kesler ed. 1987); J. Shklar, *Publius and the Science of the Past*, 86 Yale L.J. 1286, 1288–89 (1977); C. Sunstein, *supra* note 3, at 35–38. Publius accepted this theme of reciprocity but differed from the antifederalists on the character of the science of politics and on the art of political construction supported by that science.

19 The Federalist No. 49, at 315 (J. Madison).

20 *Id.* at 317.

21 *Id.* No. 1, at 35 (A. Hamilton) (emphasis added); *id.* at 34.

22 *See* D. Epstein, *supra* note 7, at 29 (1984) ("*The Federalist*'s more fundamental argument is not a plea for trust, since the book freely admits that suspicion of men's motives is justified").

23 *See* D. Adair, *supra* note 6, at 54–55 ("The Renaissance delving in the records of Greece and Rome had been primarily a matter of specialists; now two centuries later this ancient wisdom was democratized and popularized to an amazing degree").

24 The Federalist No. 22, at 152 (A. Hamilton).

25 *See, e.g.,* M. Foster, The Political Philosophies of Plato and Hegel 128 n.1 (1965) ("It is notorious that the conception, and the very name, of will was lacking to Greek ethics").

26 The best expression of this view is found in Plato's parody, in Book VIII of *The Republic,* of a democratic polity, in which the slaves consider themselves the equal of their masters, children of their teachers, and even animals of their owners.

27 *See* A. Tocqueville, quoted *supra* note 13 (describing need to educate democracy with new science of politics).

28 *See* J. Rousseau, The Social Contract 67 (C. Sherover trans. 1974) (1762): "He who frames laws . . . has, or ought to have, no legislative right, and the people themselves cannot, even if they wished, divest themselves of this incommunicable right, because, according to the fundamental pact, it is only the general will that binds individuals, and we can never be sure that a particular will is conformable to the general will until it has been submitted to the free votes of the people." *See also* The Federalist No. 38, at 231 (J. Madison) (discussing role of lawgiver— "individual citizen of preeminent wisdom and approved integrity"—in prior republics).

29 The Federalist No. 10, at 77 (J. Madison).

30 On the possible virtues of a nondemocratic political order, see J. Wilson, *Speech Delivered on 26th November, 1787, in the Convention of Pennsylvania,* in 2 The Works of James Wilson, 759, 771 (R. McClosky ed. 1967) (1804) ("The advantages of a monarchy are, strength, despatch, secrecy, unity of counsel. . . . The advantages of aristocracy are, wisdom, arising from experience and education").

31 The Federalist No. 39, at 240 (J. Madison).

32 *Id.* No. 10, at 84 (J. Madison).

33 J. Wilson, *supra* note 30, at 762.

34 *Id.* at 768; *id.* at 771.

35 *Id.* at 768; *id.* at 760.

36 J. Wilson, *Lectures on Law,* in 1 The Works of James Wilson, *supra* note 30, at 67, 72. *See also* S. Conrad, *Metaphor and Imagination in James Wilson's Theory of Federal Union,* 13 Law & Soc. Inq. 1 (1988); R. Hills, *The Reconciliation of Law and Liberty in James Wilson,* 12 Harv. J.L. & Pub. Pol'y 891 (1989).

37 J. Wilson, *Speech on Choosing the Members of the Senate by Electors; Delivered on 31st December, 1789, in the Convention of Pennsylvania,* in 2 The Works of James Wilson, *supra* note 30, at 781, 785; *id.* at 788.

38 J. Wilson, *Lectures on Law, supra* note 36, at 87; The Federalist No. 51, at 322 (J. Madison).

39 It has often been suggested that the model of political construction in *The Federalist* is a Newtonian model of natural mechanical principles. *See, e.g.,* M. Kammen, A Machine That Would Go of Itself 17 (1986) ("[T]he notion of a constitution as some sort of machine or engine, had its origins in Newtonian science"). The Newtonian analogy is accurate in its suggestion that there are universal principles of political science. It fails, however, to distinguish nature and artifact. Wilson captures the model of making when he writes that "[f]rom [the people's] authority the constitution originates . . . it is as clay in the hands of the potter." J. Wilson, *Lectures on Law, supra* note 36, at 304.

40 The Federalist No. 10, at 77 (J. Madison).

41 "There is no maxim in my opinion, which is more liable to be misapplied, and which, therefore, more needs elucidation, than the current one, that the interest of the majority is the political standard of right and wrong." Letter from James Madison to James Monroe (Oct. 5, 1786), *reprinted in* D. Adair, *supra* note 6, at 107–08.

42 The Federalist No. 10, at 81 (J. Madison); *id.* No. 39, at 241 (J. Madison).

43 *Id.* No. 10, at 81 (J. Madison). The passage continues: "A common passion or interest will, in almost every case, be felt by a majority of the whole; a communication and concert results from the form of government itself; and there is nothing to check the inducements to sacrifice the weaker party or an obnoxious individual."

44 *Id.* No. 49, at 315 (J. Madison).

45 *See id.* No. 37, at 230 (J. Madison) ("[A]lthough this variety of [private] interests . . . may have a salutary influence on the administration of the government when formed, yet every one must be sensible of the contrary influence which must have been experienced in the task of forming it").

46 *Id.* No. 55, at 346 (J. Madison); *id.* No. 10, at 80 (J. Madison); *id.* at 83 (emphasis added).

47 *See* H. Powell, *The Original Understanding of Original Intent,* 98 Harv. L. Rev. 885, 927–41 (1985) (discussing Virginia and Kentucky resolutions and role of public usage in constitutional interpretation).

48 Calder v. Bull, 3 U.S. (3 Dall.) 386, 399 (1798) (Iredell, J.).

49 5 U.S. (1 Cranch) 137 (1803).

50 5 U.S. at 175. Marshall, for example, gives little attention to the exceptions clause of article III, which specifically grants Congress the authority to make exceptions to the appellate jurisdiction of the Supreme Court. Similarly, his reading of section 13 of the act assumes that the mandamus provision is an attempt to create jurisdiction, rather than a cause of action or a remedy in cases in which jurisdiction otherwise exists. 5 U.S. at 173–76. These criticisms are now virtually commonplaces in the teaching of constitutional law. *See generally* W. Van Alstyne, *A Critical Guide to* Marbury v. Madison, Duke L.J. 1 (1969). Yet in 1833, Story could describe Marshall's opinions as "victories of a mind accustomed to grapple with difficulties, capable of unfolding the . . . simplicity, and severe logic." J. Story, Commentaries on the Constitution, iii (1833). *See also* Chancellor James Kent, 1 Commentaries 453 (1826) (*Marbury* "approaches to the precisions and certainty of a mathematical demonstration").

51 5 U.S. at 176–77.

52 *Id.* at 177.

53 *Id.* at 178.

54 *See* The Federalist No. 78 (A. Hamilton).

55 5 U.S. at 178.

56 *Id.* at 179–80; *id.* at 180.

57 17 U.S. (4 Wheat.) 316, 400 (1819). Another example of this pattern of argument is found in Fletcher v. Peck, 10 U.S. (6 Cranch) 87 (1810), in which Marshall considers the power of a state legislature to disturb a previous contractual obligation. He examines the issue first from the perspective of "certain great principles of justice, whose authority is universally acknowledged," and then confirms the result of that inquiry by offering a "fair construction" of the contract clause. *Id.* at 133, 137. *See also* Dartmouth College v. Woodward, 17 U.S. (4 Wheat.) 518, 636–38 (1819) (developing a theory of "artificial being" of corporation before turning to contract clause).

For a different but related view of the methodological framework established by *Marbury,* see W. Nelson, *The Eighteenth-Century Background of John Marshall's Constitutional Jurisprudence,* 76 Mich. L. Rev. 893, 936–42 (1978). Nelson agrees that "Marshall . . . strove to reconcile popular will and legal principle" but believes that reconciliation was achieved by distinguishing the domain of law from that of politics. *Id.* at 935.

58 17 U.S. at 411 (emphasis added); *id.* at 430–31 (emphasis added).

59 *Id.* at 403–08.

60 *Id.* at 426; *id.* at 429.

61 *Id.* at 432. Even the structural statements are confirmed by a reference to the supremacy clause of article VI. *Id.* at 433.

62 *Id.* at 405–06.

63 *Id.* at 408. *But see infra* chapter 2 (discussion of Marshall's attitude toward treatment of slavery in Constitution).

64 A vivid symbol is the secret convention at which the initial work of rational

deliberation and construction of the scientific model was done. Only the success of, not the writing of, *The Federalist* moves science from outside to within the community.

65 *See* R. Newmyer, Supreme Court Justice Joseph Story 115 (1985) ("[T]he [Marshall] Court's grand exposition transformed the Constitution from a 'noble' but precarious 'experiment' in republican government to the final source of republican principles to which all parties turned for legitimation").

CHAPTER TWO: Maintenance and the Organism of the State

1 A. Lincoln, *The Perpetuation of Our Political Institutions: Address before the Young Men's Lyceum of Springfield, Illinois, January 27, 1838*, in Abraham Lincoln: His Speeches and Writings 76–85 (R. Basler ed. 1946). For an excellent discussion of this speech and its claim to be representative of the generation's political psychology, see G. Forgie, Patricide in the House Divided 55–87 (1979).

2 *See* J. Story, Commentaries on the Constitution of the United States 718 (R. Rotunda & J. Nowek eds. 1987) (Boston 1833); J. Calhoun, A Disquisition on Government and a Discourse on the Constitution and Government 239 (R. Cralle ed. 1854).

3 Speech in the Constitutional Convention, June 6, 1787, *reprinted in* The Mind of the Founder 72 (M. Meyers ed. 1981).

4 The Antelope, 23 U.S. (10 Wheat.) 66, 120 (1825). *See also* Dred Scott v. Sandford, 60 U.S. (19 How.) 393, 624 (1857) (Curtis, J., dissenting) ("Slavery, being contrary to natural right, is created only by municipal law"); R. Ferguson, Law and Letters in American Culture 232 (1984) ("Thomas Jefferson's *Notes on the State of Virginia* first formalized intellectual debate over the relations of slavery, law, and morality in the republic. Jefferson found the situation impossible not because the law failed to handle slavery—there was a considerable body of slave law in the southern states even in 1787—but because laws on slavery could never rest upon the higher morality of natural law. Since subsequent theorists also justified their jurisprudence as an extension of higher law, they could never reconcile republican principles with the institution of slavery. This was the contradiction that gradually infected the entire culture"). The best account of the treatment of slavery in the antebellum courts is R. Cover, Justice Accused (1975).

5 The arbitrariness of this compromise is evident in the reliance on mathematical specificity: slaves were counted as three-fifths of a person for purposes of apportionment (art. I, sec. 2), and importation of slaves was protected from congressional action until 1808 (art. I, sec. 9). *Cf.* The Federalist No. 55, at 342 (J. Madison) ("Nothing can be more fallacious than to found our political calculations on arithmetical principles").

6 The Federalist No. 54, at 340 (J. Madison).

7 *See, e.g., id.* No. 1, at 33–34 (A. Hamilton); *id.* No. 10, at 78–79 (J. Madison).

8 Prigg v. Pennsylvania, 41 U.S. (16 Pet.) 539, 610 (1842).

9 For a historical description of the development of this confrontation, see R. Cover, *supra* note 4, at 159–93 (tracing growth of a particular positivist reading of the Constitution, which protected slaveholding interests); E. Foner, Free Soil,

Free Labor, Free Men 73–102 (1970) (tracing growing political acceptance of Salmon P. Chase's antislavery reading of the Constitution); J. Tenbroeck, Equal under Law 66–93 (1965) (describing constitutional theory of radical abolitionists).

10 *See* H. Powell, *Joseph Story's Commentaries on the Constitution: A Belated Review,* 94 Yale L.J. 1285, 1307 (1985).

11 Characteristic of the states' rights version of republicanism, in addition to Calhoun's *Discourse* and the Virginia and Kentucky resolutions, is Madison's 1800 report explaining the earlier Virginia resolutions. *See* J. Madison, *Report on the Virginia Resolutions,* in 4 Letters and Other Writings of James Madison 515 (Philadelphia 1867); S. Roane, *Hampden,* in John Marshall's Defense of *McCulloch v. Maryland* 106, 142–43 (G. Gunther ed. 1969). Characteristic of the nationalist views beyond Marshall and Story are D. Webster, *The Constitution Not a Compact between Sovereign States,* in 3 The Works of Daniel Webster 448, 479–86 (Boston 1851); A. Lincoln, *Message to Congress in Special Session, July 4, 1861,* in Abraham Lincoln, *supra* note 1, at 594. For insightful discussion of this conflict, see A. Amar, *Of Sovereignty and Federalism,* 96 Yale L.J. 1425, 1451–55 (1987); H. Powell, *The Original Understanding of Original Intent,* 98 Harv. L. Rev. 885, 944–46 (1985).

12 *See* H. Powell, *supra* note 11, at 931 ("[S]trict construction was justified by reference to the 'maxim of political law' that a sovereign can be deprived of any of its powers only by its express consent narrowly construed").

13 J. Story, *supra* note 2, at 112.

14 *Id.* at 118.

15 *Id.* at 117; *id.* at 118.

16 1 J. Story, Commentaries on the Constitution of the United States 287–88 (3d ed. 1858). *See also* J. Story, *supra* note 2, at 142 ("[T]he text was adopted by the people in its obvious, and general sense").

17 J. Story, *supra* note 2, at 119–22.

18 *Id.* at 125; *id.* at 127.

19 *Id.* at 132–33; *id.* at 133; *id.* at 130.

20 *Id.* at 717.

21 *Id.* at 135.

22 *Id.* at 143.

23 *Id.* at 718. *See also id.* at 2 ("affections" are to be enlisted on side of the Constitution).

24 *See id.* at 143–46.

25 *Id.* at 719 (the people are the "keepers" of the Constitution). Interestingly, Story does not attempt to ground the affection of the individual for the Constitution on the protection of rights. In a work of some seven hundred pages, he devotes only about twenty to the Bill of Rights.

26 *Quoted in* M. Peterson, The Great Triumvirate 409 (1987).

27 To these he adds abolitionism, but this is a substantive manifestation of the structural changes he identifies.

28 J. Calhoun, *supra* note 2, at 169; *id.* at 244.

29 *Id.* at 121–22; *id.* at 122.

30 *Id.* at 162.

31 *Id.* at 113; *id.* at 116; *id.* at 136.

32 *Id.* at 126; *id.* at 128.

33 60 U.S. (19 How.) 393 (1857).

34 From this perspective, Chief Justice Rehnquist, despite his protestations, is the direct descendant of Chief Justice Taney. *See* W. Rehnquist, *The Notion of a Living Constitution*, 54 Tex. L. Rev. 693 (1976). His protestations may be found in *id.* at 700–02; the intellectual inheritance is clear in his description of judges as "keepers of the covenant." *Id.* at 698. *Compare* 60 U.S. at 426.

35 Taney excuses the Court's delay in resolving the issues (the case was argued twice) by noting that "the questions in controversy are of the highest importance" requiring "a more deliberate consideration." 60 U.S. at 399–400. *See also* 60 U.S. at 633 (Curtis, J., dissenting) ("These questions are numerous, and the grave importance of some of them required me to exhibit fully the grounds of my opinion").

36 *See* D. Currie, The Constitution in the Supreme Court 264 (1985) ("*Scott* has been widely lamented as bad policy and bad judicial politics. What may not be so well recollected is that it was also bad law"). For a detailed analysis of the opinions in the case, see D. Fehrenbacher, The *Dred Scott* Case (1978).

37 60 U.S. (19 How.) at 405.

38 Taney was not alone in this historical orientation. *See also* 60 U.S. at 454 (Wayne, J., concurring) (role of Court is to reflect intent of framers). On the significance of this theme generally in the pre–Civil War period, see G. Forgie, *supra* note 1.

39 60 U.S. (19 How.) at 410 (emphasis added).

40 *See* D. Fehrenbacher, *supra* note 36, at 340–41; R. Burt, *What Was Wrong with Dred Scott, What's Right about* Brown, 42 Wash. & Lee L. Rev. 1, 3 (1985).

41 60 U.S. (19 How.) at 407; *id.* at 426.

42 *Id.* at 410.

43 *Id.* at 411; *id.* at 451.

44 *Id.* at 416; *id.* at 417.

45 *Id.* at 426.

46 *Id.*

47 See E. Corwin, *The* Dred Scott *Decision, in the Light of Contemporary Legal Doctrines*, 17 Am. Hist. Rev. 52, 63 (1911) (describing nineteenth-century move from constitutional law founded on natural rights to "the doctrine of 'popular sovereignty,' which insisted in the first place upon tracing the sanctity of the written Constitution, not to a supposed relation to fundamental rights but to its character as the immediate enactment of the sovereign people").

48 This shift in constitutional worldviews was limited neither to the Court nor to the proslavery faction. *See* H. Powell, *supra* note 11, at 947 ("By the outbreak of the Civil War, intentionalism in the modern sense reigned supreme in the rhetoric of constitutional interpretation").

49 60 U.S. (19 How.) at 409.

50 *See* D. Fehrenbacher, *supra* note 36, at 343.

51 60 U.S. at 415 ("[The African race] forms no part of the sovereignty of the State, and is not therefore called on to uphold and defend it").

52 For a modern development of this idea that the state is embodied through violence, see E. Scarry, The Body in Pain (1985).

53 A. Lincoln, *Address Delivered at the Dedication of the Cemetery at Gettysburg, November 19, 1863*, in Abraham Lincoln: His Speeches and Writings, *supra* note 1, at 734.

54 H. Jaffa, Crisis of the House Divided 227 (1982).

55 A. Lincoln, *Speech in Reply to Douglas at Chicago, Illinois, July 10, 1858,* in Abraham Lincoln: His Speeches and Writings, *supra* note 1, at 385, 401–02.

56 A. Lincoln, *Letter to Horace Greeley (August 22, 1862),* in Abraham Lincoln: His Speeches and Writings, *supra* note 1, at 651, 652 ("If I could save the Union without freeing *any* slave I would do it, and if I could save it by freeing *all* the slaves, I would do it").

57 See Lincoln's distinction of action in the territories from action in the existing states, in The Lincoln-Douglas Debates of 1858, at 315 (R. Johannsen ed. 1965).

58 *Id.* at 131 (Douglas accuses Lincoln of undermining "fraternal feeling of the whole country" by abandoning "our fathers"); *id.* at 312 (Lincoln accuses Douglas of abandoning the fathers).

59 *Id.* at 311.

60 *Id.* at 132.

61 *Id.*

62 *Id.* at 319.

63 *Id.* at 44.

64 To this, Douglas adds a materialistic strand, arguing that the union has been the key to individual prosperity. Douglas would turn the nation from the great public controversy over slavery to the private value of self-interested accumulation. Satisfaction of these material interests requires territorial expansion, but to expand, the country must first overcome the moral quandary posed by Lincoln. *See, e.g., id.* at 130.

65 A. Lincoln, *Second Inaugural Address, March 4, 1865,* in Abraham Lincoln: His Speeches and Writings, *supra* note 1, at 792, 793.

66 J. Wilson, *Lectures on Law,* in 1 The Works of James Wilson 78–80 (R. McClosky ed. 1967) (1804).

67 D. Webster, *The Completion of the Bunker Hill Monument,* in 1 The Works of Daniel Webster, *supra* note 11, at 83, 106–07. On the changing character of Webster's own constitutionalism, moving from reason to reverence and maintenance, see R. Ferguson, *supra* note 4, at 231–33.

68 On myth in general, see E. Cassirer, The Myth of the State (1946); 2 E. Cassirer, The Philosophy of Symbolic Forms (1955). My use of the term *myth* and my characterization of the force of myth in public order in the United States is far more benign than his analysis of the force of myth in modern politics—particularly his analysis of the Third Reich. On the relation between myth and political philosophy as different efforts to deal with time, see J. Gunnell, Political Philosophy and Time (1968).

69 Cassirer, for example, describes the mythical framework as follows: "By a first act of identification man asserts his fundamental unity with his human or animal ancestors—by a second act he identifies his own life with the life of nature." E. Cassirer, Myth, *supra* note 68, at 39.

70 Describing this attitude toward origins found in mythical consciousness, Cassirer writes: "The past itself has no 'why': it *is* the why of things. What distinguishes mythical time from historical time is that for mythical time there is an absolute past, which neither requires nor is susceptible of any further explanation." E. Cassirer, Philosophy, *supra* note 68, at 106.

71 D. Webster, *Adams and Jefferson,* in 1 The Works of Daniel Webster, *supra* note 11, at 115.

72 On the massive psychological trauma caused by this denial of political freedom in the nineteenth-century United States, see G. Forgie, *supra* note 1.

73 John Gunnell describes the social life of a society organized around myth as follows: "The life of society was an active participation in the poetic truth of the origin or foundation." J. Gunnell, *supra* note 68, at 30.

74 *See* E. Cassirer, An Essay on Man 89 (1970) ("[Myth's] view of life is a synthetic, not an analytical one").

75 Traditionally, education into civic life has been largely the shaping of character by the dominant political myths of the culture. Patriotism and nationalism, for example, are forces that deeply subvert any effort to divorce subject and object in political life. *See, e.g.,* B. Crick, In Defense of Politics 69–86 (2d ed. 1982); J. Schumpeter, Capitalism, Socialism, and Democracy, at 262–68 (3d ed. 1950).

CHAPTER THREE: The Evolving Unwritten Constitution

1 P. Paludan, A Covenant with Death 21 (1975).

2 *See* M. Curtis, No State Shall Abridge (1986).

3 Cong. Globe, 39th Cong., 1st Sess. 1088 (1866); *id.* at 1054 (Cong. W. Higby); *id.* at 255–56 app. (Cong. J. Baker). *See also id.* at 1034 (Cong. J. Bingham: "Every word of the proposed amendment is to-day in the Constitution of our country, save the words conferring the express grant of power upon the Congress of the United States").

4 32 U.S. (7 Pet.) 243 (1833) (Bill of Rights does not apply to the states).

5 Slaughter-House Cases, 83 U.S. (16 Wall.) 36, 78 (1872).

6 *See* T. Peebles, *A Call to High Debate: The Organic Constitution in Its Formative Era, 1890–1920,* 52 Univ. of Col. L. Rev. 49, 53–55 (1980) (listing common law, Darwin, Burke, and German historical school as contributing to development of an evolutionary constitutionalism).

7 J. Pomeroy, An Introduction to Municipal Law (1864). On Pomeroy in general, see 15 Dictionary of American Biography 52–53 (1935).

8 *See* P. Paludan, *supra* note 1, at 246–47 (describing letter from Chief Justice Chase to Pomeroy, acknowledging latter's influence on the Court).

9 J. Pomeroy, An Introduction to the Constitutional Law of the United States 21 (1868).

10 *Id.* at 22; *id.* at 24; *id.* at 25.

11 *Id.* at 78–79.

12 *Id.* at 10; *id.* at 102.

13 *Id.* at 94; *id.* at 118; *id.* at 119.

14 *Id.* at 11; *id.* at 14.

15 *Id.* at 13; *id.* at 16.

16 S. Fisher, Trial of the Constitution 61–62 (1862).

17 *See, e.g.,* H. Binney, *The Privilege of the Writ of Habeas Corpus under the Constitution,* in Campbell's Pamphlets s.2 (1862); J. Parker, *Habeas Corpus and Martial*

Law, in *id.* at s.17; F. Lieber, *What Is Our Constitution*, in 2 Miscellaneous Writings 87 (1881).

18 S. Fisher, *supra* note 16, at 55.

19 *Id.* at 96; *id.* at 39; *id.* at 53.

20 *Id.* at 30.

21 *Id.* at 18.

22 *Id.* at 55.

23 *Id.* at 18.

24 *Id.* at 21.

25 On the political direction of Cooley's thought, see B. Twiss, Lawyers and the Constitution: How Laissez Faire Came to the Supreme Court 34–37 (1942); C. Jacobs, Law Writers and the Courts: The Influence of Thomas M. Cooley, Christopher G. Tiedeman, and John F. Dillon upon American Constitutional Law 27–30 (1954).

26 T. Cooley, A Treatise on the Constitutional Limitations Which Rest upon the Legislative Power of the States of the American Union iv (1868).

27 Cooley's work in constitutional law is a precursor and model for the work on the common law that Langdell and his followers later do at Harvard.

28 When Cooley writes on interpretive methodology, he fails to understand the implications of his own work. His chapter on the construction of state constitutions, for example, makes only the standard points about the need "*to give effect to the intent of the people in adopting [the Constitution]*. In the case of all written laws, it is the intent of the lawgiver that is to be enforced." T. Cooley, *supra* note 26, at 55.

29 T. Cooley, *Limits to State Control of Private Business*, Princeton Rev. 233, 247 (1878).

30 T. Cooley, *supra* note 26, at 3.

31 *Id.* at 175; *see also id.* at 60–61.

32 *Id.* at 572; *id.* at 21.

33 Cooley offers such general maxims as "[T]he regulations must have reference to the comfort, safety, or welfare of society." *Id.* at 577.

34 The common meaning of these terms was noted earlier by Story, who cited Lord Coke. *See* J. Story, Commentaries on the Constitution of the United States 663 (R. Rotunda & J. Nowek eds. 1987) (Boston, 1833).

35 T. Cooley, *supra* note 26, at 354; *id.* at 356; *id.* at 357–58.

36 On Cooley's identification of vested rights, equity, and justice, see *id.* at 378 ("a naked legal right, which it is usually unjust to insist upon" is "coupled with no equity," and "no constitutional provision was ever designed to protect [it]").

37 *Id.* at 355.

38 T. Cooley, *Labor and Capital before the Law*, 139 N. Am. Rev. 503, 503 (Dec. 1884). *See also* T. Cooley, *The Uncertainty of the Law*, 22 Am. L. Rev. (1888), *quoted in* A. Jones, The Constitutional Conservatism of Thomas McIntyre Cooley 240 (1960): "Much of legal right was conventional in its origin; but legal rules long observed created a reason for themselves, and the citizen conforms to them without question as he does to the laws of nature whose operations he perceives about him."

39 T. Cooley, *The Lawyer's Duty to the State*, Proceedings of the Bar Assoc. of Tenn. 79 (1886), *quoted in* A. Jones, *supra* note 38, at 240.

40 T. Cooley, *supra* note 26, at 174; *id.* at 60–61.

41 *See generally* C. Jacobs, *supra* note 25, at 58–63; B. Twiss, *supra* note 25, at 110; D. Mayer, *The Jurisprudence of Christopher G. Tiedeman: A Study in the Failure of Laissez-Faire Constitutionalism*, 55 Missouri L. Rev. 93, 98 (1990).

42 C. Tiedeman, A Treatise on the Limitations of Police Power in the United States (1886).

43 C. Tiedeman, The Unwritten Constitution of the United States (1890).

44 Tiedeman studied in Germany in the 1870s. Equally important, he taught in Saint Louis from 1881 to 1891, during which time the Saint Louis Hegelians were an active philosophical community. *See* 3 Encylopedia of Philosophy 416–17 (1967) (article on W. Harris). On the German influence on Tiedeman generally, see D. Mayer, *supra* note 41, at 103–08. Mayer emphasizes the influence of Rudolf von Jhering, with whom Tiedeman studied in Germany. In fact, the claims for von Jhering's influence are quite weak. The Continental influence on Tiedeman is more general and links him as much to Savigny as to von Jhering.

45 C. Tiedeman, *supra* note 43, at 21; *id.* at 93.

46 *Id.* at 16; *id.* at 116; *id.* at 122; *id.* at 150.

47 *Id.* at 19.

48 *Id.* at 113; *id.* at 15.

49 *Id.* at 9; *id.* at 45; *id.* at 21.

50 *Id.* at 7; *id.* at 5; *id.* at 164.

51 *Id.* at 144.

52 *Id.* at 2–3.

53 *Id.* at 156. *See also id.* at 125. Tiedeman cites von Jhering for the general idea of social progress through "a vigorous contest between opposing forces." *Id.* at 12. On the Spencerian roots of this idea, see R. Hofstader, Social Darwinism in American Thought 36–37 (1959).

54 C. Tiedeman, *supra* note 43, at 78; *id.* at 80.

55 *Id.* at 76, 81. Tiedeman avoids contradiction here by developing a theory of the historical character of natural rights: there are no timeless, abstract natural rights; but at a given moment in social evolution, certain rights will be seen as so basic as to appear natural.

56 For examples of racism in thinkers of this period, see, e.g., 1 J. Burgess, Political Science and Comparative Constitutional Law 44 (1891) ("Teutonic nations are particularly endowed with the capacity for establishing national states. . . . [T]he Teutonic element, when dominant, should never surrender the balance of political power . . . Under certain circumstances it should not even permit participation of the other elements"); J. Hare, American Constitutional Law 748 (1889).

57 *But cf.* J. Thayer and W. Wilson, discussed below.

58 F. Wharton, Commentaries on Law, Embracing Chapters on the Nature, the Source, and the History of Law; on International Law, Public and Private; and on Constitutional and Statutory Law (1884). On Wharton generally, see 20 Dictionary of American Biography 27–28 (1936).

59 F. Wharton, Commentaries, *supra* note 58, at iii–iv.

60 *Id.* at iii.

61 *Id.* at 13 n.4 (quoting Pollock's inaugural lecture of 1883 at Oxford) (omissions in original).

62 *Id.* at 167; *id.* at 568 (footnote omitted).

63 *Id.* at 23; *Id.* at 94; *id.* at 95.

64 *Id.* at 29; *id.* at 30; *id.* at 29.

65 *Id.* at 63; *id.* at 64.

66 *Id.* at 61.

67 *See* T. Peebles, *supra* note 6 (describing changing political views of evolutionary constitutionalists).

68 The contrast in institutional focus that I discuss here does not quite track the more traditional division of social Darwinists and reform Darwinists in this period. *See* H. Hovenkamp, *Evolutionary Models in Jurisprudence,* 64 Texas L. Rev. 645, 654–56 (1985).

69 *See* M. Howe, Justice Oliver Wendell Holmes, The Shaping Years, 1841–1870, at 246–48 (1957).

70 *See* H. Hirsch, The Enigma of Felix Frankfurter 128–29 (1981).

71 M. Howe, *supra* note 69, at 247 (quoting Holmes).

72 J. Thayer, *The Origin and Scope of the American Doctrine of Constitutional Law,* in Legal Essays 1, 11 (1908). The paper was delivered in 1893 at the Chicago World's Fair. It was first printed in 7 Harv. L. Rev. 129 (1893).

73 *Id.* at 4.

74 *Id.* at 28.

75 J. Thayer, *Our New Possessions,* in Essays, *supra* note 72, at 153, 167.

76 J. Thayer, John Marshall 85–86 (1967).

77 *Id.* at 87; *id.* at 88.

78 J. Thayer, *supra* note 72, at 38–39 (footnote omitted); *id.* at 39.

79 *See* Munn v. Illinois, 94 U.S. 113 (1876).

80 J. Thayer, *supra* note 76, at 86.

81 J. Thayer, *supra* note 72, at 38.

82 *Id.* at 30 (emphasis omitted); *id.* at 30 n.2 (quoting J. Thayer, *The Insular Tariff Cases,* 15 Harv. L. Rev. 164); *id.* at 12–13.

83 *Id.* at 22; *id.* at 21.

84 *See supra* note 71 and accompanying text.

85 198 U.S. 45, 76 (1905).

86 Gompers v. United States, 233 U.S. 604, 610 (1914); *see also* Missouri v. Holland, 252 U.S. 416, 433 (1920).

87 T. Peebles, *supra* note 6, at 89.

88 W. Wilson, Congressional Government 52 (1890); *id.* at 10.

89 *Id.* at 4–5.

90 *Id.* at 6; *id.* at 7.

91 *Id.* at 284.

92 *Id.* at 311; *id.* at 312; *id.* at 285.

93 W. Wilson, Constitutional Government in the United States 1 (1911).

94 *Id.* at 54–55; *id.* at 56; *id.* at 57.

95 *Id.* at 57; *id.* at 53 (emphasis added).

96 This expanded view of constitutionalism brings the U.S. and British constitutions together—again, a move typical of other theorists of this period. Instead of offering a ground for critical comparison, as in his earlier work, the British model

now appears as simply an alternative form of self-government in the fourth stage. Indeed, the two have a common root: "The Constitution of the United States, as framed by the constitutional convention of 1787, was intended to be a copy of the government of England, with such changes as seemed . . . necessary." *Id.* at 42.

97 *Id.* at 2; *id.* at 3; *id.* at 4.

98 *Id.* at 14.

99 *Id.* at 68.

100 *Id.* at 109.

101 *Id.* at 16; *id.* at 17–18.

102 *Id.* at 22–23; *id.* at 143.

103 *Id.* at 147; *id.* at 152. For a modern version of this Wilsonian idea, see O. Fiss, *The Supreme Court 1978 Term Foreword: The Forms of Justice*, 93 Harv. L. Rev. 1 (1979).

104 W. Wilson, *supra* note 93, at 157; *id.* at 158.

105 *Id.* at 172.

106 *See, e.g.*, J. Carter, Law, Its Origin, Growth and Function (1907); R. Venable, *Growth or Evolution of Law*, 23 A.B.A. Rep. 278 (1900).

CHAPTER FOUR: The Forum of Science in the Constitutional Order

1 *See, e.g.*, M. Horwitz, *History and Theory*, 96 Yale L.J. 1825, 1827–30 (1987) (discussing dominance of the progressive interpretation of the *Lochner* Court); B. Ackerman, *The Storrs Lectures: Discovering the Constitution*, 93 Yale L.J. 1013, 1052–55 (1984) (describing informal constitutional amendments).

2 78 U.S. (11 Wall.) 113 (1871).

3 17 U.S. (4 Wheat.) 316 (1819).

4 78 U.S. (11 Wall.) at 124; *id.* at 127.

5 *Id.* at 127.

6 *Id.* at 126.

7 Tarble's Case, 80 U.S. (13 Wall.) 397 (1872); Crandall v. Nevada, 73 U.S. (6 Wall.) 35, 43 (1868). Although *Tarble* builds upon the prewar opinion of Chief Justice Taney in *Ableman v. Booth*, 62 U.S. (21 How.) 506 (1859), it contains little of the originalist reasoning upon which Taney relied.

8 87 U.S. (20 Wall.) 655, 663 (1875); *id.* at 664; *id.* at 662. The argument is actually a bit more complicated because in turning to a public purpose standard, the Court points to "the course and usage of the government, the objects for which taxes have been customarily and by long course of legislation levied." *Id.* at 665. This suggests an analysis something like that of Cooley, who argues that to understand the character of a constitutional grant of public authority—here the power of taxation—one must look to the common-law background. This language, however, plays no operative role in the decision; immediately after this statement, an abstract line is drawn between all private businesses—with the possible exception of transport businesses—and public purposes.

9 75 U.S. (8 Wall.) 603, 625 (1870); *id.* at 622; *id.*

10 83 U.S. (16 Wall.) 36, 68 (1873); *id.* at 67–68.

11 Justice Miller believed that the difference in approach might be justified because *Loan Association* arose under federal diversity jurisdiction. *See* Davidson v. New Orleans, 96 U.S. 97, 105 (1878). This distinction does not account for the actual pattern of cases. *See* L. Tribe, American Constitutional Law 564–65 (2d ed. 1988).

12 83 U.S. (16 Wall.) at 68; *id.* at 71; *id.* at 68; *id.* at 72.

13 *Id.* at 82.

14 The former Justice John Campbell, who argued the case for the unsuccessful parties in *Slaughter-House*, made ample use of the common-law disapproval of monopolies in his arguments. *See* B. Twiss, Lawyers and the Constitution 46–47 (1962).

15 83 U.S. (16 Wall.) at 123 (Bradley, J., dissenting); *id.* at 101 (Field, J., dissenting).

16 *Id.* at 96–97 (Field, J., dissenting). *See also id.* at 114 (Bradley, J., dissenting) ("But there are certain fundamental rights which this right of [state] regulation cannot infringe. . . . I speak now of the rights of citizens of any free government").

17 *Id.* at 114 (Bradley, J., dissenting); *id.* at 116; *id.* at 104 (Field, J., dissenting).

18 *Id.* at 104 (Field, J., dissenting); *id.* at 115 (Bradley, J., dissenting).

19 *Id.* at 115 (Bradley, J., dissenting).

20 The temporal dimensions of the *Lochner* Court cannot be specified exactly. The Court emerged gradually, but its views were fully crystallized in *Lochner v. New York*, 198 U.S. 45 (1905). Its death is often marked by *West Coast Hotel Co. v. Parrish*, 300 U.S. 379 (1937), but here again exactness is not possible.

21 A notable exception to this model is *Pollock v. Farmers' Loan and Trust Co.*, 158 U.S. 601 (1895), in which the Court relied upon an originalist methodology to declare the federal income tax unconstitutional. It is not an accident that the decision was rendered irrelevant by a new expression of popular will in the form of the Sixteenth Amendment. The Court literally invited an amendment in its opinion in that case. *See id.* at 635 ("If it be true that the Constitution should have been so framed that a tax of this kind could be laid, the instrument defines the way for its amendment"). Such invitations were completely out of place when the Court acted as a scientific decision maker.

22 *See* W. Nelson, The Roots of American Bureaucracy 82–112 (1982) (discussing general emergence of a scientific morality and its application to public and private institutions at the turn of the century).

23 94 U.S. 113, 125 (1877).

24 *Id.* at 125–26; *id.* at 124–25 ("One should use one's own property in such a manner as not to injure that of another"). *See* C. Tiedeman, A Treatise on the Limitations of Police Power in the United States 4 (1886). On this point, the dissent is in entire agreement with the majority. *See* 94 U.S. at 145 (Field, J., dissenting). The disagreement between majority and dissent pertains to the particular application of the common-law rule, not the basic model of constitutionalism.

25 94 U.S. at 133.

26 *Id.* at 134.

27 110 U.S. 516, 529 (1884).

28 *Id.* at 530.

29 *Id.*; *id.* at 531.

30 *Id.* at 535; *id.* at 536.

31 *Cf.* T. Peebles, *A Call to High Debate: The Organic Constitution in Its Formative Era, 1890–1920*, 52 U. Colo. L. Rev. 49 (1980); S. Fine, Laissez Faire and the General-Welfare State 143–45 (1956) (distinguishing *Munn* from *Lochner*).

32 198 U.S. at 54; *id.* at 53.

33 165 U.S. 578, 589 (1897) (emphasis added).

34 111 U.S. 746, 762 (1884) (discussing common-law sources of a constitutional prohibition on state-created monopolies); 127 U.S. 678, 684 (1888) (assenting to the "general proposition" that everyone has a constitutional right to pursue an ordinary calling or trade).

35 *Allgeyer*, 165 U.S. at 590.

36 169 U.S. 366, 385 (1898); *id.* at 387.

37 165 U.S. at 589.

38 154 U.S. 362, 399 (1894).

39 198 U.S. at 53. For a critique of the constitutionalizing of the common law in *Lochner*, see C. Sunstein, Lochner's Legacy, 87 Colum. L. Rev. 873 (1987). More recently, a claim has been made that *Lochner* failed to go as far as it should have in constitutionalizing the common law of contract. *See* R. Epstein, *Race and the Police Power*, 46 Wash. & Lee L. Rev. 741, 752 (1989).

40 198 U.S. at 53.

41 *Id.*

42 *See* T. Grey, *Langdell's Orthodoxy*, 45 U. Pitt. L. Rev. 1 (1983).

43 *See* G. Gilmore, The Ages of American Law 42 (1977).

44 198 U.S. at 55.

45 *Id.*

46 An appropriate analogy to the *Lochner* Court's understanding of liberty of contract would be the understanding of freedom of speech today. The general rule of noninterference with speech admits of exceptions: for example, obscenity, libel, fighting words, and time-place-and-manner restrictions. One day these exceptions may be seen as so arbitrary as to undermine the claim that there is a general rule.

47 *See* T. Grey, *supra* note 42, at 28–32.

48 198 U.S. at 56. *See also id.* at 53 (on "reasonable conditions . . . in the exercise of those powers").

49 *Id.* at 57.

50 *Id.*

51 Muller v. Oregon, 208 U.S. 412, 421–22 (1908).

52 *See Lochner*, 198 U.S. at 57 (discussing wards of the state, including children and mentally incompetent people). *See also* Muller v. Oregon, *supra* note 51 (upholding regulations protecting working women); Holden v. Hardy, 169 U.S. 366, 397 (1898) (questioning capacity of mine employees to recognize their own self-interest).

53 *Lochner*, 198 U.S. at 56–57.

54 *Id.* at 59.

55 *Id.* at 61; *id.* at 62.

56 *Id.* at 75 (Holmes, J., dissenting).

57 Writing in the same year that *Lochner* was decided, for example, James Carter, one of the leading practitioners before the Court and one of the most theoretically inclined, described the "last stage of legal study" as a "part of the field, not strictly of Law but of Sociology." J. Carter, Law: Its Origin, Growth and Function 2 (1907).

58 People v. Walsh, 117 N.Y. 34, 47 (appended to decision in People v. Budd, 117 N.Y. 1 [1889]), 22 N.E. 682, 687 (1889) (Peckham, J., dissenting); *id.* at 69, 22 N.E. at 694. For an earlier yet extremely influential statement of the connection between the common-law right of contract and the science of social evolution, see *Matter of Jacobs*, 98 N.Y. 98, 104-06 (1885).

59 Thus, the *Lochner* Court did not consistently rule in favor of corporate interests. *See* H. Hovenkamp, *The Political Economy of Substantive Due Process*, 40 Stan. L. Rev. 379, 386-89 (1988) (rejecting claim that *Lochner* Court was protecting large economic interests); O. Fiss, The Supreme Court and the Rise of the Modern State, 1888-1910 (forthcoming).

60 *See, e.g.*, Meyer v. Nebraska, 262 U.S. 390 (1923); Pierce v. Society of Sisters, 268 U.S. 510 (1925).

61 Godcharles and Co. v. Wigeman, 113 Pa. 431, 437 (1886). *See* S. Fine, *supra* note 31, at 159-62 (discussing case law).

62 *See, e.g.*, J. Burgess, *Private Corporations from the Point of View of Political Science*, 13 Pol. Sci. Q. 201, 210-12 (1898). *See generally* R. Hofstader, Social Darwinism in American Thought (1955); S. Fine, *supra* note 31, at 91-95.

63 198 U.S. 45, 72 (1905) (Harlan, J., dissenting) (citation omitted).

64 *Id.* at 70-71; *id.* at 59 (opinion of the Court). It is not surprising, therefore, to find the *Lochner* Court responding positively to efforts made in "Brandeis briefs" to marshal the best available social science evidence to support controverted state interventions. *See, e.g.*, Muller v. Oregon, *supra* note 51; McLean v. Arkansas, 211 U.S. 539 (1909) (upholding regulation of wages paid to miners); Bunting v. Oregon, 243 U.S. 426 (1917) (upholding ten-hour work day for manufacturing employees).

65 198 U.S. at 76 (Holmes, J., dissenting).

66 *Id. See* Abrams v. United States, 250 U.S. 616, 630 (1919) (Holmes, J., dissenting) (on competition of ideas).

67 R. Hofstader, *supra* note 62, at 168-69.

68 On Darwin's own ambiguity in linking social evolution to progress rather than mere adaptation, see S. Gould, Wonderful Life 257-58 (1989).

69 *See* J. Frank, Law and the Modern Mind, x-xii (1963).

70 M. Cohen, Law and the Social Order 139 (1933). *See also* M. Cohen, The Faith of a Liberal 180-81 (1946).

71 C. Beard, An Economic Interpretation of the Constitution of the United States 6 (1965).

72 *Id.* at 7-8; *id.* at 9.

73 *Id.* at 17-18.

74 *See, e.g.*, K. Llewellyn, *The Constitution as an Institution*, 34 Colum. L. Rev. 1 (1934), which builds on the similar claims made by nineteenth-century theorists who supported the idea of an unwritten evolving constitution.

75 C. Beard, *supra* note 71, at 4.

76 C. Beard, *Historiography and the Constitution*, in The Constitution Reconsidered 159, 160 (C. Read rev. ed. 1968).

77 *Id.* at 163.

78 *Id.* at 165-66.

79 *Id.* at 161.

80 J. Frank, *supra* note 69, at 158; *id.* at n.27.

81 *Id.* at 126.
82 *Id.* at 22; *id.* at 109. In support of this proposition, Frank cites J. Dewey, *Logical Method and Law*, 10 Cornell L.Q. 17, 20 (1924), and then writes that "[i]t is of interest that the best available description of the logical method employed by judges is from the pen, not of a lawyer, but of a psychologist." *Id.* at 369 n.1.
83 *Id.* at 112; *id.* at 119-20.
84 *Id.* at 123-24; *id.* at 148.
85 *See* R. Pound, *The Scope and Purpose of Sociological Jurisprudence*, 24 Harv. L. Rev. 591 (1911); R. Pound, *The Need of a Sociological Jurisprudence*, 19 Green Bag 607 (1907).
86 R. Pound, *Liberty of Contract*, 18 Yale L.J. 454, 455 (1909).
87 R. Pound, *Mechanical Jurisprudence*, 8 Colum. L. Rev. 605, 608 (1908).
88 *Id.* at 606-07.
89 R. Pound, *supra* note 86, at 457. For this reason, Pound is concerned to show both the recent origin of the doctrine of liberty of contract and its time-bound appropriateness. *Id.* at 455-56. Pound offers a theory of the four-stage evolution of the idea of political liberty. Liberty of contract belongs to the third stage. While the rest of the country, as well as political science, has moved on to the final stage, the courts are still "working out the last extreme deductions from the older conception." *Id.* at 460.
90 *Id.* at 462; *id.* at 466-67 (citation omitted).
91 R. Pound, *supra* note 87, at 605 (quoting F. Pollock, A First Book of Jurisprudence for Students of the Common Law 56 [1896]).
92 *Id.* at 608.
93 *Id.* at 609.
94 R. Pound, *supra* note 86, at 454.
95 *Id.* at 469.
96 R. Pound, *Common Law and Legislation*, 21 Harv. L. Rev. 383, 384 (1908).
97 R. Pound, *supra* note 86, at 469.
98 R. Pound, *supra* note 96, at 406 (citation omitted).
99 R. Pound, *supra* note 86, at 470.
100 *See* R. Pound, *The Call for a Realist Jurisprudence*, 44 Harvard L. Rev. 697 (1931).
101 *See* O. Fiss, *The Death of the Law?* 72 Cornell L. Rev. 1 (1986).
102 *See, e.g.,* J. Alsop, The 168 Days (1973).
103 169 U.S. 466, 526 (1898); *see id.* at 528.
104 United States v. Carolene Products Co., 304 U.S. 144, 152 (1938); *id.* at 154.
105 291 U.S. 502, 525 (1934).
106 291 U.S. at 516.
107 The dissent captures this shift perfectly when it asks: "Are federal rights subject to extinction by reports of committees?" *Id.* at 548-49 (McReynolds, J., dissenting). The answer was yes.
108 *Id.* at 530 (opinion of the Court).
109 *Id.* at 537.
110 *Id.* at 531 ("[W]e are told that because the law essays to control prices it denies due process").
111 *Id.* at 537. The Court confronted exactly the same problem a few years later in *West Coast Hotel Co. v. Parrish*, 300 U.S. 379 (1937), with respect to a distinction

between regulation of hours of employment and regulation of wages. Again, the majority, adopting an economic perspective, could see no difference: "The bargain is equally affected whichever half you regulate." *Id.* at 396 (quoting Adkins v. Children's Hospital, 261 U.S. 525, 569 [1923] [Holmes, J., dissenting]).

112   *Nebbia,* 291 U.S. at 523.

113   300 U.S. at 399.

114   *Nebbia,* 291 U.S. at 533; *id.* at 555 (McReynolds, J., dissenting).

115   301 U.S. 1 (1937).

116   Carter v. Carter Coal, 298 U.S. 238, 307–08 (1936).

117   *Id.* at 308.

118   301 U.S at 32.

119   *Id.* at 41; *id.* at 32.

120   See H. Hovenkamp, *Evolutionary Models in Jurisprudence,* 64 Tex. L. Rev. 645, 673–74 (1985) (describing decline of social Darwinists and rise of reform Darwinists in U.S. universities in first decades of twentieth century).

CHAPTER FIVE: The Locus of Will in Modern Constitutional Theory

1   On their being opposed, see, e.g., R. Wolff, In Defense of Anarchism 38–42 (1976).

2   See R. Jackson, The Struggle for Judicial Supremacy (1941), for a transitional work that maintains both critiques. Jackson argues that the *Lochner* Court was inconsistent with a modern progressive democracy and that the institutional form of the lawsuit was not capable of utilizing or evaluating new forms of expert knowledge about the social order.

3   *See* J. Balkin, *The Footnote,* 83 Nw. U.L. Rev. 275, 288 (1989).

4   *See* G. Peller, *Neutral Principles in the 1950s,* 21 U. Mich. J.L. Ref. 561 (1988).

5   L. Hand, The Bill of Rights 1 (1958).

6   *Id.* at 14.

7   *Id.* at 7; *id.* at 9–10.

8   *Id.* at 14.

9   *Id.* at 15.

10   See *id.* at 49 (on nondelegation); Youngstown Sheet and Tube Co. v. Sawyer, 343 U.S. 579 (1952).

11   L. Hand, *supra* note 5, at 51.

12   *Id.* at 73; *id.* at 72.

13   *Id.* at 73–74.

14   H. Wechsler, *Toward Neutral Principles of Constitutional Law,* 73 Harv. L. Rev. 1 (1959) at 2; *id.* at 1.

15   *Id.* at 16 (citation omitted).

16   *See* A. Amar, *Law Story* (Book Review), 102 Harv. L. Rev. 688 (1989).

17   Wechsler is not committed to these methodologies as exhaustive. History, text, and precedent are all backward looking, but Wechsler supports an evolving constitution: "I cannot find it in my heart to regret that interpretation did not ground itself in ancient history but rather has perceived in these provisions a compendious

affirmation of the basic values of a free society ... [which] leave room for adaptation and adjustment if and when competing values, also having constitutional dimension, enter on the scene." H. Wechsler, *supra* note 14, at 19.

18 *Id.* at 17.

19 It fails, for example, to recognize a place for exceptions to rules, an idea traditionally expressed in the approach of equity.

20 Perhaps for this reason, Wechsler begins his article with a textual derivation of judicial review, relying upon the supremacy clause. This entire argument turns on a concession that Hand seems to have inadvertently made—that under the supremacy clause, state courts might be called upon to review the constitutionality of federal statutes. H. Wechsler, *supra* note 14, at 3. If so, their decisions are subject to appellate review by the Supreme Court. Yet there was no reason for Hand to make this concession, and indeed, it seems inconsistent with his larger argument.

21 *See, e.g.,* O. Fiss, *Groups and the Equal Protection Clause,* in Equality and Preferential Treatment 84 (1977).

22 For an example of a complex discussion over the "correct" principle by which to interpret the equal protection clause, see id. For an effort to resolve the problem of neutral derivation of principles, see R. Bork, *Neutral Principles and Some First Amendment Problems,* 47 Ind. L.J. 1 (1971) (historical inquiry into original intent is the only neutral method of determining substantive principles).

23 347 U.S. 483 (1954).

24 Various political theorists have, since Wechsler, tried to generate a model of justice based upon the idea of giving neutral reasons. *See, e.g.,* J. Rawls, A Theory of Justice (1971); B. Ackerman, Social Justice in the Liberal State (1980). There is, however, a large difference between basing a theory of justice upon neutral principles and arguing that the Constitution embodies neutral principles.

25 A. Bickel, The Least Dangerous Branch 261 (2d ed. 1986). *Cf.* The Federalist No. 22, at 152 (A. Hamilton) ("The fabric of American empire ought to rest on the solid basis of THE CONSENT OF THE PEOPLE ... that pure, original fountain of all legitimate authority").

26 A. Bickel, *supra* note 25, at 199; *id.* at 29.

27 See the discussion of Chief Justice Marshall, *supra* chapter 1.

28 Bickel's project and Thayer's work are obviously connected. *See supra* chapter 3. Bickel is frank to acknowledge the importance of Thayer's work. *See* A. Bickel, *supra* note 25, at 35–45.

29 A. Bickel, *supra* note 25, at 24.

30 *Id.* at 25–26.

31 *Id.* at 239. For this reason, most of *The Least Dangerous Branch* is devoted to the techniques by which the Court can manage its institutional and representative role vis-à-vis the other political branches and the community.

32 Bickel takes this idea from E. Rostow, *The Democratic Character of Judicial Review,* 66 Harv. L. Rev. 193, 208 (1952).

33 A. Bickel, *supra* note 25, at 30.

34 *See* G. Gunther, *The Subtle Vices of the "Passive Virtues,"* 64 Colum. L. Rev. 1, 5 (1964) (Bickel's claims "rest on faulty perceptions of the adjudicatory process; and they yield guidelines which invite not accommodation but surrender of principle to expediency").

35 United States v. Carolene Products Co., 304 U.S. 144, 152–53 n.4 (1938); J. Ely, Democracy and Distrust (1980).

36 304 U.S. at 152–53 n.4.

37 J. Ely, *supra* note 35, at 103. A pure process remedy may not be available if the problem requiring judicial intervention is prejudice. Even, then, the Court must attempt to find a remedy that replicates the value choices that would be made by a perfected process. *See id.* at 169.

38 *See, e.g., id.* at 102–03, 151–53 (accepting pluralist model); *see id.* at 79–83 (accepting the Madisonian idea).

39 For a succinct and effective critique of Ely's work, see L. Tribe, *The Puzzling Persistence of Process-Based Constitutional Theories,* 89 Yale L.J. 1063 (1980).

40 *See* L. Brilmayer, Carolene, *Conflicts, and the Fate of the "Inside-Outsider,"* 134 U. Pa. L. Rev. 1291, 1305–06 (1986).

41 *See* M. Ball, *Judicial Protection of Powerless Minorities,* 59 Iowa L. Rev. 1059 (1974); C. Black, *The Unfinished Business of the Warren Court,* 46 Wash. L. Rev. 3, 8–9 (1970); P. Brest, *The Supreme Court, 1975 Term—Foreword: In Defense of the Antidiscrimination Principle,* 90 Harv. L. Rev. 1, 6–12 (1976); O. Fiss, *supra* note 21, at 130–31; L. Powell, Carolene Products *Revisited,* 82 Colum. L. Rev. 1087 (1982).

42 J. Ely, *supra* note 35, at 73.

43 On the concern with speech and press rights, see, e.g., *Cohen v. California,* 403 U.S. 15 (1971); *Brandenburg v. Ohio,* 395 U.S. 444 (1969); *New York Times Co. v. Sullivan,* 376 U.S. 254 (1964). On the concern with rights of candidates, see, e.g., *William v. Rhodes,* 393 U.S. 23 (1968). On the concern with voting and apportionment issues, see, e.g., *Baker v. Carr,* 369 U.S. 186 (1962); *Reynolds v. Sims,* 377 U.S. 533 (1964). On the concern with the effects of prejudice, see, e.g., *Brown v. Board of Educ.,* 347 U.S. 483 (1954) (race); *Reed v. Reed,* 404 U.S. 71 (1971) (gender); *Graham v. Richardson,* 403 U.S. 365 (1971) (alienage).

44 Ely, who has the most articulate and complete theory based upon *Carolene Products,* was also an early opponent of *Roe v. Wade. See* J. Ely, *The Wages of Crying Wolf: A Comment on* Roe v. Wade, 82 Yale L.J. 920 (1973).

45 347 U.S. 483, 492 (1954) (footnote omitted).

46 163 U.S. 537 (1896).

47 B. Ackerman, *Constitutional Politics / Constitutional Law,* 99 Yale L.J. 453, 531 (1989).

48 347 U.S. at 492.

49 *Id.* at 494–95; *id.* at 494 (quoting a finding of the lower court).

50 O. Fiss, *supra* note 21, at 131.

51 P. Brest, *supra* note 41, at 6.

52 *See* C. Sunstein, *Naked Preferences and the Constitution,* 84 Colum. L. Rev. 1689, 1689 (1984).

53 *See* Mayor of Baltimore v. Dawson, 350 U.S. 877 (1955) (beaches); Holmes v. Atlanta, 350 U.S. 879 (1955) (golf courses); Gayle v. Browder, 352 U.S. 903 (1956) (buses); New Orleans City Park Improvement Ass'n v. Detiege, 358 U.S. 54 (1958) (parks).

54 *See supra* chapter 2.

55 Roe v. Wade, 410 U.S. 113 (1973); *see also* Thornburgh v. American College of Obstetricians and Gynecologists, 476 U.S. 747, 777 n.5 (1986) (Stevens, J., concurring) (citation omitted).

56 *See, e.g.,* P. Brown, The Body and Society (1988) (discussing early Christian community's struggle to break the link between the body and the state). Although the Court discusses a state interest in potential life, it recognizes that interest only after the point of viability—i.e., actual life—has been reached. *Roe,* 410 U.S. at 163.

57 It is no accident that the traditional claim of the state upon the male body through the army is simultaneously repudiated in the move to a volunteer army.

58 381 U.S. 479, 484 (1965).

59 *Id.* at 486.

60 *See* J. Rubenfeld, *The Right of Privacy,* 102 Harv. L. Rev. 737, 755–56 (1989).

61 410 U.S. at 153.

62 Allgeyer v. Louisiana, 165 U.S. 578, 589 (1897). *See supra* chapter 4.

63 *See* 410 U.S. at 132–39.

64 Bowers v. Hardwick, 478 U.S. 186, 204 (1986) (Blackmun, J., dissenting); *id.* at 205; *id.* (citation omitted).

65 *Id.* at 205.

66 *See, e.g.,* Griswold v. Connecticut, 381 U.S. 479 (1965); Eisenstat v. Baird, 405 U.S. 438 (1972) (unmarried persons have same right to contraceptives as married); Roe v. Wade, 410 U.S. 113 (1973); Moore v. City of East Cleveland, 431 U.S. 494 (1977) (invalidating zoning ordinance barring residence of nonnuclear families); Wisconsin v. Yoder, 406 U.S. 205 (1972) (Amish cannot be compelled to send their children to school beyond the eighth grade); Tinker v. Des Moines Indep. Community School Dist., 393 U.S. 503 (1969) (students cannot be prohibited from expressing independent political views); Shapiro v. Thompson, 394 U.S. 618 (1969) (protecting right to change one's residence).

67 Akron v. Akron Center for Reproductive Health, 462 U.S. 416, 439–40 (1983); Bellotti v. Baird, 443 U.S. 622, 643–44, 647–48 (1979) (opinion of Powell, J.); Planned Parenthood v. Danforth, 428 U.S. 52, 72–75 (1976).

68 *Bellotti,* 443 U.S. at 644; *Akron,* 462 U.S. at 440.

69 *See* Parham v. J.R., 442 U.S. 584, 606–07 (1979).

70 *See* Cruzan v. Director, Mo. Dept. of Health, 110 S.Ct. 2841 (1990).

71 Wisconsin v. Yoder, 406 U.S. 205, 231 (1972) (protecting Amish); Moore v. City of East Cleveland, 431 U.S. 494, 499 (1977) (protecting unconventional family).

72 *See* Abood v. Detroit Bd. of Educ., 431 U.S. 209 (1977) (union shop arrangements cannot compel contributions for political speech); Elrod v. Burns, 427 U.S. 347 (1976) (striking down patronage practices); Roberts v. United States Jaycees, 468 U.S. 609 (1984) (upholding state antidiscrimination ordinance applied to private club).

73 *See, e.g.,* F. Michelman, *In Pursuit of Constitutional Welfare Rights,* 121 U. Pa. L. Rev. 962 (1973); M. Perry, The Constitution, the Courts, and Human Rights (1982); D. Richards, Toleration and the Constitution (1986).

74 *See* H. Wellington, *Common Law Rules and Constitutional Double Standards: Some Notes on Adjudication,* 83 Yale L.J. 221 (1973).

75 *See, e.g.,* T. Aleinikoff, *Constitutional Law in the Age of Balancing,* 96 Yale L.J. 943 (1987).

76 Similar concerns underlie the renewed interest in the doctrine of unconstitutional conditions. *See, e.g.,* Sherbert v. Verner, 374 U.S. 398 (1963) (state must extend unemployment benefits to those who refuse to work for religious reasons).

77 *See* Reynolds v. Sims, 377 U.S. 533 (1964).

78 *See* Brown v. Board of Educ., 347 U.S. 483 (1954); Hernandez v. Texas, 347 U.S. 475 (1954) (protecting Mexican Americans); Graham v. Richardson, 403 U.S. 365 (1971) (protecting resident aliens); Levy v. Louisiana, 391 U.S. 68 (1968) (protecting illegitimate children); Reed v. Reed, 404 U.S. 71 (1971) (protecting women); Bellotti v. Baird, 443 U.S. 622 (1979) (protecting minors' access to abortions); Elrod v. Burns, 427 U.S. 347 (1976) (protecting politically affiliated); City of Cleburne v. Cleburne Living Center, 473 U.S. 432 (1985) (protecting mentally retarded); Harper v. Virginia Bd. of Elections, 383 U.S. 663 (1966) (protecting poor); Widmar v. Vincent, 454 U.S. 263 (1981) (protecting religious groups).

79 Weber v. Aetna Cas. & Sur. Co., 406 U.S. 164, 175 (1972).

80 *See* B. Ackerman, *Beyond* Carolene Products, 98 Harv. L. Rev. 713 (1985).

81 *See, e.g.,* Frontiero v. Richardson, 411 U.S. 677 (1973) (rejecting sex-based classification with respect to dependency allowances for wives of servicemen); Caban v. Mohammad, 441 U.S. 380 (1979) (rejecting sex-based classification in allocating natural parents' rights in adoption proceedings).

82 University of California Regents v. Bakke, 438 U.S. 265, 289 (1978) (opinion of Powell, J.) (quoting Shelly v. Kraemer, 334 U.S. 1, 22 [1948]).

83 *Id.* at 318; *id.* at 317.

84 394 U.S. 618 (1969).

85 457 U.S. 55, 70 (1982) (Brennan, J., concurring).

86 Dunn v. Blumstein, 405 U.S. 330 (1972).

87 Reynolds v. Sims, 377 U.S. 533, 579–80 (1964) (footnote omitted). The Court allowed some tolerance for deviations caused by recognition of local governmental units, but because these units are used in the efficient rendering of services, not because they are historically valuable groupings. *See id.* at 580–81.

88 *Id.* at 561. *See, e.g.,* R. Sickels, *Dragons, Bacon Strips and Dumbbells—Who's Afraid of Reapportionment?* 75 Yale L.J. 1300 (1966).

89 377 U.S. at 580. *See* A. Bickel, The Supreme Court and the Idea of Progress, 156–62 (1970).

90 397 U.S. 254, 264–65 (1970); *id.* at 265.

91 *Id.* at 267–68. *See also id.* at 265 ("most terminations are accepted without challenge").

92 *Id.* at 279 (Black, J., dissenting).

93 *See* Bell v. Burson, 402 U.S. 535 (1971) (driver's license); Perry v. Sindermann, 408 U.S. 593 (1972) (teacher at a state school); Morrissey v. Brewer, 408 U.S. 471 (1972) (parolee); Goss v. Lopez, 419 U.S. 565 (1975) (high school students); Fuentes v. Shevin, 407 U.S. 67 (1972) (debtors).

94 Vlandis v. Kline, 412 U.S. 441, 452 (1973).

95 *Id.*

96 Cleveland Bd. of Educ. v. LaFleur, 414 U.S. 632 (1974) (pregnancy leave); *see also* Shapiro v. Thompson, 394 U.S. 618, 631 (1969).

97 Gideon v. Wainwright, 372 U.S. 335 (1963) (on the right to appointed counsel); Miranda v. Arizona, 384 U.S. 436 (1966) (on procedural safeguards for Fifth Amendment protections).

98 372 U.S. at 344.

99 316 U.S. 455, 472 (1942).

100 384 U.S. at 457 (footnote omitted); *id.* at 460.

101 *Id.* at 517 (Harlan, J., dissenting); *id.* at 539 (citation omitted) (White, J., dissenting).

102 *See* Furman v. Georgia, 408 U.S. 238 (1972) (invalidating standardless death penalty); Woodson v. North Carolina, 428 U.S. 280 (1976) (invalidating mandatory death penalty).

103 Woodson v. North Carolina, 428 U.S. 280, 304 (1976).

104 Lockett v. Ohio, 438 U.S. 586 (1978); Gardner v. Florida, 430 U.S. 349 (1977).

105 *See, e.g.,* Pulley v. Harris, 465 U.S. 37, 54 (1984) ("Any capital sentencing scheme may occasionally produce aberrational outcomes"); McCleskey v. Kemp, 481 U.S. 279 (1987) (rejecting statistical argument to support claim of equal protection violation in administration of death penalty).

CHAPTER SIX: Community in Contemporary Constitutional Theory

1 *See, e.g.,* B. Barber, Strong Democracy: Participatory Politics for a New Age (1984); M. Sandel, Liberalism and the Limits of Justice (1982); A. MacIntyre, After Virtue (1981); J. Pocock, The Machiavellian Moment (1975).

2 *See* B. Ackerman, *Beyond* Carolene Products, 98 Harv. L. Rev. 713 (1985) [hereinafter *Carolene*]; B. Ackerman, *The Storrs Lectures: Discovering the Constitution,* 93 Yale L.J. 1013 (1984) [hereinafter *Storrs*].

3 *See* B. Ackerman, *Storrs, supra* note 2, at 1038.

4 Ackerman labels Ely the "archetypical" leveler. *Id.* at 1047.

5 To the leveler, politics is merely an alternative to a market mechanism for coordinating diverse, conflicting private interests. *See, e.g.,* R. Dahl, A Preface to Democratic Theory (1956); J. Schumpeter, Capitalism, Socialism, and Democracy 250–83 (3d ed. 1950); D. Truman, The Governmental Process: Political Interests and Public Opinion (2d ed. 1971); A. Becker, *A Theory of Competition among Pressure Groups for Political Influence,* 98 Q.J. Econ. 371 (1983).

6 B. Ackerman, *Storrs, supra* note 2, at 1020.

7 *Id.* at 1022. Ackerman goes on to write that "[n]ormal politics must be tolerated in the name of individual liberty." *Id.* The important word here is *individual,* not *liberty.* Liberty is essentially contested: constitutional politics makes an equal claim to liberty, but it is no longer an "individual" liberty.

8 *Id.* at 1039.

9 *Id.* at 1041; *id.* at 1050; *id.* at 1072; B. Ackerman, *Constitutional Politics / Constitutional Law,* 99 Yale L.J. 453, 477 (1989).

10 B. Ackerman, *Storrs, supra* note 2, at 1043. Ackerman's idea is clear here, even though he fails to recognize the communal character of the Christian tradition, which offered an alternative to the community of the state, not simply a domain of private salvation. *See* E. Pagels, Adam, Eve and the Serpent (1988); P. Hanson, "The People Called": The Growth of Community in the Bible (1986). At various points in the Christian tradition, the Church itself used the state to impose "salvation" upon citizens. *See generally* P. Johnson, A History of Christianity 191–264 (1976).

11 B. Ackerman, *Storrs, supra* note 2, at 1022–23 (footnote omitted).

12 B. Ackerman, *supra* note 9, at 465.

13 Ackerman pursues this dualist conception of politics in his description of the individual, whom he characterizes as a "private citizen." The private citizen is contrasted with both the "perfectly private person" and the "perfectly public citizen." B. Ackerman, *Storrs, supra* note 2, at 1042–43.

14 B. Ackerman, *supra* note 9, at 461; B. Ackerman, *Storrs, supra* note 2, at 1016.

15 *See* L. Simon, *The Authority of the Framers of the Constitution*, 73 Cal. L. Rev. 1482, 1498 n.44 (1985) (only 2.5 percent of population voted in favor of ratification of Constitution).

16 *See* J. James, The Framing of the Fourteenth Amendment (1956); J. James, *Is the Fourteenth Amendment Constitutional?* 50 Soc. Sci. 3 (1975).

17 B. Ackerman, *supra* note 9, at 545.

18 *See* B. Ackerman, *Storrs, supra* note 2, at 1042–43.

19 Given the growth of the population of the United States, the problem identified in the text is not just a problem arising from less-than-complete participation in a national dialogue in the past. A current minority is quite likely to be larger than a past majority.

20 Ackerman comes closest to acknowledging the implied-consent basis of his argument in describing the meaning of a judicial decision holding a statute unconstitutional: "[T]he Court's backward-looking exercise in judicial review is an essential part of a vital present-oriented project by which the mass of today's private citizenry can modulate the democratic authority they accord to the elected representatives who speak in their name." B. Ackerman, *Storrs, supra* note 2, at 1050. Because the usual answer of the people to the Court is "no answer," the operative effect of this statement is to understand a failure "to modulate" as implied consent to continue as before.

21 *Id.* at 1034.

22 *See, e.g.*, F. Michelman, *The Supreme Court, 1968 Term—Foreword: On Protecting the Poor through the Fourteenth Amendment*, 83 Harv. L. Rev. 7 (1969); F. Michelman, *In Pursuit of Constitutional Welfare Rights: One View of Rawls' Theory of Justice*, 121 U. Pa. L. Rev. 962 (1973); F. Michelman, *Welfare Rights in a Constitutional Democracy*, 1979 Wash. U.L.Q. 659; F. Michelman, *The Supreme Court, 1985 Term—Foreword: Traces of Self-Government*, 100 Harv. L. Rev. 4 (1986) [hereinafter *Traces*]; F. Michelman, *Law's Republic*, 97 Yale L.J. 1493 (1988).

23 F. Michelman, *Traces, supra* note 22, at 16. In making this claim, Michelman asserts that he is offering "merely [an] elabora[tion] on the work of Bruce Ackerman." *Id.* at 16 n.65.

24 J. Rousseau, *The Social Contract* 83 (C. Sherover trans. 1974).

25 *See* F. Michelman, *Traces, supra* note 22, at 65. ("In the final analysis, the People vanish, abstracted into a story written by none of us"). *See also* F. Michelman, *Law's Republic, supra* note 22, at 1520 (criticizing Ackerman's historical account of republican politics as leading to an "authoritarian jurisprudence").

26 F. Michelman, *Traces, supra* note 22, at 24 (footnotes omitted); *id.* at 25. For an elaboration of the distinction between negative and positive freedom, see I. Berlin, *Two Concepts of Liberty*, in Four Essays on Liberty 118 (1969); C. Taylor, *Kant's Theory of Freedom*, in 2 Philosophy and the Human Sciences: Philosophical Papers 318 (1985).

27 F. Michelman, *Traces, supra* note 22, at 33–35.

28 *Id.* at 27.

29 *Id.* at 17.

30 *Id.* at 56; *id.* at 57. Michelman presents this description of constitutional history as a summary of the views put forth in G. Stone et al., Constitutional Law (1986). *Id.* at 19. Yet he seems to embrace it. *See id.* at 74.

31 F. Michelman, *Traces, supra* note 22, at 65. *See also id.* at 16 ("My reading of the republican tradition, and its relation to American constitutionalism . . . confirms that, however Bickel's difficulty may or may not be resolved, the Court is, vis-à-vis the people, irredeemably an undemocratic institution").

32 *Id.* at 74.

33 *Id.* at 75.

34 For an alternative vision of the Court's role in a dialogic community, see R. Burt, *Constitutional Law and the Teaching of the Parables,* 93 Yale L.J. 455, 482 (1984) (Court should follow "pedagogic strategy" of ensuring inclusion of all minority viewpoints in communal discourse), and The Constitution in Conflict (1992).

35 F. Michelman, *Traces, supra* note 22, at 74.

36 Michelman himself recognizes this in his later work. *See* F. Michelman, *Law's Republic, supra* note 22.

37 For example, this line is at issue in much federalism jurisprudence; *see, e.g.,* FERC v. Mississippi, 456 U.S. 742, 788 (1982) (O'Connor, J., concurring in part and dissenting in part) (arguing for state freedom from federal control because states "serve as laboratories for the development of new social, economic, and political ideas"). It is also at issue in cases involving the autonomy of alternative, nonpolitical communities. *See, e.g.,* Moore v. City of East Cleveland, 431 U.S. 494 (1977) (protecting private choice as to makeup of family from authoritative state regulation); Wisconsin v. Yoder, 406 U.S. 205 (1972) (protecting idiosyncratic religious community from uniform state regulation).

38 F. Michelman, *Traces, supra* note 22, at 75.

39 *Id.*

40 On the elitism associated with traditional republicanism, see J. Appleby, Capitalism and a New Social Order: The Republican Vision of the 1790s, 8-19 (1984). For a skeptical account of the new republicanism, raising the problem of elitism from a contemporary perspective, see M. Fitts, *Look before You Leap: Some Cautionary Notes on Civic Republicanism,* 97 Yale L.J. 1651 (1988).

41 C. Sunstein, *Interest Groups in American Public Law,* 38 Stan. L. Rev. 29, 37 (1985). *See also* C. Sunstein, *Beyond the Republican Revival,* 97 Yale L.J. 1539, 1558-60 (1988).

42 C. Sunstein, *Interest Groups, supra* note 41, at 41.

43 *See generally* C. Sunstein, *Naked Preferences and the Constitution,* 84 Colum. L. Rev. 1689 (1984).

44 *Id.* at 1693.

45 *See, e.g.,* C. Sunstein, *Republican Revival, supra* note 41, at 1558 ("There can be little doubt that elements of both pluralist and republican thought played a role during the period of the constitutional framing").

46 *See* C. Sunstein, *supra* note 43, at 1691.

47 C. Sunstein, *Interest Groups, supra* note 41, at 31-32 (footnote omitted). "Practical reason" is the epistemological correlate of an objective public good. *See also id.* at

42 (speaking of "something like an objective public good"); C. Sunstein, *Republican Revival, supra* note 41, at 1154–55.

48 *See* C. Sunstein, *supra* note 43, at 1698–99 (distinguishing weak and strong views of prohibition on government distributions based on raw political power, but recognizing dominance of weak view).

49 *See id.* at 1728 ("For practical purposes, the line between public value and naked preference is quite thin, since attempts to protect particular groups are usually justifiable as responsive to some public value"); *see also* J. Ely, Democracy and Distrust, 129 (1980) (expressing skepticism "that a method of forcing articulation of [legislative] purposes can be developed that will be both workable and helpful").

50 This point is graphically made in Sunstein's choice of United States R.R. Retirement Bd. v. Fritz, 449 U.S. 166 (1980) to illustrate the republican model of legislative behavior. In *Fritz*, one group of beneficiaries was harmed through legislative ignorance: "Congress was unaware of that harm and indeed had sought to prevent it." C. Sunstein, *Interest Groups, supra* note 41, at 71. No one will disagree that a Congress that acts in ignorance and on the basis of misrepresentation is unlikely to accomplish the ends it sets for itself.

51 F. Michelman, *Traces, supra* note 22, at 75.

52 R. Cover, *The Supreme Court, 1982 Term—Foreword:* Nomos *and Narrative,* 97 Harv. L. Rev. 4 (1983); O. Fiss, *Objectivity and Interpretation,* 34 Stan. L. Rev. 739 (1982); O. Fiss, *Conventionalism,* 58 S. Cal. L. Rev. 177 (1985).

53 *See* R. Dworkin, Law's Empire (1986).

54 O. Fiss, *Objectivity, supra* note 52, at 739; *id.* at 742.

55 *Id.* at 744. Fiss himself recognizes the larger theoretical context within which he is writing: "[Interpretation] has emerged in recent decades as an attractive method for studying all social activity." *Id.* at 739 (citing C. Taylor, *Interpretation and the Sciences of Man,* 25 Rev. Metaphysics 3 [1971], and *Understanding in Human Science,* 34 Rev. Metaphysics 25 [1980]).

56 O. Fiss, *Objectivity, supra* note 52, at 745.

57 *Id.*

58 *Id.* at 746. Fiss acknowledges his debt to the work of Clifford Geertz in addition to the work of Charles Taylor. *See id.* at 739 n.2 (citing C. Geertz, Negara: The Theatre State in Nineteenth-Century Bali (1980); C. Geertz, *Deep Play: Notes on the Balinese Cockfight,* in The Interpretation of Cultures 412 [1973]).

59 O. Fiss, *Conventionalism, supra* note 52, at 183. Fiss is unclear on whether this community is the same for all adjudication. For example, do state bars, which are responsible for the articulation and development of state law, constitute separate communities?

60 *See, e.g.,* O. Fiss, *Objectivity, supra* note 52, at 747 ("Nothing I have said denies the possibility of disagreement in legal interpretation").

61 For an interesting example of such a dissynchronization, see H. Hovenkamp, *The Political Economy of Substantive Due Process,* 40 Stan. L. Rev. 379 (1988) (discussing conflict between political economy of the Court at the turn of the century and the state of professional economics).

62 O. Fiss, *Conventionalism, supra* note 52, at 182.

63 O. Fiss, *Objectivity, supra* note 52, at 746.

64 *See* A. Hirschman, Exit, Voice, and Loyalty (1970).

65 O. Fiss, *Objectivity, supra* note 52, at 753.

66 *Id.* at 740.

67 *Id.* at 757.

68 *Id.* at 751.

69 *Id.* at 747.

70 *See, e.g.,* K. Llewellyn, *Some Realism about Realism,* in Jurisprudence: Realism in Theory and Practice 42, 58 (1962) ("[T]he line of inquiry [of the legal realists] has come close to demonstrating that in any case doubtful enough to make litigation respectable the available authoritative premises—i.e., premises legitimate and impeccable under the traditional legal techniques—are at least two, and that the two are mutually contradictory as applied to the case in hand").

71 O. Fiss, *Objectivity, supra* note 52, at 745; O. Fiss, *Conventionalism, supra* note 52, at 185.

72 *Cf.* R. Fallon, *A Constructivist Coherence Theory of Constitutional Interpretation,* 100 Harv. L. Rev. 1189 (1987) (in most cases various kinds of constitutional arguments prescribe the same results, but when arguments fail to do so, they are hierarchically ordered).

73 O. Fiss, *Objectivity, supra* note 52, at 748.

74 *See* S. Carter, *Constitutional Adjudication and the Indeterminate Text: A Preliminary Defense of an Imperfect Muddle,* 94 Yale L.J. 821, 835–36 (1985) (Fiss's claim of authority does not rest on interpretation).

75 R. Cover, *supra* note 52, at 4; *id.* at 5.

76 *Id.* at 5.

77 *Id.* at 10.

78 *See, e.g., id.* at 8 ("Legal precepts and principles are . . . signs by which each of us communicates with others"); *id.* at 9 ("A legal tradition . . . includes not only a corpus juris, but also a language and a mythos—narratives in which the corpus juris is located").

79 *Id.* at 11; *id.* at 5; *id.* at 8. Cover explicitly rejects Fiss: "[M]y position differs fundamentally from [that] of Fiss . . . in that I accord no privileged character to the work of the judges. I would have judges act on the basis of a committed constitutionalism in a world in which each of many communities acts out its own *nomos* and is prepared to resist the work of the judges in many instances." *Id.* at 57 n.158). *See also* R. Cover, O. Fiss & J. Resnik, Procedure 729, 730 (1988) (previously unpublished note of Cover's, accusing Fiss of having a "romantic" notion of a "community of interpretation that is national in character").

80 R. Cover, *supra* note 52, at 16.

81 *See* S. Levinson, Constitutional Faith (1988) (developing theological analogy). Levinson's contrast of the Catholic and Protestant approaches to the constitutional text, *id.* at 27–30, is a fair approximation of the contrast between the arguments of Fiss and Cover. Fiss sees the constitutional world of meaning through an institutional hierarchy; Cover insists on an unmediated relation of each community to the constitutional text, which parallels the Protestant belief that sects can freely multiply as new claims to truth are made.

82 R. Cover, *supra* note 52, at 17 (footnotes omitted). On the image of Babel, Cover writes, "It suggests not incoherence but a multiplicity of coherent systems and a problem of intelligibility among communities." *Id.* at 17 n.45.

83 *Id.* at 17 (quoting W. Gallie, Philosophy and the Historical Understanding 157–91 [1964]).

84 R. Cover, *supra* note 52, at 18.

85 R. Cover, *The Bonds of Constitutional Interpretation: Of the Word, the Deed, and the Role,* 20 Ga. L. Rev. 815, 817 (1986).

86 R. Cover, *supra* note 52, at 60.

87 *Id.* at 53.

88 *See* R. Nisbet, The Quest for Community (1953) (on simultaneous and linked development of centralized state and autonomous, private individual).

89 R. Dworkin, *supra* note 53, at 65–66.

90 *Id.* at 66.

91 *Id.* at 67. For more elaborate explanations of this theory of the character of social criticism, see M. Walzer, Interpretation and Social Criticism (1987); J. White, *Introduction: Is Cultural Criticism Possible?* 84 Mich. L. Rev. 1373 (1986).

92 R. Dworkin, *supra* note 53, at 66.

93 *Id.* at 93; *id.* at 109.

94 *Id.* at 164–65. Dworkin does not mean this to be a comprehensive list.

95 *Id.* at 167.

96 *See id.* at 172–73 (discussing attitude of many contemporary Germans toward Jews, and white Americans toward black Americans).

97 *But see* P. Soper, *Dworkin's Domain* (Book Review), 100 Harv. L. Rev. 1166, 1182 (1987) ("'[L]aw as integrity' . . . fits only one particular society").

98 R. Dworkin, *supra* note 53, at 189.

99 *Id.* at 58.

100 *Id.* at 191; *id.* at 195–96.

101 *Id.* at 196–98. *See generally* R. Dworkin, *"Natural" Law Revisited,* 34 U. Fla. L. Rev. 165 (1982).

102 R. Dworkin, *supra* note 53, at 188.

103 *Id.* at 199–201.

104 *Id.* at 211.

105 *Id.* at 214.

106 I focus on this fourth condition—equality—because it is the one with which Dworkin is most concerned and because it is the only substantive condition among the four. One may legitimately question, however, the ground—and meaning—of his second and third conditions as well: direct interpersonal concern with the general well-being of each member. These conditions suggest a concern with something like Kant's categorical imperative that each person be treated as an end, rather than a means, but Dworkin fails to explain the link between such a moral rule and obligations of role within a community.

107 R. Dworkin, *supra* note 53, at 190.

108 *Id.* at 189.

109 F. Bradley, Ethical Studies 73 (2d ed. 1927).

110 R. Dworkin, *supra* note 53, at 203–05.

111 *See* H. Hirsch, *The Threnody of Liberalism: Constitutional Liberty and the Renewal of Community,* 14 Pol. Theory 423, 424–25 (1986) (community requires policing

of "borders" and protection of "frontier"); I. Young, *Polity and Group Difference: A Critique of the Ideal of Universal Citizenship*, 99 Ethics 250, 257 (1989) ("People necessarily and properly consider public issues in terms influenced by their situated experience and perception of social relations").

112   R. Dworkin, *supra* note 53, at 202.

113   *Id.* at 215.

Index